AF251507

Marie passed away October 2, 2008, at home surrounded by her family.

To honor her WWII service as a US Air Force Pilot, as a member of the Women's Air Force Service Pilots (WASP), Marie was awarded the ***Congressional Gold Medal*** in 2010.

In August 2012 the military uniforms with a number of artifacts related to both the military and civilian services of John Alden Clark and Marie Mountain Clark were placed in separate display cases as part of the permanent collection at the Yankee Air Museum, Willow Run Airport, Ypsilanti, Michigan.   John Alden Clark, Jan. 2013

Dear Mother and Daddy:

World War II Letters Home from a WASP
An Autobiography
by
Marie Mountain Clark
Women's Air Force Service Pilots (WASP)
Class 44-1

First Page Publications

First Page Publications

12103 Merriman • Livonia • MI • 48150
1-800-343-3034 • Fax 734-525-4420
www.firstpagepublications.com

All proceeds from the sale of this book will be donated to the WASP Collection at the Texas Woman's University, Denton, Texas and the WASP National Museum at Avenger Field, Sweetwater, Texas.

Library of Congress Control Number: 2005904217

Dear Mother and Daddy / Marie Mountain Clark
ISBN # 1-928623-63-8

Summary: Letters from a WWII WASP pilot home to her family during the period of her service, and autobiographical memoir.

First Page Publications
12103 Merriman Road
Livonia, MI 48150

Marie Mountain Clark, 1944

Marie Mountain Clark, 1944

Dedication

I wish to dedicate this memoir to my family, and to the memory of the WASPs killed in training and during active duty, 1942–45:

My husband since 1945, John Alden Clark: loving husband, father, grandfather, great-grandfather, professor of mechanical engineering, engineering consultant, author, sailor, B-17G combat pilot World War II with the 100th Bomb Group, Eighth Air Force, 1944–45, Citizen-Patriot;

My son, David W. Clark: engineer, pilot, aircraft designer and builder, clarinetist;

My daughter, Eloise-Marie Clark McKenzie, MD: physician, professional musician, violinist, and performer;

My son-in-law, Philip D. McKenzie: chief executive officer, management consultant, professional musician, oboist, and performer;

My grandchildren, Susan and C. J. Clark, and my great grandson, Curtis;
May they face the future with some understanding of the past.

And, our three sons, Alan (1946), Merrill (1946), and Peter (1988); and our grandson, Philip John Alan McKenzie (1995), whose souls rest with God.

Also, to the memory of the thirty-eight WASPs who made the ultimate sacrifice in the service of their country in World War II. *R.J.P.*

For He will command His angels concerning you,
To guard you in all your ways. -Psalm 91:11

Table of Contents

Author's Preface

During the fiftieth anniversary celebrations commemorating the Second World War, 1989–95, a renewed interest in that war emerged and my husband and I were asked to give presentations to veterans groups, civic clubs, and various service organizations about our World War II flying experiences. I had served as an Air Force pilot as a member of the Women's Air Force Service Pilots (WASP), and my husband had flown combat missions over Germany in a B-17, the famous "Flying Fortress," as a pilot with the Eighth Air Force. After two or three years of giving talks and slide presentations, it became increasingly apparent to us that we ought to record our experiences in some permanent form so that these experiences would be readily available to our families, to historians, and as archival reference regarding the pioneering role of the women pilots in WWII. We realized, too, that our own shadows were lengthening, and if we were to do this, it should be done soon.

We were married in July 1945, and my husband was released from the Air Force that month. The WASP had been deactivated six months earlier in December 1944.

After the war, we devoted our lives almost exclusively to our educations, rearing our children, developing professional careers, and finding our places in society. Of course, the war was permanently fixed in our memories, but it was family responsibilities that dominated our lives. Since we rarely mentioned our war service at home, our children and families knew very little about it. By the 1990s, however, the pace of our lives had slowed somewhat, and we had both the time and resources to consider the publication of our experiences.

My husband had kept a war diary of each of his combat missions and had hundreds of photographs from both his war service and his post-war flying with the Michigan Air National Guard. Using these resources, he published a book in 2001 titled *An Eighth Air Force Combat Diary.* While researching this book, he discovered all the letters I had written home to my parents during my flight training at Sweetwater, Texas, and service as a WASP Air Force pilot at the Las Vegas Army Air Base in Nevada. My husband then encouraged me to write my own book describing my service, using these letters as the centerpiece. I also had a large number of photographs, certificates, documents, etc., from this period, so a book seemed to be a realistic project. As the year 2005 marks the sixtieth anniversary of the end of WWII, it also seemed to be an appropriate time to publish my wartime experiences.

I had begun each of my letters with "Dear Mother and Daddy," so I decided to use those words as the book's title. Fortunately, my husband's publisher, First Page Publications of Livonia, Michigan, believed the subject matter would have broad appeal and agreed to publish my material. So, in the fall of 2004, I began to prepare the manuscript.

I am now ninety years old, have greatly diminished eyesight and hearing, and am virtually an invalid from several broken hips, heart problems, and other ailments too numerous to mention. Because of these limitations, I depended almost completely on my husband of sixty years to record these events for me as I related them to him. He has intimate familiarity with my WASP experiences as he went through Air Force pilot training himself at about the same time as I did, and we met and flew together in Las Vegas in 1944. He has attended all the WASP reunions with me since 1976, knows all my WASP friends, and has assembled and read a large number of books regarding the WASP. Because his active collaboration derives from both interest and knowledge, I am able to produce a faithful and accurate account of my WWII service. I greatly appreciate his assistance.

To support the maintenance of the WASP history in perpetuity, I am donating the proceeds from the sale of this book to the WASP collection at the Texas Woman's University, Denton, Texas, and the WASP National Museum at Avenger Field, Sweetwater, Texas. The TWU collection contains books, documents, and other WASP artifacts and has been designated as the official depository of WASP memorabilia. The WASP bylaws stipulate that any remaining funds in the WASP treasury, at dissolution, shall be donated to the WASP Endowment of the Texas Woman's University Foundation.

I wish to thank my sister, Eloise Mountain Wright, for her help in checking the facts of my early history and providing additional photographs. Also, I gratefully acknowledge the assistance of the staff at First Page Publications who made essential contributions to this book. They are:

Mr. Joe Aller, president;

Ms. Marian Nelson, marketing director;

Ms. Sarah J. Hart, acquisitions manager; who tirelessly, and with great patience, reviewed the manuscript, made many valued suggestions on style and content, and professionally managed the manuscript to publication. I am especially grateful for her help and guidance;

Ms. Elizabeth Brown-Striks, who typed all my letters and diary entries—from fading, hard to read, aging, handwritten, sixty-year-old manuscripts—with accuracy;

Ms. Kimberly Franzen, graphic designer who laid out and designed the book.

I have made every effort to present the facts and circumstances in this book as accurately as possible, but I know it cannot be done perfectly. Any errors are regretted and acknowledged with the pledge that they will be corrected at my first opportunity.

Ann Arbor, Michigan
February 2005

Marie Mountain Clark
WASP, Class 44-1

OFFICERS MESS
LAS VEGAS ARMY AIR FIELD
LAS VEGAS, NEVADA

Introduction

During the four decades following the Wright brothers' successful powered flight in 1903, women had almost no role in aviation. Women were expected to marry, bear and rear children, manage the home, and generally focus their efforts inward to husband and family. This is still, in my judgment, a noble, virtuous, often sacrificial, and critically important role for women today. However, in the past century, changes in public attitudes have allowed for a broader participation of women in society without denying their domesticating instincts. Meanwhile, men, who doubtless found aviation and the new flying machines to be a source of fulfillment for their natural masculine impulses, dominated aviation.

There were exceptions, of course, to the male preeminence in aviation. As early as 1911, Harriet Quimby, a writer, demonstrated her flying ability by piloting her aircraft around the Long Island, New York, airfield of the Aero Club of America. On landing, she was granted a license as an Aeronaut, the first woman to be so recognized. She was also the first woman to die in an aircraft accident. Less than a year after being awarded her aeronaut rating, she crashed to her death in Dorchester Bay near Boston during an air show. The English flyer Beryl Markham, author of *West with the Night*, made headlines in the 1930s with her record breaking flights in Africa and Europe and made the first solo flight from Europe to North America. In 1928, the American aviatrix, Amelia Earhart, became the first woman to fly the North Atlantic from west to east. In that flight she was the copilot, but four years later she flew as the pilot from Canada to Ireland, becoming the first woman to fly solo across the North Atlantic to Europe. Ms. Earhart was lost in 1937 in the western Pacific Ocean during an attempt to circumnavigate the earth by air. Ms. Jacqueline Cochran, probably the most famous American aviatrix, learned to fly in 1932, and in the next few years set many speed records in the National Air Races. In the 1938 Bendix Transcontinental Air Race she took first place. Ms. Cochran later served as the Director of Women Pilots for the WASP in World War II. After the war she became the first woman to pilot an aircraft at supersonic speeds. She flew a

Lockheed F-104 Starfighter at 1,273 MPH on April 12, 1963. Ms. Cochran died on August 9, 1980, at her home in Indio, California.

Although they were not gaining fame from spectacular feats, other American women were earning their civilian pilot licenses in the 1920s and 1930s by private instruction on small, low-powered, single-engine aircraft. A few women, mostly from affluent families, were able to fly larger aircraft—in rare cases, even multi-engine airplanes. However, in virtually all cases, the aircraft flown by these women were much less powerful than even the smallest flight trainers then used by the Army Air Corps.

At this time, military aviation was simply not accessible to women pilots, both by official order and because the cultural view of women did not permit it. Military flying was viewed as exclusively a male domain. The onset of the Second World War, however, brought great changes to the place of women in society, including their role in aviation.

With the war, the demand for qualified pilots in the military expanded enormously, far in excess of the availability of such pilots. The United States, like most of the democratic countries, had neglected military preparedness in all areas—especially in their Air Forces. As a result, the US Army Air Corps suffered a critical shortage of pilots. The USAAF flight training schools in 1940 could produce at most three hundred pilots a year, yet thousands were needed. An obvious solution was to consider the possibility that women could serve as Air Corps pilots, thereby releasing male pilots for combat assignments.

Women pilots in the military were considered a pioneering, perhaps even an extravagant experiment in 1941. Women served in this role in England and Russia, but in the US, it was a step into the unknown. To assess the practicality of using women pilots, a study was ordered in the summer of 1941 by General Henry H. "Hap" Arnold, Commanding General of the USAAF. Ms. Jacqueline Cochran, who had encouraged the use of women pilots, was asked to direct the study. At the beginning of the war, there were approximately three thousand women in the US holding private pilot's licenses, but it was found that most would require formal flight training to qualify as Air Corps pilots. There were only one hundred women from this group who had had sufficient experience to be considered for direct admission to military flying duty. A further assessment of these women winnowed their number to twenty-eight. Ms. Cochran recommended that those women with the least experience be recruited for full Air Corps flight training and the more experienced ones be used immediately in a military ferrying capacity. However, the implementation of Ms. Cochran's recommendations had to be delayed almost a year because of a shortage of aircraft.

By September 1942, more aircraft had been produced and were available so that the twenty-eight more experienced women could be invited to serve with the Ferry Division of the USAAF Air Transport Command. They were based at the Newcastle Army Air Base in Delaware, named the Women's Auxiliary Flying Squadron (WAFS), and placed under the direction of Ms. Nancy Harkness Love, one of the most experienced of the licensed women pilots. Their initial duties involved ferrying small training aircraft from the factory to AAF bases in the US. At the same time, women from the less qualified group were invited to Houston, Texas, to enter formal flight training similar to that given to male USAAF aviation cadets. In the spring of 1943, all flight training for women was moved to Avenger Field, Sweetwater, Texas. The women pilots were consolidated into a single organization in mid-1943 and named the Women's Air Force Service Pilots (WASP), headed by Ms. Jacqueline Cochran, as Director of Women Pilots.

This was the situation when I joined the WASP in August 1943, in the class 44-1. I drove to Sweetwater, Texas, from my home in West Des Moines, Iowa, on August 5, and reported for flight training, as ordered, on August 9. I spent the next seven months in USAAF flight training, completing each of the three training phases: Primary, PT-19 trainer with 175 HP, Basic, BT-13 trainer with 450 HP, and Advanced, AT-6 trainer with 600 HP. In training I once parachuted from an aircraft in an emergency, thus becoming a member of the exclusive Caterpillar Club. I received the coveted silver WASP pilot wings on February 11, 1944 and was assigned to active duty as an Air Force pilot at the Las Vegas Army Air Base in Nevada. My total flight time was then 315 hours. I served at Las Vegas until the WASP was deactivated on December 20, 1944, flying all the aircraft on the base, including the P-39 and P-63 fighters. My total flying time had by then increased to 844 hours.

The WASP program had the characteristics of an exclusive sorority because, of the 25,000 young American women who applied, only 1,074 earned their wings. During training, four out of ten were unable to meet Air Force flight standards and were "washed out."

In the end, Ms. Cochran's "experiment" was an unqualified success. It demonstrated that women were capable of flying every aircraft in the USAAF inventory, including the new jet fighter and the B-29 bomber. Thirty-eight women were killed in training or on active duty, but the overall WASP accident record was better than that of the male pilots. The WASP experience led the way for women to participate as pilots in all the branches of the military services. I am proud to have been a member of this pioneering group. I am also deeply grateful for having had the opportunity to fly powerful military aircraft while also serving my country in time of war. It was truly an "opportunity of a lifetime."

There is a large body of literature giving

an extensive and detailed account of the WASP in training, active service, and their post-war activities. I have cited many of these in the section of the book titled "Selected Reading."

My wartime flying experiences are described in this book through the letters I wrote to my parents from Sweetwater and Las Vegas and in my diary, which I kept for a short period after arriving in Sweetwater. These intimate, personal accounts are the central focus of the book. I hope they will give the reader an inside glimpse of the life and times of a woman military pilot of that period.

The book is, in a sense, a love story, too, for it describes my love both of flying and for a man, also an Air Force pilot, whom I met and flew with in 1944. We shall celebrate our sixtieth wedding anniversary together in July 2005.

I have included many photographs and documents from my files that will provide a better understanding of the narrative. To provide a framework for my wartime experiences, I have added a chapter on my historical background, a description of my life immediately following deactivation of the WASP, and an epilogue recounting my life since the end of the war. To complete the record, I am reproducing excerpts from my flight log from the beginning of my civilian flying to my flight training and active duty as a WASP.

I hope the reader will find my book both enjoyable and informative.

A Brief Personal History, 1915 to 1943

My life began in a small Iowa farmhouse, about mid-morning, on a cold and blustery day during the first week of February 1915. World War I was raging in Europe. No doctor was in attendance because in those days it was difficult to make timely arrangements for medical help. Although there was a party-line telephone in the house, communication by that means was unreliable. There was no hospital nearby either and, anyway, travel was slow and difficult with snow often blocking the roads in winter. So, my family did as most farm people were accustomed to doing: family members worked together as best they could to bring the new baby into the world. It was my father and his parents who took care of my birth. Later in the day, when they were able to get word to the doctor, he did come out to the farm and looked me over. I fear I was not much to see, as my birth weight was only five pounds and I was barely seventeen inches long. My chances for survival did not at all

My birth farmhouse at West Liberty, Iowa, February 1915.

5

My mother and me. West Liberty, summer 1915.

Daddy and me. West Liberty, summer 1915.

seem good, but with the loving care of my parents and grandparents, I slowly grew stronger. I was named Ethel Marie after my mother. In later years I became known simply as Marie, but my original name has appeared all my life on various documents.

The farmhouse in which I was born was owned by my paternal grandparents, Ross and Celina Arvesta Mountain. It was about three miles north of the village of West Liberty in Cedar County, on the west side of what is now Garfield Avenue, and approximately two miles south of the present Interstate 80. Springdale, where John Brown of Harper's Ferry notoriety spent some time in the late 1850s, is three miles north, and West Branch, the birthplace of President Herbert Hoover, is about five miles farther west. My sister Eloise Mountain Wright and her husband John R. Wright have owned the adjacent farm of 160 acres south of my birthplace since 1963. Today, my grandfather's farmhouse is gone, though certain vestiges remain, such as parts of the foundation and two or three of the original trees that shaded the house.

My parents, Charles Ross Mountain and Ethel Pearson Mountain, were married in 1912 and lived with my grandparents in order to help with the operation of the farm. They raised, bred, and milked Guernsey cattle, selling the milk to distributors. My grandfather grew corn, beans, and hay to support the livestock. The families of both my paternal and maternal grandparents had migrated to Iowa shortly before the Civil

Eloise and me with Daddy, Clover Hills, summer 1917.

My sister, Eloise, on the left, and me, 1920.

War when rail and water transportation made the westward movement of the US population possible to an unprecedented degree. There were also genuine opportunities for successful farming in Iowa, particularly in the southern tier of counties where the soil is especially rich.

My many cousins were reared on nearby farms and today their families own and operate hundreds of acres of farmland in Cedar County. They produce corn, beans, hay, oats, and other grains. My mother's sister, her husband, and their children, two boys and two girls, operated a very large Hereford cattle feeding business. They shipped their cattle to the Chicago and New York markets. All family members became prominent and respected citizens of Cedar County—actively contributing to the cultural, agricultural, and business interests there. My mother's grandfather, John F. Pearson, her father, Albannus Pearson, and her brother-in-law, Fred Hinkhouse, became presidents of the West Branch State Bank, and my cousin, Bill Hinkhouse, served on its board of directors. Albannus's wife, Mary Fogg Pearson, was a teacher in the Springdale School, the first school to be accredited in Iowa. Another cousin, Herbert Hinkhouse, after service in World War II, was elected to the Iowa Legislature from his district.

A year after my birth, my parents relocated their farming activity to a 160-acre farm (a quarter section) in the small community of Clover Hills, west of Des Moines, where later my father served thirteen years as mayor. This move to the metropolitan area of Des Moines provided a larger market for dairy products than was afforded by the rural regions around West Liberty. My sister, Eloise, was born here in 1916. Clover Hills subsequently changed its name to the city of West Des Moines.

My father's older brother, Dr. Elmer Mountain, a physician and later an insurance company executive, had established a medical practice in Des Moines. In 1927, Grandfather and Grandmother Mountain also settled in Des Moines, a move which brought their family together and enabled them to help care for Uncle Elmer's son, Billy, who had become seriously ill with a blood infection that year. Billy died the next year. Billy's mother, my aunt Maple, was close to our family, and we spent many happy times together. Aunt Maple and Mother enjoyed an especially good relationship and talked by telephone almost every day.

My father devoted his efforts to the breeding and development of purebred Guernsey cattle for milk production. Eventually, his stock of milking animals grew to around one hundred head. To market the milk and cream, my father established a full dairy operation with home delivery and named it the *Iowanola Dairy*. The milk that we sold was unpasturized—something that probably could not be done today. Guernsey milk is of high butterfat content and very nutritious. The quality of his cows' milk was vastly superior to that available in stores, and mothers especially favored it for their young children. The cows were frequently tested for disease by the Department of Agriculture in order to secure the purity of the milk.

To assist him in the operation of the dairy, my father invited his brother, Clark Mountain, and his family to join him in the business. My father built a house for each of the two families, giving the larger house to his brother, who had six children. The full story of this arrangement need not be told here, but it was not a satisfactory one for my family. Clark Mountain was in poor health most of the time and could only be of marginal help. He died in 1932 of a lung disease, probably caused by a lifelong habit

The Ross Mountain family: Back Row, L-R: Clark, Elmer, Charles; front row: Celina and Ross Mountain. January 1904.

The **Iowanola Dairy** *showing the grazing Guernsey cows, cow barn, farm buildings, and the milk house, looking SW, 1930.*

The milk house and cow barn, looking SE, 1930.

The **Iowanola Dairy** *looking NW, 1940.*

of smoking cigarettes. However, my father was a dedicated Christian and had a deep sense of responsibility to his brother and his family, and he put these beliefs into practice in all his actions. In later years I have realized that whatever we may have lost in terms of material comforts and benefits were more than amply compensated for by the splendid example my father set for his own family and all those who knew him.

My father, who was very creative, designed and built a large cow barn, a milk house, and several auxiliary buildings to serve the needs of the *Iowanola Dairy*. The fields were planted with corn, alfalfa, and beans to provide fodder for the livestock. Home deliveries of dairy products were made in the early years by horse and wagon. Later, as business improved and better equipment became available, these deliveries were made using a gasoline-powered truck with the *Iowanola Dairy* name and logo painted on its sides. When I was a child, it was a great, but rare, thrill for me to accompany my father on his daily dairy rounds.

As his business grew, my father added full-time employees to his work force. There was a permanent herdsman who lived with his family in the milk house, and usually two or three other workers who provided general farm labor such as field-work and care for the cattle. At mealtimes the single workers usually ate with our

***Daddy and Duke with a Guernsey cow beside the cow barn.
Published in* Successful Farming. *March 1943.***

family. At harvest time there were several more workers to be fed. Throughout the year, Mother spent a great deal of her day in planning, preparing, and serving meals—and then cleaning up afterward.

Some of my early memories include the annual picnics my parents held for their dairy customers. With particular fondness I remember the heaping bowls of strawberry shortcake that we would have for dessert.

Although the farm work was hard and the cattle needed daily attention, my parents tried to find time for vacations. Usually we were able to get away for a week or two of camping in the summer. One summer we took a long trip east and visited the nation's capital. Daddy loved to fish, so more often these vacation breaks took us to north central Minnesota. Mother and Daddy began these (fishing) vacations in the early 1920s, and they continued for the next fifty years. Both my own family and my sister's carried on with this tradition, and each of our families has kept it going for the subsequent fifty years. Most of this time was spent together at Woman Lake near Longville, Minnesota. Our children and grandchildren considered a month at the cottage a normal part of their summer. For the younger generations, however, boating, swimming, scuba diving, and water skiing replaced fishing as the sport of choice.

I loved living in the open spaces of the farm. On clear nights the sky was ablaze with stars and when the moon was full the entire landscape was bathed in its soft light. I developed a keen and lasting interest in astronomy and learned the names of many of the stars. In later years, I understood the spiritual significance of the opening verse of Psalm 19, "The Heavens declare the glory of God; the skies proclaim the work of His hands." Farm living naturally put us in touch with the natural processes of the earth, plants, and animals. I grew to know and love many creatures, especially birds. For the rest of my life, I have greatly enjoyed studying and watching birds.

Ross and Celina Mountain on their fiftieth wedding anniversary, with their children and grandchildren. January 12, 1922.

Each of my parents gave generously of their time to community service. My father served as president of several civic and service organizations and was a leader in our church as a deacon and elder. He was selected as the recipient of the 1957 Outstanding Citizen Award of West Des Moines. In 1936, he served as the president of the Iowa State Guernsey Breeders Association. During the 1960s and 1970s he served as a member and chairman of the Polk County Grand Jury. Mother, likewise, gave much of her time to community and church activities, serving as the 1924–25 president of the Polk County Federation of Women Clubs, superintendent of the Junior Department at church, and a leader in school organizations. I still have the 1924–25 yearbook of the Federation of Women Clubs. She was instrumental in the establishment of the Polk County 4-H Girls' Club. As I matured, I became increasingly aware of how important the standards set by my parents were to developing the character and values of my sister and me. I am deeply grateful for this influence of home and hearth.

In 1930 my father sold eighty acres, which was the western half of the farm, to the Resthaven Cemetery Association. The two houses in which we and the Clark Mountain family lived at the time were located on this half of the farm. Both families had to be relocated. This move resulted in an improvement in our living situation because we installed running water and improved plumbing. Owing to Uncle Clark's rapidly deteriorating health, his family decided to move to West Des Moines. Our family then relocated to the larger house. This house, at 1614 Ashworth

The family home at 1614 Ashworth Road, West Des Moines. August 1967. The address was changed in the 1950s to 1700 Ashworth Road.

The "grand staircase" in the family home. September 1967.

Road, West Des Moines, became our family home for the next forty years. The address was changed to 1700 Ashworth Road in the 1950s. In 1970, my parents moved into retirement quarters at Muscatine, Iowa, and the place was sold.

As part of the 1930 sales agreement with Resthaven Cemetery, we received about two dozen burial lots in a choice location in the central mall. Mother and Daddy were buried there in 1977 and 1979, respectively, and my husband, John, and I have our burial sites adjacent to those of my parents, with our markers in place. Our three sons, Alan (1946), Merrill (1946), and Peter Mountain Clark (1988) are buried there. At Resthaven Cemetery, the bronze plaques marking all the graves are set level with the ground, which allows for a broad, lawn-like appearance. There are many trees and flowering shrubs scattered across the gently rolling ground. This arrangement presents a beautiful and restful landscape. When the time comes, we shall finally rest next to my family home and in ground that was once a part of our family farm.

The Great Depression, which began with the stock market crash in October 1929, did not affect us in Iowa as severely as it did the rest of the country. However, its impact was felt. Our dairy business slowed and money became harder to keep. My parents found it necessary to introduce economic constraints in their business operations and household expenses, even beyond those of the generally frugal ways they had always lived. I believe my younger sister Eloise and I received a good practical education in the importance of patience, thrift, and savings during these times. During 1934, when the economic downturn was the worst, my father suffered two of his own business setbacks. A

The Campfire Girls in our Indian theme costumes, 1930. I am third from the left.

fire of suspicious origin in a rented barn nearby destroyed twelve cattle and two stud bulls he owned. Later that year, during a road show tour of our cattle, seventeen out of twenty-one prize Guernsey cows became infected with tuberculosis from exposure to a sick animal. The diseased cows had to be destroyed. Each of these cows was valued at about one thousand dollars, but the insurance paid only twenty-five dollars per animal. These 1934 losses were severe, and, combined with the drought that hit the country that year, put great strains on the continued operations of my family's dairy business. I believe that it is only my father's great faith, his strong character, and his outstanding talent as a dairyman that pulled us through those difficult times. Of course, Mother was a source of great emotional support and service as well.

My Campfire Girls group, about 1930. Mrs. Sharp is in the center, back row, and I am in the center, front row.

In spite of these difficulties,

my father established a growing reputation among Iowa farmers and was chosen as an Iowa Master Farmer in 1938. The Iowa and National Purebred Guernsey Cattle Clubs awarded his cattle many honors as both Iowa Grand Champions and National Grand Champions. Each year he showed his prized cows at the Iowa State Fair and won many blue ribbons and trophies.

I want to mention the Campfire Girls, an organization that made an important contribution to my life. I joined them when I was about twelve years old and was active for four years. Mrs. Mabel Sharp of West Des Moines organized the group. The Campfire Girls emphasized integrity, honesty, and loyalty, traits of character that I was taught at home and in church. This reinforcement of standards strengthened our personal development in those difficult teenage years when we were experiencing both physiological and emotional changes and were becoming aware of our responsibilities in society.

Over the next twenty years, up to my entry into the US Air Force WASP pilot training program in 1943, I put aside my interest in aviation and devoted my efforts to my education and my growing interest in music. My parents were very determined that my sister and I get the best possible education. Daddy had wanted to attend college, and his parents had promised to cover all the costs. Unfortunately, after many years of reading in poorly lit rooms, his eyesight deteriorated to the point that sustained reading was impossible. Mother spent two and a half years at William Penn College at Oskaloosa, Iowa, before marrying Daddy. Rather than sending us to the one-room schoolhouse in Clover Hills, they paid tuition for us to attend the more comprehensive schools in Valley Junction. Valley Junction later changed its name to West Des Moines. We walked the mile and a half to school in all kinds of weather, although on days of especially severe weather Daddy would drive us. I always enjoyed school, and I put my best efforts to learning and understanding the subjects. I earned high grades, often the best in the class. My favorite subjects were Latin, ancient history, physics, math (especially geometry), and music. I attended high school at Valley High in West Des Moines and was there for three years.

As I matured, music began to occupy an increasingly important role in my life. When I was about nine years old I became interested in the flute, and began taking lessons from Mr. Alonzo Leach, a teacher and the owner of a music store in Des Moines. That was the beginning of a lifelong vocation for me, which has included many significant positions in symphony orchestras, trios, and quartets, as well as performances as a soloist. Two years before I started flute lessons, I had private piano lessons weekly from Miss Genevieve Westerman, a music teacher in Des Moines. In 1913, on their first wedding anniversary, Daddy had given Mother a piano and it became a focal point of our home. My sister still has this piano in her home. Mother played the piano well, and she helped and encouraged me in my practice sessions. Daddy had a fine tenor voice and we spent many happy evenings at home singing around the piano while Mother played. Both my sister, who became an accomplished violinist, and I are blessed with absolute, or perfect, musical pitch. This ability helped me a great deal in my musical studies and performances. In later years, as a result of a firecracker explosion near my ear when I was about ten and exposure to the high sound intensities from the powerful engines of the military aircraft I flew during World War II, my ears suffered disabling damage. As music is one of the great loves of my life, this loss of hearing sensitivity has been very distressing.

We had a hand-cranked phonograph at home, and one of my childhood duties was to wind it so Daddy could put a record on to play. Over the years we collected a large number of fine classical music records. This was one of the ways my parents encouraged both my sister and me to become acquainted with classical music. We learned early to enjoy it.

My senior year of high school was spent at Roosevelt High School in Des Moines. The director of instrumental music at Roosevelt, Mr. Alvin Edgar, wanted me to participate in their musical programs as the principal flute and soloist in the symphony orchestra and concert band. He convinced my parents that this transfer to the Des Moines high school would be in my best

Getting started on the flute. My best friend, Katherine Kiester, is on the right. Summer 1924.

interest musically and well worth the additional tuition they would have to pay. He even offered to provide transportation! By that time, I had become well known in the Des Moines area as a flutist because of my many performances with the West Des Moines school orchestras and before various clubs, civic groups, and associations.

During my sophomore year in high school I tied for first place in flute performance at the Iowa High School Music Competition. The next year, as a junior, I won first place in the state flute competition. I also entered the National Music Competition in my junior and senior years of high school and won second place in the flute competitions both years. These competitions were held in Tulsa, Oklahoma, and Marion, Ohio. On these occasions I was assisted by Mrs. Ella Zopf Woods, a professional piano accompanist. While a

My photograph when I joined the Drake University Omega Chapter of Mu Phi Epsilon, National Honorary Music Sorority 1937.

Graduation from Drake University June 1939.

junior at Valley High School in West Des Moines and later, as a senior at Roosevelt High School, I served as the principal flute in the Des Moines Symphony. On two occasions I soloed with the orchestra, playing "The Dance of the Blessed Spirits" by Gluck and "The Flight of the Bumble Bee" by Rimsky-Korsakov. The "Bee" is always a great favorite of audiences.

In June 1932, I graduated from Roosevelt High School with an excellent academic

Giving a flute lesson to Doris Van Fossen, one of my private students 1942.

record. At the honors assembly that year, I was presented with the award for the outstanding student in instrumental music. Normally, I would have gone on to college, but because this additional expense was beyond my family's budget at that time, I delayed college for a year. However, I used this period to advance my musical studies and proficiency in flute.

After a year away from formal studies, I enrolled at William Penn College in the fall of 1933. I decided to study there partly because Mother had attended Penn College before her marriage, and therefore I was familiar with the study program. I soon found, however, that the curriculum was unchallenging and lacked much of what I desired, particularly in music. I left after a year.

I started at Drake University in Des Moines for their winter term in 1935. I lived at home. At Drake, the music depart-

ment had inspiring and comprehensive study programs, and I could play in both the symphony orchestra and the concert band as the principal flute. As an undergraduate, I also served as the flute instructor in the music department. I rejoined the Des Moines Symphony as the principal flute as well.

Drake had a high school outreach program to provide musical instruction and lessons to students. I participated in this as the flute teacher and assembled a group of students. This was my first experience in what eventually developed into my private practice in flute instruction. Over the next few years, the group grew to several dozen students. In the meantime, I gave recitals and performances to alumni groups and at school assemblies. In the fall of 1937, while still an undergraduate at Drake, Mr. Lorrain Waters, Director of Music of the Des Moines Public Schools, asked me to join their faculty as the flute teacher, which I did on a part-time basis until graduation.

I graduated from Drake University in June 1939 with the degree of Bachelor of Fine Arts. That fall, I continued teaching flute in the Des Moines Public Schools and maintained a group of private students.

In 1937, I was honored to become a member of Pi Kappa Lambda, an honorary music fraternity, and the Drake University Omega Chapter of Mu Phi Epsilon, a national honorary musical sorority. Membership in this sorority is by invitation only to women undergraduates having high scholastic achievement and demonstrated

Professor Georges Barrère at his studio, Woodstock, New York, summer 1939.

accomplishments in music. During the following decades, Mu Phi Epsilon became an important professional and social focus, enabling me to associate with likeminded women wherever I lived. I have enjoyed and benefited from these friendships and connections with talented sisters in alumni chapters in Des Moines, Ann Arbor, and Boston. In 1980, my husband became a patron of the Ann Arbor Alumni Chapter.

I was invited to perform as a regional soloist at the 1940 Mu Phi Epsilon National Convention in Cincinnati, Ohio, where I played Griffth's "Poem" for flute with piano accompaniment. Sixty-three years later, at the 2003 Mu Phi Epsilon National Convention, also held in Cincinnati, it was my pleasure to sponsor several young musi-

cians in this same program. Although I was eighty-eight years old, physically handicapped, and failing in both eyesight and hearing, I was thrilled to attend as a sponsor of these young musicians.

During the summers of 1939 and 1940, I enjoyed the great privilege of having private flute lessons with the world's most eminent flutist, Georges Barrère, at his summer studio and residence in Woodstock, New York. Mr. Barrère was professor of flute at the Julliard School of Music in New York City. During these two summers, I improved my playing techniques greatly, deepened my understanding of the significance of the music, and was exposed to a vastly broader array of flute literature. At the end of the summer of 1939, I visited the World's Fair in New York City for a few days on my way home.

My involvement with aviation began at an early age. The Des Moines Airport authorities placed a radio navigation tower on our property in order to provide guidance for aircraft approaching the airport. For several years, it was the duty of my sister and me to turn on a light on the top of the tower a half an hour before dark, and turn it off after dawn. As I recall, we were paid a few dollars each year for this service.

As a youth I was always interested in aircraft and aviation. Perhaps growing up on a farm encouraged my natural affinity for mechanical equipment and engines, and an interest in their operation. Since aircraft are also machines with engines and mechanical equipment, I developed a desire to extend these experiences to the new domain of flight. My generation was very air-minded, and flying presented a new challenge, much as space travel challenges the present generation of young people. In the 1930s, an organization known as the Junior Birdmen of America was formed to encourage youths to become interested in aviation. Many joined, though they were mostly boys. Aviation was the new frontier, inviting adventuresome youths such as myself to explore and maybe conquer the challenges of flight.

At the Iowa State Fairs, an air show with demonstrations of aerobatics and exciting stunts was always featured. Our farm was only a couple of miles northwest of the Des Moines Airport. Airplanes landing or taking off frequently flew low over the farm, giving me a clear view of them. These experiences excited my enthusiasm for flying. Daddy and Mother knew of my growing interest in aviation and always found ways to encourage me. They took me to the Iowa State Fair Air Shows and sometimes to the Des Moines Airport to watch the planes. Flying was, of course, an activity quite separated from farming by both cost and opportunity. Daddy appreciated the technical advancements necessary for flight, but this understanding did not translate into actually taking flying lessons. His farm and dairy business responsibilities also prevented him from involvement outside the farm, community, and church. My sister

Preparing to start the engine of the Piper J-5 "Cub," 1941.

I am on the right in front of the Piper J-5 "Cub" shortly after landing at Omaha, Nebraska, November 1941.

was always interested in new things, although she focused her activities on music, becoming very proficient on the violin. I was the one family member who gave serious attention to aviation.

During the 1930s, however, money was scarce and learning to fly was expensive. I had to put a hold on my dreams of flying, although they were always in my mind. I did not consider flying as a vocation, but as an interest, something more than a hobby. I was determined that should any opportunity come along to learn to fly, I would grab it.

In the pilot's seat of a Piper J-5 "Cub" at Omaha, Nebraska, November 1941.

However, in September 1939, with the beginning of World War II, everything changed, including the opportunity for young Americans to learn to fly. After the dramatic aerial victories of the German Luftwaffe in Poland and France in 1939–40, the US military realized that the country was woefully unprepared to meet the challenges of modern aerial warfare. The US Army Air Corps had a shortage of adequately trained pilots, and their aircraft were antiquated. To increase the pool of trained pilots, the Civil Aeronautics Administration of the Department of Commerce established the Civilian Pilot Training Program (CPT) in 1940. This came exactly at the right time for me. My early ambitions to learn to fly had been frustrated by lack of money, and this CPT program, financed by the government, offered me an excellent opportunity to take flying lessons. I immediately applied to the CPT program at Drake University, my alma mater.

My application was rejected. I was told they were not accepting women! The traditional role of women in the early 1940s did not include such dangerous activities as flying airplanes. I was, of course, very disappointed by this discriminatory rejection. My parents, despite their full support of my endeavors, were probably less disappointed than I! However, Dowling College, a school for osteopathic medicine in Des Moines, also had a CPT program, and they accepted me. Hence, in October 1940, I began my flying instruction with a CAA-certified flight instructor with the Des Moines Flying Service at the municipal airport in Des Moines.

The course of instruction covered both ground and flight training. The ground training included overall familiarization with the aircraft, its controls, instruments, starting procedures, etc. The aircraft I flew was a Piper J-3 "Cub" powered by a 65 HP Franklin engine.

My first flight with an instructor was on October 17, 1940, for thirty minutes. After this first lesson, my instructor rated me in my logbook as "tense, eager to learn, and alert"—not bad for a beginning, I thought then. Finally, on October 31, after nine hours and fifteen minutes of dual instruction, I was cleared to solo! My instructor rated me at this point as "relaxed, good control touch, careful, consistent, and ready for solo." My first flight alone that day was for ten minutes and consisted of taking off, circling the airport, and making a landing. I did this twice as my instructor watched

My Private Pilot Certificate, CAA, dated June 4, 1941.

intently from beside the runway. After completing this lesson, he wrote in my logbook "solo OK." I was exhilarated! I had left the ground and had flown by myself!

For the next two months I became competent in the basic disciplines of flight maneuvers: coordinated turns, stalls, spins, side-slips, holding a constant altitude, power-on and power-off landings, and making strange field landings, among others. By the end of December 1940, I had completed about nine hours of solo flight and had advanced to the point of taking a cross-country flight, first with my instructor, and then solo. The knowledge I required for this included proficiency in the use of aerial charts to identify objects on the ground, the capacity to plan a flight path and establish the compass heading to a destination (allowing for wind drift), and the ability to determine the time of arrival based on ground speed and distance. My first solo cross-country flight was on December 29: a round trip from Des Moines via Ames and Jefferson. It took three hours, which brought my solo flight time up to twelve hours. I successfully passed the CAA Private Pilot's flight test on January 24, 1941, having completed about twenty-six hours of dual instruction and fifteen hours solo. I continued flying the Piper J-3 "Cub" during the next six months, and by June 1941, my total time was about fifty hours, of which twenty-one hours were solo.

I was awarded my Private Pilot Certificate by the Civil Aeronautics Administration June 4, 1941.

After receiving my certificate, I applied for the CAA Private Pilot Advanced Course, but my application was denied. Their reason was that the physical stresses involved in the acrobatic maneuvers in the course could cause damage to the reproductive organs of a female. This, of course, was nonsense—but the ruling stuck. Later, as a WASP flying military fighters, I endured far greater "internal stresses" than would ever have been experienced in the small private aircraft, and I still managed to have babies later without any trouble!

During my CPT ground school studies I did very well, so at the conclusion of my flight training, the director of the Dowling College CPT Program asked me if I would teach their ground school courses in meteorology, aerial navigation, and two or three other subjects. I was glad to accept this assignment, and spent the next two years teaching these courses. Actually, this experience helped me greatly with my own understanding of these subjects, which also helped me later during my WASP training.

I continued flying solo for the next two years as the weather and my budget permitted. My flight instruction in the CPT program was without cost to me. However, once my pilot's license was obtained, I had to pay for the flights myself. I was earning a living then from teaching flute, so I could afford the rental cost of the airplanes. Normally I flew the 65 HP Piper J-3 "Cub." Occasionally I flew the Piper J-5 "Cub" with its slightly higher-powered engine at 75 HP. I made these flights primarily to maintain proficiency and was periodically checked by an instructor. I took a couple of cross-country flights, too, in rented airplanes, including one to Omaha, Nebraska, to visit my sister in November 1941. My last flight as a private pilot was on March 13, 1943. By this time, I had seventy-six and one quarter hours of flight experience.

At the onset of World War II, there were critical shortages of both material and human resources in the United States. The nation had been preoccupied with other matters between the wars, perhaps believing that World War I really was "the war to end all wars." In the late 1930s, the democracies of Europe were in the same situation. In terms of air power, the US was woefully unprepared to fight another war. During the years 1940 to 1942, the US Army Air Force actually had more pilots and aviation cadets than aircraft for them to fly, although the total number of aircraft was grossly inadequate to fight a global war, and the equipment was outdated. On June 20, 1941, the Army Air Corps formally became the United States Army Air Force (USAAF or AAF). To increase the pool of qualified military pilots and relieve male pilots for combat duty, the Air Force instituted a survey in the summer of 1941 to determine the number of women who might be able to be Air Force pilots. The sole source of qualified women pilots was those holding valid CAA private pilot licenses, numbering about three thousand. Of these, less than a hundred had sufficient flight experience to meet USAAF ferrying duty standards without further training. The flight experiences of the remaining 2,900 were inadequate in terms of flying hours and type of aircraft flown to qualify to fly even the Air Force training aircraft. Since my Private Pilot's Certificate was dated June 1941, I was included in the group that would require further training.

A plan, developed by Jacqueline Cochran, (whom we always called Miss Cochran), to use trained women pilots and to train others was submitted in 1941 to General Henry H. "Hap" Arnold, Commanding General of the USAAF. He accepted it and ordered its implementation. Because of the shortage of aircraft, this plan was delayed until mid-1942 when sufficient aircraft became available for training. Only twenty-eight women pilots from the CAA pool were qualified for immediate duty. In September 1942, these women were assigned to the Air Transport Command Base in Newcastle, Delaware, under Nancy Harkness Love. They were called the Women's Auxiliary Flying Squadron (WAFS). A second group, known as the Women's Flying Training Detachment (WFT), was used to initiate a pilot training program that met US Army Air Force standards. They were first assigned to a contract school at the municipal airport in Houston, Texas, and later to Avenger Field, Sweetwater, Texas, where all training was conducted after May 1943. To provide a more comprehensive experience, including the full range of aircraft in the Air Force inventory, and to allow a more inclusive test of women's flying abilities, these two women's groups were consolidated into the Women's Air Force Service Pilots (WASP)

on June 28, 1943. Jacqueline Cochran, the famous American aviatrix, was appointed Director of Women Pilots.

In the spring of 1943 I received notice that opportunities for Army Air Force flight training—similar to that given to male aviation cadets—was open to qualified women who had a Private Pilot's Certificate and at least thirty-five hours of flight time. I was invited to an interview conducted in Des Moines early that summer with Mrs. Ethel A. Sheehy, the WASP recruiting officer for Miss Cochran and an experienced pilot in her own right. Immediately following this interview, I applied for admission to the WASP program, as I had more than the minimum qualifications necessary to do so. My application was accepted. I received a letter dated July 13, 1943, from Headquarters, AAF Flying Training Command, Fort Worth, Texas, inviting me to join the WASP program. I was ordered to report for training to the WASP training base at Avenger Field, Sweetwater, Texas, at 10:00AM, August 9, 1943.

This was the beginning of my opportunity of a lifetime! For the past several years, I'd had my heart set on advancing my flying career as an avocation, and the WASP training program seemed like an ideal way to do it. I also wanted to serve my country in the war, as did most young people at the time, and flying for the USAF was a perfect way to serve. My parents encouraged me in this, but I believe they thought they would never see me again!

**HEADQUARTERS
ARMY AIR FORCES FLYING TRAINING COMMAND
FORT WORTH, TEXAS**

In reply
refer to: 201-Mountain, Marie

40G

18 JUL 1943

Miss Marie Mountain
1014 Ashworth Ave., West
.Des Moines, Iowa

Dear Miss Mountain:

Your application for admission to the Women's Flying Training program has received favorable consideration.

It is desired that you report at your own expense at 10:00 a.m., 9 August 1943, to the Commanding Officer, 318th AAFFTD, Avenger Field, Sweetwater, Texas. Due to a change in curriculum the entrance dates for the remainder of the calendar year have been changed and the class scheduled to enter training 29 July will enter 9 August. Sufficient allowance should be made for possible delays, as transportation difficulties will not be accepted as an excuse for late arrival. Bus leaves Blue Bonnet hotel at 9:30 a.m. on reporting date.

You should bring with you this letter, Social Security card(if you hold such), current CAA pilot license, and your logbook.

Provisions have been made for your employment on Civil Service status at the rate of $150 per month during your satisfactory pursuance of flying instruction under Army control. Upon completion of the Army instruction course, and if physically qualified, you will be eligible for employment as a utility pilot at the rate of $250 per month, subject to your satisfactory performance of the duties assigned you.

No allowance is made for your subsistence and maintenance during the term of this appointment.

Please acknowledge receipt of these instructions and your intention to report as directed, addressing such acknowledgement to the Commanding General of this Headquarters. Failure to acknowledge within ten days from entrance date intention to report as directed, or submission of valid reason why it is impossible to report, automatically cancels your application for entrance to Women's Flying Training.

For the Commanding General:

Incl-1
Handbook

CHESTER R. KEOWN,
Captain A.G.D.,
Assistant Adjutant General

Acceptance letter to the WASP training program, July 13, 1943.

Part I

Letters and Diary from Avenger Field, Sweetwater, Texas

This part of the book contains letters I wrote home to my parents in West Des Moines, Iowa, from Avenger Field, Sweetwater, Texas, where I was assigned for WASP Air Force flight training. There are forty-four letters in all, including one from the pastor of the church I attended in Sweetwater and one from an insurance company. For the first three months I kept a diary, and these diary entries are included. I did not keep the diary after November 1, 1943, probably because I was simply too tired after busy days flying and in ground school.

At the end, I give a brief account of my graduation from WASP flight school at Sweetwater and of my automobile trip with my parents to southern California before reporting for duty at the Las Vegas Army Air Base.

Diary

August 5, 1943

At 1:45 PM, Madelon Burcham, Jean Sidwell, and I started for Avenger Field, Sweetwater, Texas. We spent the night at Snapps Hotel in the hilly, disarranged resort town of Excelsior Springs.

Comment

Madelon Burcham and Jean Sidwell both came from Des Moines. I met them at the Des Moines airport, and we were members of a women's flying club. Madelon was the daughter of a prominent Des Moines physician, and we both served at the Las Vegas AAB when we completed training. She married Lt. Jack Hill, a pilot at Las Vegas, and we are lifelong friends. Jean did not complete training.

Postcard

August 6, 1943, 6:50 PM
Dear Mother and Daddy:

We are waiting for our dinners in Tulsa. We are discussing driving all night and arriving in Sweetwater for graduation tomorrow. Jean wants to and Madelon doesn't want to. I am neutral. It is 94 here and we hadn't realized it.

Our road was 69 to Vinita, Oklahoma. Now we are on 66. We intend to drive at least to Okla. C. tonight. The road—most of it—has been so straight and nice. We had a detour yesterday on the southern edge of Iowa.

The dinners have arrived now. We are having a nice time together. We drive 2 hours at a stretch for each. We have seen several planes constantly all day. There are so many flight schools all along. Be careful. Does the L.R. [living room] look nice now? Tell Dickey "Hello."

Love,

Marie

We are averaging 22½ miles/gallon

Diary

August 6, 1943

At 8:45 AM we started on toward Sweetwater going through K.C., MO, and K.C., Kansas in the rain and then on south. We saw many, many Army planes through southern Kansas and Oklahoma. We ate in Tulsa and decided to drive all night to arrive in time for graduation Saturday morning.

Letter 1

Sweetwater, Texas

August 7, 1943
Saturday Evening, 6:00

Dear Mother and Daddy:
We all went to bed in the Blue Bonnet Hotel at 3:30 this afternoon and I have just awakened. Madelon is awake but still in bed. This is certainly a hot place, but the breeze is swell. The fan in the ceiling of our room goes constantly.

We did drive all night—55 to 60 miles/hour—during the night and got here at 8:30. We got a room at the Blue Bonnet and got cleaned up and ate breakfast and went out to Avenger Field about 10:45 and found a girl whom Jean knows who received her wings today. We saw the field and watched 112 girls graduate and all the girls on the field march. The band—all men—led the parade. We were thrilled to death and all the girls on the field must be crazy about it. They all look so enthusiastic. We like their appearance. We ate lunch with Jane Loban, from Waterloo, who has been writing to Madelon. Their food is served cafeteria style on divided trays and it is wonderful and loads of it. Guess I certainly won't starve to death.

A Fairfield girl is rooming with us. She arrived about the time we did by train. She has been with us the rest of the time and the 4 of us intend to be together in a room. There are six to a room. The lockers are wood and have quite a lot of room. The beds are just metal cots and ticks.

The 112 girls who graduated started out 160 girls! Jane was to have graduated today. She is the one who had whooping cough and expected to be sent home. But she is still here and expects to be assigned to another class—perhaps the next class to graduate. The girl from Fairfield is

Darlene Haskins. She remembers Johnny. [John R. Wright, who married my sister, Eloise.]

I had the car greased—oil changed—gas tank filled—at the Buick shop which is also Chevrolet. The garage man was so nice. He invited us to patronize his garage while we were here. He offered us $1,000 for the car. He said he would sell it for $1,100. He was swell.

It was beautiful driving into this county at sunup. Our backs were to the sun and everything was bathed in sunshine. Isn't this the most godforsaken country? But it is beautiful. I love it and the towns are so open and so clean. I love the roughness of the ground.

Everyone is awake now and Jane has brought us limeades and grape juice and is telling about the training. Jane says we will need more dresses, so I would appreci-ate the new dress. How about ordering name tapes for me by telephone and having them send them to me? They are in notions dept. if you didn't know. If it will take more than a week, don't do it.

How are you all? Please rest and take care of yourselves. How do the rooms look now? Are they about finished?

We think we can move into barracks tomorrow.

Loads of Love,
Marie

Aunt Maple can read this.

The jackrabbits were thick as grasshop-pers on the road this morning. We hit one.

The administration building at Avenger Field with the Fifinella logo on the roof. August 1943.

The Fifinella logo, designed by Walt Disney especially for the WASP.

Diary

August 7, 1943

Driving all night in 2-hour shifts was fun. Hardly a soul was on the straight, smooth roads of Texas. Just before dawn jackrab-

bits were thick as grasshoppers on the road. In the gray of dawn we were conscious of ghostly scrubby trees over the landscape. Then, just after sunup, the skyscrapers of distant Abilene rose out of the plain bathed in sunshine. We rolled on over plains and hills surrounded by mountainous, flat topped hills into Sweetwater at 8:30 AM. We obtained a room at a nice Blue Bonnet Hotel and met Darlene Haskins of Fairfield. After dressing and eating breakfast we started on west to Avenger Field. The first glimpse of the vast array of grounds—clinging sunshiny buildings on the distant hill, an unforgettable thrill to future Avengerettes. From atop hangar one, we watched all trainees in dress uniform march according to classes out on the ramp, led by an Army band from Big Springs. On the reviewing stand were Jacqueline Cochran, Ethel Sheehey, Army officers, and other notables. At the end of the graduation ceremonies the girls received well-earned diplomas and <u>wings</u>. Jane Loban from Waterloo showed us the grounds and then we ate dinner with her in the mess hall. It was delicious. Saturday evening Jane took us to dinner, then to the Avengerette Club and to the U.S.O., where lemonade was served. Men from Camp Barclay spend weekends in Sweetwater and the town is full of uniforms. We 4 spent the night at the Blue Bonnet.

Letter 2

Sweetwater, Texas

August 8, 1943
Sunday morning, 10:30

Dear Mother and Daddy:

How are you this morning? We all slept like tops for nine whole hours. This is a very nice hotel—sort of new I would say. We had the fan on, but in the night I was stuffed up and got up and turned it up. I am quite worried about my nose. I sneeze and get stuffed up about twice a day and the drops then clear it out. I wish you would talk to someone about it. Will George be gone long? [Dr. George Mountain, my cousin in Des Moines.] *I wouldn't care so much if the Eustachian tubes wouldn't be affected so my ears wouldn't stop up in flying. But I wouldn't doubt if they are affected too. Wish I had taken Dr. Burcham's offer of x-ray treatment. I am afraid to let the flight surgeon know. He would as sure send me home.*

I hope you get this in time not to order that name tape. We bought some India ink last night. (We just heard that we can't move to the field until tomorrow.)

Did you go to church this morning? Madelon went but the rest of us went to eat breakfast. I am writing now after that.

Johnny Tucker, a boy Darlene knew at Ottumwa—he was in her CPT class—is up here now. He instructs instructors at our field. So it is nice knowing him. They all have something on this PM—all Ottumwa people. They are all leaving now.

Last night Jane took us to see the girls' own club downtown and the USA fellows come here from Camp Barkley at Abilene every weekend, it seems, and the town is just full of uniformed men.

Well, must save a little to say next time. I'll send this airmail in hopes that it will ward off the name tag order.

Love,
Marie

Diary

August 8, 1943
The day was spent mostly in letter writing. In the evening Jane and Mary Connor directed us to Sweetwater Lake and then back for supper and another night at Blue Bonnet. Oh, in the evening, when we took Jane and Mary back to the post, we received special permission to hear Miss Cochran and all about the uniforms. [Miss Jacqueline Cochran, Director of WASP women pilots.]

My class relaxing between ground school sessions outside the school building. Note the turbans for our hair, an idea from our commanding officer, Major Robert K. Urban. They were promptly named "Urban Turbans." August 1943.

Letter 3

Sweetwater, Texas

August 9, 1943
Monday, 9:35 PM

Dear Mother and Daddy:
Lights have to be out in 20 minutes. Last night Jane and Mary (another veteran) directed us to Sweetwater Lake a few miles out of town. You wouldn't imagine that there was such a lake around. In spite of what I said the country is quite rough—a

bit mountainous. Then we drove them to the field and had special permission to hear Jacqueline Cochran talk to the girls.

We moved to the field this morning along with all the other girls in our class. We are all assigned to two barracks which face each other. There are 8 bays [rooms] in each barracks and six girls in a bay. All the rooms open outside on a porch. All 4 of us Iowa girls are in a different bay. Madelon is across from me and down one.

All day we have spent getting settled, having meetings, and filling out about 10 forms with loads of questions. The food is wonderful.

Tonight some upperclassmen serenaded us with field songs.

We are divided into Flight 1 and 2. Our bay is in 2 and we fly tomorrow at 7:00 and go to ground school and physical training in the afternoon. Flight 1 turns the schedule around.

We have just carried our beds outdoors. It is cool there.

A light moment between classes. I am in the back row standing at the left. August 1943.

I found such a lovely looking little book in my trunk. Thank you so much for my other shorts. We wear them in the evenings.

Love,
Marie

A view of our barracks with its porch. August 1943.

Diary

August 9, 1943

Finally! Arrived at the field soon after 9:30 and spent the day in lectures, barracks assignments, filling out myriads of forms, unpacking, and getting acquainted. Miss Cochran talked to us today. Lights out at 10:00.

The Fairchild PT-19 trainer used in Primary Flight Training. I am sitting on the wing. August 1943.

I am standing in front of a PT-19 wearing a "zoot-suit," ordinary Army issue men's overalls, which is all that was available at the time. August 1943.

I am about to climb into the cockpit of a PT-19. The parachute I am wearing is the one I used when I parachuted a few days later. I still have the ripcord, the handle of which is seen below my left elbow. August 1943.

Diary

August 10, 1943

Up at 6:00! Flight line at 7:05. Met our instructors. Mine Clark Rowe. Flew 33 minutes in my first Army plane. Fairchild PT-19-A. Not so hot. Ground school started in math, airplane structures, physics. No PT (physical training) today. Bought 3 pairs uniform trousers in evening.

Diary

August 11, 1943

Flying a little better today. Ground school horribly easy. Saw movie on parachute jumping and story [movie] on training of famous aviator. Madelon and I stood watching PTs [Primary Trainers] from end of barracks and thrilled over everything that had happened, our opportunity, etc.

Diary

August 12, 1943

My flying is consistently better every day. Landing [crosswind] still bad. My instructor is marvelous. Stalls better coordinated. Housemother met us tonight.

Letter 4
EMM
Sweetwater, Texas

August 13, 1943
Friday, 10:20 AM

Dear Mother and Daddy:
We are on the flight line. We have a lovely new hangar for the Primary students. We came into it just Wednesday. We have nice study tables in the ready room where we can do anything we wish just so we are available at all times unless specially excused. I flew this morning during second period—8:30 to 9:30. We started flying on Tuesday in Fairchild PT 19-A [Primary Trainer] 175 H.P. It is the same type as the Howards' at home. Low wing, open cockpit, silver. A real Army ship with stars on the wings! Madelon and I stood, Wednesday night, at the end of our barracks which overlooks the ramps leading into the PT hangar and just thrilled at how wonderful it all is and what a wonderful opportunity we have. We have such wonderful meals and loads to eat. Our barracks are nice—sea green walls with a cream near the bottom and ivory ceilings—and Venetian blinds. The buildings—all on the field—are cream colored with blue near the ground and blue roofs. Everything is very pretty.

We certainly get the very best of everything. I understand why you civilians are living without.

I like the girls better every day. I feel as though I really belong. You should see us in our zoot-suits [coveralls]. We sort of took what was left. Many of us have size forty-two. We stood and laughed at each other at first. We don't mind. It is just all so funny. We are to have new slick ones—specially designed for us—in blue soon along with our other new blue uniforms.

My instructor, Clark Rowe, is wonderful. There is one instructor to 5 students. I have 2 hrs. and 58 minutes so far. Everyday I get consistently better which makes me very happy. But don't worry, (I can just hear mother) that doesn't mean I think I am good. I am just making steady improvement.

Our days are rather full but I don't feel rushed as some students do. We get up at 6:00, breakfast formation at 6:35, breakfast at 6:40, flight formation at 7:05, flight line at 7:40, recall at 12:00 if you don't fly last period (12:30 if you fly last period), lunch formation at 12:40, lunch (I mean dinner) at 12:45, ground school formation at 1:25, ground school 1:30 to 4:30. Physical training at 4:45 to 5:45. Supper formation 6:55, supper at 7:00. We march in formation whenever we go to any of these scheduled things. Every evening there has been something we have had to do (bed at 10:00).

Ground school is so, so simple. There just isn't much studying to do. Most of the girls are kept pretty busy. Ahem! We have marvelous ground school instructors (men). Our subjects so far are math, physics, and airplane structures. The girls spend the time in the ready room on the flight time studying, writing letters, and everything. Chattering, hangar-flying, and stuff. Everyone is nice on the field. Regulations are strict, of course, and if you don't conform, you receive demerits. But regulations are not bad. They still leave lots of freedom. We just know what they are and conform and think nothing of it. There

are no more than are necessary for efficiency in organization.

How is everything at home? Are you taking good care of each other? I still haven't heard from you. Doris sent a letter Wednesday. What are you doing? How does the house look? What do you hear from Eloise and Johnny and Suzanne? [My sister, her husband, and their daughter.] Whenever you are finished with the Kodak I shall have a picture of me and my zoot-suit taken. Pictures naturally are limited in subject, and they have to be cleared at the intelligence office, but there are still many things I can show you. Don't forget those pictures you are to take when you all get together. Tell Dickey hello and everybody else and Aunt Maple and Uncle Elmer. I certainly make constant use of the notebook. Everything people gave me is very essential. I could use more shorts—that rainbow pair—and more letters too.

Love,
Marie

P.S. The pen works swell, but the air is dry, and if I stop to listen to someone a bit, it dries slightly naturally. So please excuse the spots where it is slightly dry.

Me

You may let Aunt Maple read this.
We were assigned to barracks alphabetically. And the whole squadron of new girls is divided into two flights alphabetically. One flight flies while the other goes to

My instructor, Mr. Clark Rowe, and me. August 1943.

Mr. Clark Rowe and his Primary students. L-R: Myra Stockton, Marge Logan, Edie Keene, and me. August 1943. Edie was killed in an air crash in April 1944.

ground school. So I never see Madelon except in evenings. Our meals are even at different times.

Bye now.

Diary

August 13, 1943

Received 100% in Airplane Structures test today and 100% in physics too. Ground school is so simple. Washed and ironed on top of the lockers. Started cleaning for inspectors.

Diary

August 14, 1943

Had our first formal inspection today and didn't get any gigs. We were quite proud. Then had the rest of the day off. Slept, read, played ping pong. Did my hair all by myself. We have a swell bay. All kids with a marvelous sense of humor. Lucky! Had roast buffalo meat today.

Letter 5
EMM
Sweetwater, Texas

August 15, 1943
Sunday afternoon, 5:10

Dear Mother and Daddy:
How are you both today? I still haven't heard from you. Are Eloise and Johnny still in the country?

We are confined to the post this weekend, so without any flying and ground school we have amused ourselves. We have slept, played ping pong in the recreation hall, read, listened to the radio (New York Philharmonic this afternoon), etc. I haven't studied yet, and this is the first letter. I took a sunbath, washed my zoot-suit and other clothes, and ironed. We iron on top of our lockers on towels, and I can do an O.K. job on my shirts.

It seems such a silly waste of time. Two days of seven just wasted as far as training is concerned. That is certainly winning the war fast, isn't it?

We had formal inspection yesterday morning by Lt. McAnany, our intelligence officer. We cleaned and scrubbed and made our beds and arranged our lockers and everything according to regulations. We dressed in our dress uniforms of khaki slacks and white shirts and brown shoes and socks and stood at attention at the heads of our beds. He didn't find any dust or a thing out of place. We get demerits whenever we break regulations.

Two of my bay mates just came back from a whole afternoon of ping pong. We have such a nice group in our bay. Everyone has a sense of humor and is easy to get along with. Everyone understands and cooperates. We are so thankful that we happened this way because there are some very undesirables in our class. Our bays are so large (about 20x20) and lovely.

We miss the sound of planes today. All day and most of the night there is a con-stant roar. It is certainly an interesting place. We used to think it wonderful to see one of these planes take off or go overhead, didn't we? Now we hear and see them con-stantly. It is hard to realize.

The girls carry their beds outdoors to sleep at night. The first night was enough for me. The wind kept me awake. But the heat is rather bad inside. It is very hot here, but the humidity must be low, because we don't mind. We pour off sweat constantly, but no one thinks about it because everyone does perspire. I heard someone say it is 116° today, but that is hard to believe.

It is almost time to eat. Bet I gain. I eat so much. Many girls have been ill includ-ing Jean S., but Madelon and I have

In our dress uniforms for inspection. I am on the right and Kay Murphy is on the left. August 1943.

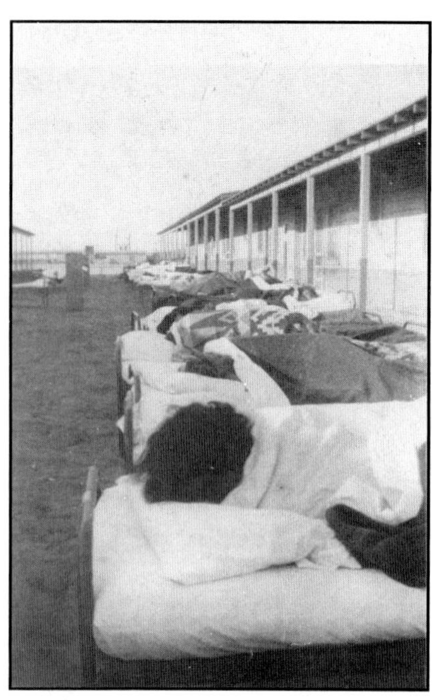

On hot nights some of the girls took their cots outside until a rattlesnake decided to join the group. August 1943

escaped. They think it is heat prostration and too many iced drinks. It will be nice to hear from you. Isn't Helene's stationery nice?

Lots and lots of love,
Marie

I started this letter to tell you how much I am enjoying the book and the note in the front. I am sure I shall need and use the little personal note after. I am starting the readings today. Thank you so much.

Please call King's Pharmacy and ask them to send prescription no. 1771473 (nose drops) to me, and ask them not to label the outside. Pretty please.

Diary
August 15, 1943
Confined to post—whole class.

Letter 6
EMM
Sweetwater, Texas

August 17, 1943
Tuesday, 9:30 PM

Dear Mother and Daddy:
Gee, but you sound busy and the house must look beautiful. Wish I could see it. Please, don't overdo, Mother, and you too, Daddy. Wilbur Chandler, new vocal teacher, was in Des Moines until last year. He was at Washington Irving (school) last.

The damp grass sounds nice. I read that about the washing drying in spite of wet grass to the kids. We had one of the famous Texas dust storms today and they said this one wasn't bad. The wind was too strong too, so we couldn't fly. Our bay was coated thickly with dust. It was a mess. I drew the job of sweeping—almost scooping—out the dust. Our hair is gray. In spite of not flying we went to the flight line for half the afternoon and our instructors talked each to his own group of students. I wouldn't be surprised if one in my group of 4 doesn't make it. She doesn't seem to understand instructions. We certainly have a wonderful instructor.

This week our schedule is switched. We go to ground school and physical training *in the morning and fly in the afternoon—when the air is full of bumps. The night flyers are roaring overhead. It sounds wonderful. They keep that up until 2 or 3 o'clock.*

Ground school is going O.K. I have received 100% in all tests so far. Our section had the most marvelous instructors. There are instructors in other sections which are not so hot from all information. We are lucky.

There is a very sweet girl whom I have suddenly become conscious of this week, so tonight I sat beside her at supper. Isn't it funny that sometimes—in fact often—the worthwhile ones are not obvious at first? They are often the quiet ones. Her name is Jo Keating. Another one which I think I shall like, but is quiet and hard to become acquainted with is Martha Ann Wilkins. But she is loosening up. One evidently just has to wait for her to come around. I shall have to be worthy of them, won't I? I have to watch me. Isn't it strange how first impressions change? The obvious at first are not now the highest in my opinion. It will be fun to watch it change. One has to keep an open mind, doesn't one? I hope I never let myself get too old for that. It seems to have rolled around to 9:50 and taps will soon sound.

Madelon and I went for a long walk tonight. The air is almost chilly for a change.

Keep the letters coming.

Love,
Marie

Letter 7
EMM
Sweetwater, Texas

August 20, 1943
Friday, 12:45 PM

Dear Mother and Daddy:

We are on the flight line. I was to have flown first, but my face was so burned that I requested a later hour. I flew first yesterday at 12:40; that is why the burn. I have 5 hours and 22 minutes now in a PT. Day before yesterday was a <u>bad</u> day, so I got mad at me and had a much better one yesterday. Hope I am still mad today. They are starting washouts already. Some girls had check rides yesterday and some more today. You are given a check ride after 3 daily pink unsatisfactory slips in a row. But then, you are given a chance at 3 civilian and 3 Army checks before you're washed out. We are all given check rides regularly. The first will be about 7 hours—after 7 hours, I mean. We solo between 8 and 12 hours.

One of the girls in my flight class went to see the girl in my flight who has been in the hospital since she arrived. She found out that she instructed in Iowa 1½ years before she came. Madelon and I are going to see if she is the instructor from Ames we had heard before was coming.

Jean S. told me yesterday that her husband has left her. Don't say anything about it. Isn't that a shame. I don't know whether people here know it or not.

Yesterday it turned hot again. If our bays would just cool off faster at night it wouldn't be so bad. There is a breeze but not too effective inside. It is always breezy in Texas, so one doesn't mind heat. It is hot as can be in the ready room now. They seem to be trying out the heating system—big blowers installed just below the ceiling.

I so wish you could sell the farm now that there would be another problem of finding a man. I don't want Daddy to have to work hard—I mean, any harder. He already works hard.

I broke my record of 100%. Got 93 in hydraulics test. Missed one question. Guess I am just normal now.

It was fun to read Eloise's letter. Hope she finds time to write again. We can go off the post this weekend, but we can't be gone overnight.

It is nice of Aunt Maple and Uncle Elmer to take such good care of you. I shall love to hear from Aunt Maple when she has time.

Isn't this a dumb letter? I am sleepy.

Love,
Marie

I am back from flying. I did a much smoother job. Guess I won't wash out for another 3 days anyway. Guess I am at the point where things will go better.

Letter 8
EMM
Sweetwater, Texas

August 21, 1943
Saturday, 3:00 PM

Dear Mother and Daddy:
How are you today? Are you glad tomorrow is Sunday and maybe you can be lazy? We have open post until one tonight and all the girls in our bay are gone to Sweetwater but me. One would think they had just been let out of jail. Madelon and I are going in about six and have dinner and maybe go to a show and do our little bit of shopping. Last night I asked Mrs. Deaton, who seems to be in charge of our welfare outside of the Army personnel, if there would be a place where I could practice. She told me I could use her office any time I wanted to. She was quite thrilled about it. Her mother was a piano teacher, and Mrs. Deaton grew up listening to two pianos and 4 violin practices at once. So I am going to practice this afternoon as soon as she leaves.

This morning someone called me about 6:15. The bugler hadn't sounded Reveille and there were no lights and no water. The field was in total darkness. After we were all dressed we were told to go back to bed and there would be no breakfast for a while and no Saturday morning inspection. So we went back to bed. Then about 7 we were called to breakfast, but there was still no inspection. We had swept and scrubbed the floors until there was actually no pink dust on them and cleaned out our lockers. Then we were told why. One of the girls on basic training made a crash landing into a power line in the middle of the night. She was knocked out, but not hurt. When she came to, she couldn't get the field by radio, so she flashed her landing lights.

Yesterday two girls were washed out in the class which graduates in two weeks. Two girls in Flight 1 of our class were washed out too. The others who had to take checks passed O.K. The girl in my flight who took one passed. It was decided that the fault was with the instructor in her case and she will have a new one.

My instructor complimented me on my judgment yesterday. Did I tell you? The first thing we learn here is to pivot our heads constantly to watch for other planes. We certainly learn to dodge them. Yesterday it seems that I did a good job dodging. I didn't realize until we flew that there is a farm area just west of here. Our practice area is over that area—wonderful for forced landings. The fields, the rows of stuff, follow the contours of the land. Did I tell you one of our girls soloed yesterday at 8 hours and 7 minutes? Martha Wilkins and I have 6 hours and 8 minutes.

Love,

Marie

Are they sending my laundry tags? I shall wait. Been here 2 weeks already anyway. I would love my wedgies and riding boots.

Letter 9

EMM

Sweetwater, Texas

August 23, 1943
Monday, 7:20 AM

Dear Mother and Daddy:
We have just come to the flight line and the first girls have gone to the planes. The sun has just come up and everything is nice and cool.

We had a nice weekend. Madelon (Dr.'s daughter who went with me from D.M.) and I went into town after dinner Saturday evening and did a little shopping and then went to a show (Arabian Nights). We went to the Avengerette Club for a minute and saw no one we knew except some who were leaving, and then to the USO just as it was closing, then home.

Yesterday Wanda and I went to church and then met the other girls who are all Catholic (the other 3 in my bay and Madelon) and went to Starr's for dinner— nice steak. Then we went swimming in Sweetwater's very nice pool—almost as nice as the country club. Nearly everyone there was from Avenger Field and soldiers from nearby camps. Then we ate a lunch and drove over to Abilene and bought limeades and drove back. Madelon drove back. It was 9 o'clock then. The drive was pretty. All along the way south of the road is a string of low flat-topped so-called mountains.

I am on the left, Kay Murphy on the right, and Dolores Meurer on the wing of a PT-19. August 1943.

I finally know the names of all the people in my flight. Everyone seems amazed that I do. We hardly know the other flight, because we never see them. Another of the other flight's people is up for a check today. I don't know why that happens to them more than to us. Poor kids! Our flight commander, Mr. Pool, is very nice, but it seems that theirs is "a devil." (Madelon's words.) Madelon talked to her family yesterday.

Last night we figured our mileage for the trip down. It was 980 miles on 44 gallons of gas. Almost 22½ miles to the gallon! Cheap enough, wasn't it? We hadn't been in the car since we came until Saturday evening. It runs so beautifully I would hate to sell it. It hadn't occurred to me until last night that if I washed out, I wouldn't have a car!

The flight line doesn't seem to be a very inspiring place for letter writing, does it?

This is the news anyway.

Love,
Marie

What did you do yesterday? Another nice spree, like last week? Did you go see Eloise and Johnny and Suzanne?

Comment

My car was a black 1941 Chevrolet Deluxe Coupe. It gave excellent service and lasted until 1949 when John and I replaced it with a new 1949 four-door Chevrolet sedan.

August 23, 1943
2:00 PM

We are in ground school now—math class. We are taking a test and I did mine in about 10 minutes. The other kids are still working hard and I have read your letters of yesterday all over since I finished. Mr. Kincaid just put a note in front of me; "Did you ever observe a person's facial expression while reading a letter?"!!!

I had quite a conversation with Mr. Patterson, physics and aircraft instructor, after I finished a test Tuesday. He directed the band at Sweetwater H.S. before this. He graduated from Simpson and lived at Coon Rapids and knew Mountains there? Who are they? He wants me to play on the radio, so would you please send a pack of my music, if you have time? It will be a job, I'm sorry. It is hard to tell you what to send so—how about all the music on the bottom shelf and any that might be on the rack. See if the B [Bach] is on the bottom shelf. It may be on the top. Take out all the orchestration manuscript inside the cover. Title's "Serenades" (in a blue cover) maybe on the top.

My flying was better today. I did 3 landings dual and 3 landings solo. They were crosswind, too. We ride over to the field in a bus and back. But the girls who fly 1st period get to fly over. Mr. Rowe came back solo both days and zoomed the bus and did acrobatics to thrill us all. Mr. Nesper did, too. The instructors asked me this morning if this was my 4th or 5th jump. It seems that I did it very professionally. (See later in this letter for more about this "jump.")

How is your poison oak, Daddy? It must be miserable stuff. Oh, in answer to your question, we used 11 coupons coming down—44 gallons and we did have to use them in Oklahoma and Texas.

It would be nice if something would work out with Dale Wicks. It sounds like a good idea.

Well, it is time for the next class—aircraft.

Bye, love,
Marie

P.S. Mr. Patterson takes just a little bit of credit for my jump because we had a movie on use of parachutes just a few days before.

He told Mr. Kincaid just now that I got 100% in that test.

Me

We fly almost an hour each day. Will increase soon as soon as our first 3 supervised solos are over.

Letter 10
EMM
Sweetwater, Texas

August 23, 1943
Monday Evening

Please sit down before you read!

Dear Mother and Daddy:
You have a famous daughter now as far as Avenger Field is concerned. She is a member of the Caterpillar Club—very exclusive. The only way in is to make an emergency parachute jump.

I was thrown out of the plane today on a bad spin recovery. I am certainly not proud of the spin, but I am proud of the jump. It happened so quickly that there was no time to do anything except the right things very calmly. I was trying to recover from the spin and suddenly I wasn't sitting on anything, so I looked at the ripcord and pulled it and started floating through space. The white silk looked so beautiful against the blue sky, and the skies down here are really blue. I remembered to stop the oscillations by pulling the proper shrouds and that kept me busy most of the time. I had no

Myra Stockton, Mr. Curtis C. "Scotty" Scott (an instructor), me, and Mr. Bill Harper, my Primary Training instructor, just before my parachute jump. August 1943.

sensation of falling whatsoever, even before the canopy opened. Then I remembered that you should turn around facing downwind, so I swung my feet to turn. I had often wondered if you could turn that way; I found out. Then suddenly the ground was coming right up to meet me and I fell flat on my tummy. Then I remembered to spill the 'chute so the wind wouldn't pull it and me along the ground. I hit right in the middle of a cotton field. I had lots of company all the way down. All the planes in the air including my own with my instructor circled me all the way down. I picked up my 'chute—I still had the ripcord! —and I get to keep it—and started walking south and one instructor in a circling plane hollered, "Right!" so I turned right to a road. A couple of fellows were working in the field and came to meet me and carried the 'chute the

rest of the way to the road. The fellow's wife came up to the road from the farmhouse and wanted to take me to the field, but a truck from one of the 3 auxiliary fields nearby came and took me to auxiliary No. 2, where my instructor finally came and took me home. He made me fly all the way back which was O.K., because I wasn't scared anyway. The Army always sends fellows right back up after a crash. I was afraid my instructor would scold me, but he just smiled and patted me on the shoulder and told me what a good job I did. They even sent an ambulance and a doctor over from Avenger, but they decided I was O.K. and I flew back. Everyone is so excited and have come in to see the ripcord, which my bay mates have hung from the light cord. It was really just the most marvelous fun, just sitting there in a

CATERPILLAR CLUB

IRVING AIR CHUTE CO., INC.

1670 Jefferson Avenue
BUFFALO 8, N. Y.
January 25, 1944

Marie Mountain, WASPT
44-W-1, A-7
318th AAFFTD
Sweetwater, Texas

Dear Miss Mountain:

Congratulations on your recent emergency parachute jump! It is indeed gratifying to know that parachutes are daily serving their purpose and proving their worth.

We are pleased to inform you that your experience entitles you to membership in the Caterpillar Club, and we are accordingly enrolling your name on the roster of the Club.

The Irving Air Chute Company has sponsored this Club since its inception twenty years ago, and it is our endeavor to maintain our records as complete and authentic as possible. You may be interested in knowing that there are thousands of members enrolled in this Club, which lists persons from all over the world. The war, of course, has greatly increased the membership rolls which now include personnel in training in the States, and those who used their parachutes in combat areas, as well as hundreds of pilots and their crews who have baled out over enemy territory and subsequently been taken prisoners of war.

In connection with our records, therefore, we would appreciate receiving additional information relative to the incident, which may be submitted in the form of a newspaper clipping or an affidavit of a witness, together with a short personal account giving particularly your reactions and impressions of the jump.

It is also our custom to present to each new member the official insignia of the Club, engraved with his name and the date of his emergency jump. We are having your pin made and engraved, and shall forward it to you when completed, together with the membership card of the Club.

We await further word from you with interest and welcome you into the Caterpillar Club.

Very truly yours,

IRVING AIR CHUTE CO., INC.

G. C. Krull

GK

The January 25, 1944 letter to me from the Irving Co. informing me of my membership in the Caterpillar Club.

cushioned seat hanging in midair. I picked some cotton for a souvenir. Are you still there and sitting up straight?

Love,

Marie

[Note in my father's handwriting: "She fell out 3000 ft. high."]

Diary

Fell out of a plane today and landed safely by parachute in a cotton field. Worried all the way down about an impending scolding by Mr. Rowe and about being washed out. My instructor simply patted me on the shoulder and smiled. I remembered to pull the ripcord!—and stop oscillations and to face downwind. The silk canopy was beautiful against the blue, blue Texas sky. Flew back to the field from auxiliary No. 3 where I had been taken by truck by Mr. Harper.

Comment

It was a tradition in the Army Air Corps that you could keep the ripcord if you still

My classmate, Dolores Muerer, and me by the "wishing well," resplendent in our "zoot-suits" and "turbans." August 1943.

had it in your hand when you landed after parachuting from an airplane. I still have mine. It has been hanging from a lamp in our house since 1945.

Comment

It has been the policy of the Irving Air Chute Co., the maker of the parachute I used at Sweetwater, to enroll each person who completes an emergency parachute jump in the Caterpillar Club. The letter to me from the company, dated January 25, 1944, announcing my membership in the club is included here. The membership card and pin were never sent, probably owing to the normal amount of confusion that prevails in wartime. In 1992, my husband John, as a birthday surprise for me, wrote to the Irving Air Chute Co., reminding them of their 1944 promise. Both the pin—a small caterpillar with a red dot for

an eye—and the membership card were sent promptly. I wear the pin above the right breast pocket on my WASP uniform. The caterpillar symbol is a carryover from the days when parachutes were made from silk. During World War II, our parachutes were made of nylon.

Diary

August 24, 1943

Did a pretty good job today. Mr. Rowe did a spin because I couldn't with a slightly sore right arm. He is doing everything to keep me from losing my nerve. It isn't necessary though.

Diary

August 25, 1943

Soloed today! At exactly 8 hours at aux. no. 3. Made 3 landings—not bad.

Comment

It was a tradition that when a flight student soloed, she was tossed into the "wishing well" by her classmates. I have no recollection of ever being tossed into the "wishing well" when I first soloed.

Letter 11
EMM
Sweetwater, Texas

August 26, 1943
Thursday, 8:40 AM

Dear Mother and Daddy:
We are at auxiliary field no. 2 where they

brought us to practice landings and solo. We came over yesterday first. I practiced 3 landings yesterday dual and then soloed at exactly 8 hours. A number soloed yesterday and several more today. Jean Sidwell just came down from her first solo. Mr. Rowe soloed all 4 of us students yesterday. I made 3 landings on the solo. I shall solo some more this morning at 9:30.

Mr. Rowe is going to show me this morning where I

My class marching around the "wishing well" on our way to ground school. August 1943.

landed by parachute. It's just south of this field. He has been wonderful trying everything to keep me from losing my nerve— (as if it were necessary!). I flew back to the field Monday as I have already told you. Tuesday, in spite of my slightly lame right arm (from landing), he had me do one stall and one spin (he really did it because my arm wouldn't stretch that far). He took me up Tuesday just as soon as the hospital had checked up on me, so I wouldn't have to think about it, I guess. It seems that the last girl who jumped lost her nerve for quite a while, so they took all kinds of precautions with me. Mr. Rowe said he was scared to death. He saw my 'chute streaming out when it started to open and he was afraid I had torn it. The kids said he was nervous and excited when he went back to the field. I proved to them that I didn't lose my nerve though. I did a swell job of flying Tuesday.

Yesterday, I made the official report to Mr. Elmer Riley, flight director, and he was just like a father. He sat down and tried to analyze what was wrong with my spin. He explained just what was wrong with it. And I expected to be washed out! The rumor is floating around the field that I was. But here I am.

I learned two things in that jump. Always check the safety belt before each maneuver—and that I can depend upon myself to think with an absolutely cool mind in an emergency. Mr. Riley said he was glad to have the excuse to jump on everyone to check safety belts. That is now the main cry of all instructors to their students.

I would like to have the Kodak for a little while, if I may, so I can send you some pictures. Have you found some film? I hope.

Yes, I got the addresses and laundry tape too. You may keep the shorts too. After this

A typical student flight group: Mr. H. F. Fuchs, instructor, with his primary students. Standing L-R: Jane Robbins, Mr. Fuchs, Jo Keating, and Wanda Mustain; kneeling L-R: Phyllis Ryder and Mary Rosholt. August 1943.

week we wear nothing but official uniforms except on weekends. I still would love to have the blue polka dot when you have time.

Hope you let Aunt Maple and Uncle Elmer and Eloise and Johnny read these letters because I would like them to know everything, too, but it doesn't sound so fresh to say it twice. It's so nice to hear from you all. I love it here.

Love,
Marie

Diary

August 26, 1943
Second supervised solo.

Comment

A "supervised solo" is a flight in which the pilot flies the airplane alone while the instructor watches intently from beside the runway.

Diary

August 27, 1943
Third supervised solo and last ride with Mr. Rowe. We are very sad. He gave me a swell ride of acrobatics for a good share of the period. It was wonderful.

Diary

August 30, 1943
Mr. Harper is my new instructor! We are all so happy. He doesn't yell.

Comment

One of the tribulations a flight student sometimes has to endure is instructions shouted loudly by an instructor in order to emphasize a point. These are occasionally accompanied by remarks that reflect poorly on the student's intelligence and pedigree.

Letter 12
EMM
Sweetwater, Texas

September 3, 1943
Friday, 11:15 AM

Dear Mother and Daddy:
It rained this morning! Hard! While we were in ground school. So no PT. So I helped Edie, our mail orderly, sort and deliver the mail. I got a letter from you and Ruth Peacock. I am so sorry you have to work so hard. Please, can't you get someone to help? It would be nice if you could sell immediately, then you can come see me and everybody and the field.

It is wonderful here and I love every bit and every minute of it. I feel perfectly free and happy. Everyone is crazy about it, I guess. Everyone is so nice to us.

Yesterday I got a special pass to go to Sweetwater for an osteopathic treatment on my knee. (I strained it in the fall.) I forgot to sign out, so Mrs. Shaw signed out for me. She is our mother—for our class. She drew a picture of her paratrooper to put in her scrapbook. She drew it on a note I had left for her on my desk to find (what's the matter with me?) at daily inspection. The note was an apology to "Mother Shaw" for her having to find some clothes out of place the day before. She is so sweet to me.

Love,
Marie

Diary

September 4, 1943
Barbecue at Double-Heart Ranch. Fun. Church and swimming and riding on Sunday next day.

Letter 13
EMM
Sweetwater, Texas

September 5, 1943
Sunday Evening

Dear Mother and Daddy:
The field was muddy Friday afternoon, so we were on the flight line just a short while—no flying. Then we had open post and we went to town to do our shopping and a new water pump went into the little car.

Saturday morning we were paid. I got $48+. Everything had been deducted when I got it—room and board—gym clothes, a bond, etc. I'll send about $30 for you to keep. You don't have to bother about bonds, because I have signed up for it here.

Saturday afternoon we flew to make up for Friday. I had one period dual and 2 solo periods, but the last solo was cut short because of a thunderstorm. All the little Fifinellas went scampering home like little scared rabbits in the rain. It was fun. That happened when I was flying solo that period Thursday too. We have been flying nearly two weeks from the auxiliary fields. The first students get to fly over and the last students fly back. I have had a new instructor this week—Mr. Harper. Mr. Rowe started teaching BT's this week. That is the next course. I am certainly thankful that I had him at least for 3 weeks. I have never seen a more perfect and precise flyer.

Taps!

September 6, 1943
Good Morning! 7:00

My new one (instructor) is so quick and I am appreciating more and more every day every little thing that Mr. Rowe was so particular about and every bit of hollering he did. I find myself saying to myself all the things he used to say. I hope I don't forget it.

I haven't had a civilian check yet. I asked for one every day last week. Most of the kids have been given one. I shall soon have so many hours they'll expect me to be too good. I have 21 hours and 6 minutes now. Checks started at 12 hours.

Saturday night all of Avenger Field's girls and cadets from Stamford were invited for a rodeo and barbecue and dance to calliope music at a ranch nearby. It was south 5 or 10 miles in the hills we can see south of us. It was a beautiful drive and the ranch was quite a place with bleachers, dance floor (outdoors), and everything. It was fun.

(Flight Line Formation) 11:45 AM

Yesterday I went to M. E. Church (went to the other Christian Church last Sunday,

but I didn't like the preacher). Then we had steaks at Starr's, went for a little ride, and swimming at the pond.

This morning it is too windy and dust makes visibility too bad to fly. We sat on the flight line for a couple of hours then came back to our bays. I have had a nap and read some swell letters from you, Aunt Maple, and Jim. It's cold today and our brown leather jackets were issued.

It was so sweet of Aunt Maple to take time to write to her little niece. She can't know how I loved it. I am so glad they are taking care of you in my absence. Aunt Maple told me how nice the house looks. I shall see it someday. Suzie is a smart little girl to want in the highchair when hungry. Ruth Meyerpeter, one of my bay mates, argues often over whether my niece or her godchild is cuter. It is a draw so far. Well, Aunt Maple, I want to know all about George [Dr. George Mountain, my cousin] and Jean and Mary Lea. I'll bet Mary Lea does crawl right over the fence. Hope Aunt Maple and Uncle Elmer had a very lovely anniversary.

Is Daddy better? I hope you aren't too tired, Mother. Hope Mr. Goforth comes through. We finally got a hold of 1 roll of film Friday. If you aren't using the Kodak I would like to take pictures for you. Can you find film there?

In answer to your questions, we went into the spin at 4,000 feet, and I probably fell out at 3,000 feet. It was 1½ miles south of auxiliary field No. 3, about 6 or 7 miles from the home field. It was a nice long ride down. Plenty of time to do all the necessary things and wonder if my instructor would cuss me and wonder if I would wash out for it. Mr. Harper said this morning that this student of his who fell out solo before we came finally resigned. She couldn't get back her nerve. Her experience was not so pleasant as mine. The plane followed her down (until it passed her) and frightened her. She was in the hospital, too, for several days.

Two girls who were to graduate this Saturday and their instructor, all together in an AT-17, were killed last week. With all the flying done on this field that was only the 4th fatal accident. A girl in my class had an epileptic fit last week and was given a medical discharge. She was quite bitter about it. But it is suicide, and homicide, and hard on government property for her to fly. It is certainly lucky it didn't happen in the air. I'll bet that girl lied to the flight surgeon in her physical.

I seem to be ending this with gruesome news, don't I? Don't let it worry you. It doesn't worry us. It is all in the business.

Eloise sent some swell, swell cookies and did they ever hit the spot! They didn't last very long. Wish I had some right now.

Love,
Marie

Please take good care of you for me.

P.S. Maybe you would like to know my spin recoveries have improved since I fell

out. In fact, Saturday I did some just as slick as a whistle. Wish I could say that about all the rest of my flying.

We are no longer the babies on the field. The new class arrived Saturday.

Bye,
Marie

Diary

September 6, 1943
Swimming on cold day—PT—caught cold.

Letter 14
EMM
Sweetwater, Texas

September 12, 1943
Sunday Evening

Dear Mother and Daddy:
It is just 15 minutes before taps so I shall start a note to you. We are all writing letters in bed (all except Kay who is washing) because they took our chairs out for graduation yesterday and we haven't seen them since.

We have had two new bay mates this week, we thought temporarily, but today they were told to stay. Two of our bays were emptied for the class which arrived a week ago until the class graduated yesterday. The girls in the two bays were divided among other bays. We had seven this week, but Ruth Meyerpeter in our bay was

High jinks in our PT sweat suits. L-R: Carol Wood, Dolores Muerer, Wanda Mustain, me, and Kay Murphy. September 1943.

hour dual and 2 hours solo everyday. It is wonderful. All the time I am flying solo, I work hard to make the best use of the time.

Monday morning, 9:00

It is wonderful to fly and fly so much. One day last week my instructor said if I did some nice chandelles and lazy 8s, we would do other acrobatics. (Secret!) So we did a loop, half roll, slow roll, snap roll, vertical reverse. I got to do all of them but snap roll and vertical reverse, but I followed him through on them. It is certainly funny to try to hold a plane level upside-down. I didn't hold the wings very level, the nose went down a little and I let it turn a bit! Everything looks so funny upside-down. One is just hanging on the belt. I always thought it would be so hard to hold one's feet on the rudder pedals, but you don't even think about it.

Graduation was beautiful. We all marched by squadrons and stood at parade rest during the hour-long ceremony. I carried the flag for our squadron and stood in front two paces behind and two paces to the right of our squadron commander.

We flew Saturday afternoon, and went to town and did our shopping in the evening, then I came home and practiced. Sunday morning I practiced so I couldn't go to

washed out this week, so now we are six. I liked Ruth especially well. 3 girls were washed in our flight Thursday. Seven have washed out in Flight 1 (Madelon's flight).

The insurance man came Wednesday, so now I have life ($3,000) and accident (the kind that pays so much for losing hands, feet, etc.) which covers only <u>flying accidents</u>. It cost $12.35 for half and the same amount in 3 months. I would like you to get a policy from Uncle Elmer right away, because I could have accidents when I am not flying, too.

I have 35 hours of flying now and still no 12 check. I have coaxed for it for 2 weeks, and Mr. Pond, flying commander for our flight, has promised one for tomorrow. It is time now for the 35 hour Army check. I think I really accomplished something in flying last week. We have been flying 1 *church because I played on the field radio program over on KHOH, Sweetwater, Sunday, 1:30 to 2:30. Two carloads went for a picnic to Sweetwater Lake Sunday afternoon and evening. It is large and very beautiful out there in the middle of the hills. It is a dammed up lake.*

This week we fly in the afternoon. Physical training (8:00–9:00) and ground school (9:30–12:00) this morning.

Love,
Marie

The music came Friday. Thanks so much for all the bother.

Diary

September 13, 1943
First civilian check with "Scotty." Passed—35 hours.

Letter 15
EMM
Sweetwater, Texas

September 16, 1943
Thursday morning, 8:30

Dear Mother and Daddy:
We are having no PT this morning—goody goody—so we are all writing letters and stuff. It seems as though I never get around to it. We get off the flight line about 6:30 or 6:45 and eat dinner at 7:00 and I have been practicing every evening when we don't have something else (meetings,

My class lining up for the graduation parade for Class 43-5. I am at the far right. September 1943.

etc.) until 9 o'clock, when we have to be in our bays. We are in bed and lights out at 10. Maybe I should write cards.

I have to play on the radio Sunday again. It does give me something to practice for even if I do gripe as usual about having to play somewhere. We (Flight 2) gave a party last night for Flight 1. Even though we are all 44-W-1, we never see them because our schedules are entirely different, even mess formation. We had stunts by both flights, and sang; then our ping pong champion, Ann Noggle, challenged anyone in Flight 1 and she beat them. In fact, Flight 2 won all the games, and were they ever bad! We had cakes and doughnuts for refreshment.

I finally had a civilian check ride Monday and passed! Aren't you surprised.

Mr. John "Johnny" Tucker, instructor in Basic and Advanced flying and Erwin "Doc" Ives, instructor and Basic Training Flight Commander. Both were from Fairfield, Iowa. September 1943.

The Army check pilot will get me just any day now. Then there is just one civilian check left before we finish PTs. We have just 2½ weeks left on PTs. I think my flying is going swell. I do lots of things wrong, of course, but I am eventually getting each new maneuver O.K. Yesterday I did some swell lazy 8s. The chandelles were O.K. except that I went too fast from one chandelle to the other. My instructor said so, so I won't do that anymore. The ship settles too fast, if you do, because it hasn't a chance to pick up airspeed between. My instructor tells me just what is wrong with each thing and I fix it—sometimes. Some

things naturally take practice to correct. I get so amused when we fly in the afternoons. The bumpy air tosses the ship around so that I laugh out loud to myself. When Mr. Harper is with me I still am laughing to myself because he can't hear me anyway. Instructors can talk to us through the gosports, but we can't talk to them unless we throttle back and shout. Even then they usually can't hear. One of the new girls in our bay resigned yesterday. She surely couldn't have been very serious about this all in the first place. There are just 5 of us again—4 old ones and 1 new.

I think I shall call you someday unless you call me first.

Love,
Marie

Letter 16
ℰℳℳ
Sweetwater, Texas

September 16, 1943
Thursday evening

Dear Mother and Daddy:
You must hear the news. I am really sitting on top of the world. I passed my Army progress check ride today! I sneaked around back of the truck to avoid the Army check pilots third period to go to my plane for a solo period, but our dispatcher nabbed me and sent me right up with Lieutenant Blackburn. It certainly was the

nicest way to go. No chance to worry (just like my jump). It was a very short check— 28 minutes. Some things were very good and some weren't so hot. Everyone is scared to death of Army check pilots because they are washing them out right and left in our class—mostly Flight 1. 3 more were washed out in Flight 1 today...I passed! Isn't it wonderful?

This was really my day. My instructor told me at the end of 1st period that I was really on the ball today. It was the best ride I had ever given him.

Taps!

Good morning! I don't know what I was going on to say last night. Probably wasn't important. I practiced flute last night from 8 to 9, and it sounded good. Tone was better and it was such a thrill. Did I tell you about the good accompanist Mr. Patterson found for me—Mr. Morrison, meteorology instructor here. He played for me last Sunday without practice. He is very fine. He knows Glenn Morning when they were both at Emerson Conservatory. 3 of the ground instructors were formerly band directors, Mr. Patterson, Mr. Gilligan, and Mr. Smith, whom I don't know. Mr. Gilligan is our navigation instructor now.

It is getting very cloudy now. Hope the weather doesn't get too bad to fly.

Will you please call Jim's mother and find out his address? I threw away the letter with his Pennsylvania address on it. She may have a more recent address now.

Pretty please. Ground school formation! Bye!

Load of Love,
Marie

Diary

September 16, 1943
Did first acrobatics—Army check ride— caught on spur of moment—thank goodness—passed—Lt. Blackburn.

Diary

September 17, 1943
Last civilian check with "Scotty." He said, "What I like about your flying is that you are always master of the plane!" Nice? Mr. Harper said, "That's right."

Letter 17
EMM
Sweetwater, Texas

September 20, 1943
Monday, 2:10 PM

Dear Mother and Daddy:
I just read Mother's nice letter with all the swell news. I am glad you are taking your time about the selling. I was afraid you were so tired that you would rush into it. You might as well have your price. But I wouldn't be sorry if you could make some arrangement without selling. I am glad Roy [Squires, the herdsman] *came to see you. It will be nice for all of you. Whenever*

it is convenient, please send Eloise's letters. I haven't written to her since she sent the cookies (isn't that awful) but I just haven't had time for writing, but I hope she and Johnny see my few letters to you.

The broadcast Sunday went better; in fact; the whole program was better planned and prepared. Tomorrow night we go to Roscoe, a little town under our practice area, to give a program.

Saturday I practiced in the morning for over an hour; then I helped the kids with just the finishing touches of cleaning the bay for formal inspection at 10:00; then we went to class at 10:00; then to Sweetwater at 11:00 to practice with Mr. Morrison; then lunch and flight line at 1:00. That must be the third straight Saturday of flying (goody, goody).

Saturday night we marched in a bond sale program at 7:30 in Sweetwater. Then I picked up the tire that had to be vulcanized and did just a bit of shopping and went home and practiced as long as my tired old bones could stand it.

PT formation. Bye.

8:30 PM

In ground school I found the letter that I wrote last Friday morning in my notebook. I am sorry.

Let's see, where was I? Oh, yes. Sunday morning we slept until 9:30, then ate breakfast and practiced an hour and ate dinner and went to practice at Mr. Morrison's at 12:30 and to the radio station at 1:00 and on the air from 1:30 to 2:30. Then we went home and did things in the bay, including finally looking at the magazines you sent, then to Starr's for steak and home and laundering shirts, etc.

I talked Carol Wood, my new bay mate, into singing on the radio program. She has a luscious soprano voice that just rolls out in rich, rich velvet. It sounds beautiful in the shower, I thought, so I made her very much disgusted by talking her into it. She says "never again." She is really very, very sweet.

What I am really writing for is to tell you about the last check, which was civilian, which took place last Friday. Yes, I passed. Wasn't that nice to get all checks out of the way in one week with still 15 hours to go. 4 hours are to be spent on cross-country. Outside of those 4, there is nothing to do but acrobatics! Isn't it wonderful? I have been doing acrobatics and acrobatics. I am very lucky because not many of the girls will have much time in acrobatics after their checks are finished. But here is the nicest thing of all. It is the compliment of "Scotty," my civilian check pilot. "The thing I like about your flying is that you are always master of the ship," he says with a charming little smile. He looks just like Johnny [John Wright, my brother-in-law] and we are crazy about him. But he is certainly particular and exacting. That was the nicest thing he could have said. When I told Mr. Harper, he said, "That's right."

It seems that we graduate in February, so don't expect me until then.

I didn't send the $30, because I need it.

Expenses do seem to come up with a car and insurance and stuff. I'd like to keep what I have for the weekend between Primary Training and Basic Training. We shall probably have a couple of days and we would like to go to Carlsbad.

Hope I get some money to you for my bills. I didn't really look at the bond. Was there any filling out to do? The address should be my Sweetwater address, so Sweetwater can get credit for it.

Must wash my hair. Flute practice will just have to go for tonight.

Loads and loads,
Marie

Letter 18
EMM
Sweetwater, Texas

September 22, 1943
Wednesday evening

Dear Mother and Daddy:
How are you? Still working hard? Please rest as much as you possibly can. Is Roy [Squires] still there? If he is, tell him hello for me. And give him my congratulations on being a grandfather.

Eloise sent the sweetest letter yesterday. I am so glad she wrote even though I am not very reciprocating. She said I could write the answers to her questions to you, but I shall answer her letter directly before she knows it.

Today I finished up flying time on PTs—except 5 hours of cross-country—with 2 hours of dual on half rolls, slow rolls, snap rolls, loops, 4 leaf clovers (4 loops, one in each direction), Immelmans, etc. We did lazy 8s with a snap roll at each end. Some fun! I am up first for dual cross-country tomorrow morning. Mr. Harper and I arranged it that way so that I could go solo cross-country right after, while he takes Edie Keene on dual, and we are going to fly in formation. Edie is a very fine student and Mr. Harper said she would be a good one for formation flying.

Mr. Patterson has received a navy commission of lieutenant (j.e.) as a radar officer. Isn't that wonderful? He has a master's with a math major.

We gave our program at Roscoe last night and it seemed to go very nicely. I played "Souvenir" and "Flight of the Bumblebee." I followed a blues singer, and my playing went over with more enthusiasm than her singing and the other popular numbers which had preceded her. I was so happy because it is hard to fill such a spot—classical after popular. But then, the "Bee" always gets them, doesn't it? Besides the girls from the field, were Mr. Morrison, who played a solo besides accompanying Mrs. Urban and me, Major Urban, our commanding officer, Mrs. Urban, and Lieutenant LaRue, who sang as well as being master of ceremonies, sort of. Everyone on the field is nuts about him. He is PT officer (physical training).

Tell Aunt Maple and Uncle Elmer "hello" and tell Aunt Maple I still love her letters and I shall write to her someday. Goodnight and sweet dreams!

Just your loving daughter,
Me

Comment

Edith "Edie" Clayton Keene, a member of my class, 44-1, and in my flight, was killed in the crash of an AT-6 on April 25, 1944, near Mission, Texas.

Edie was one of thirty-eight WASPs who lost their lives in training or on active duty.

Diary

September 23, 1943

Went cross-country to Harpersville with Mr. Harper today. I did a good job, I thought, and so did Mr. Harper think so. Had loads of fun illegally on the way home. (Acrobatics and low level flying, i.e., "buzzing.")

Diary

September 24, 1943

Went to Harpersville solo—first there— right on the nose. Kay Murphy, Wanda Mustain, and I came back together playing follow the leader and flying in formation. It was wonderful. We would like to go x-c everyday.

Comment

"Harpersville" was an odd shaped piece of Texas farmland that made a good destination for navigational training flights, as it required the student to maintain her alertness in identifying her position throughout the flight.

Letter 19
EMM
Sweetwater, Texas

September 27, 1943
Monday afternoon

Dear Mother and Daddy:

We had a nice rain yesterday all day and it is misty today so the ceiling is practically zero and the visibility also, and the field is gooey, so our wings are temporarily clipped. All we have today is 2 ½ of ground school (this morning). We would love the vacation, but we are afraid that the class will not be through flying PTs so we can have the weekend off. So many plans are in the air. Of course, you know we are planning on going to Carlsbad. But it looks a little doubtful now. Some of us are about through, but no one can leave, if everyone is not finished. It is quite cool and we have our gas heater going.

Last Thursday we did our dual cross-country to Harpersville, about 100 miles east, and Friday we went solo. The field is a little meadow in the middle of nowhere, no town, nothing. The only noticeable thing is its particular shape, as I have drawn in.[Sketch not included here.] I hit it right on the nose and spotted it while still several miles away. Mr. Harper and I were the first ones to arrive. On the way home he let me do anything I wanted. We hedge-hopped and buzzed cotton pickers and houses, etc., wound our way through passes between hills, and then went up higher and did acrobatics. In spite of all the play, I stayed right on the course, much to his surprise. For the first time in my life I flew by compass because most of the way there were few landmarks—just wastelands. But it was so pretty from up high. The land looks like marble with different colors winding around. In spots there are thick patches of mesquite.

On Friday when some of us went solo, the visibility was only about 4 miles, but it was enough to see our way. Landmarks were confined to immediate vicinity. Cross-country would have been more fun if we could have seen clear to the horizon many, many miles away. Of course, Thursday and Friday were the worst ones we have had here for visibility. We played on the way back Friday, too. Mr. Harper warned us about flying low over mesquite, but said it was O.K. otherwise. I led the procession of 17 kids over, because I was first off the field here. On the way back, Wanda Mustain and Kay Murphy, two bay mates, and I played follow the leader. We had so much fun we would like to go every day! Of course, this is not to be published. It is all very illegal—two feet off the ground and acrobatics 1000 feet! Two girls got lost and never did find Harpersville and on the way back 3 girls were lost. But they all got back safely. They just weren't tending to business. In spite of play, I kept my eye on instruments too. It took 1 hour each way.

We had formal inspection Saturday morning—the third since we came. We are supposed to have one every Saturday. Saturday afternoon we wrote letters and Saturday evening we had a picnic at the city park. It was misty but we stayed dry under trees. We bought steak sandwiches and potato salad and cakes at Starr's and apples and cupcakes at the grocery store and paper spoons at the ten cent store. Then Wanda and Kay and I went to a good show while Carol and Dolores and Ruth (the one who washed) went to a drinking party. Then we went to the Avengerettes Club for a little while and went home.

Sunday, Wanda and I went to the Presbyterian Church where Major and Mrs. Urban attend. Mrs. Urban sang a solo and I nearly cried it was so pretty. Lieutenant LaRue sings in the choir too. Wanda and I slept the whole afternoon and everyone else was gone somewhere. In the evening we were all at home reading and studying and I ironed shirts.

June Braun writes often asking questions which I am glad to answer, because I know how she wonders. It is hard to tell her what clothes to bring, for we are to have uniforms within two months—they think. Even now clothing regulations change occasionally. It was nice of her to call. Have you heard from Helene?

No, I haven't gained weight. It stays just the same. We are now required to be weighed at the hospital once a week, because it seems that some girls are gaining unnecessarily. Most seem very slender to me.

The insurance covers accidents even on the ground provided they are concerned with authorized aircraft. It concerns also airline accidents. I shall send the policy when it arrives and Uncle Elmer can tell just what it is then. It is so nice of Uncle Elmer to take such interest in my insurance affairs. I would love to hear from Aunt Maple again. Please tell me all about her and Uncle Elmer and George and Jean and Mary Lea and tell them "Hi" for me. It seems that hospital expense is taken care of here.

We are to be in the Army any time, but we haven't much information about it yet.

Yes, please send my magazines when it is convenient. I just drool over the clothes in Mademoiselle. We love to dress up in our clothes on weekends at least.

Eloise sent some more wonderful cookies today. We got them between code class and navigation class at ground school. I opened the package and the odor tantalized the whole class just before lunch

My original bay mates. L-R: Kay Murphy, Ruth Meyerpeter, Dolores Meurer, Wanda Mustain, and me. Ruth and Wanda did not finish. August 1943.

Mail call was always a happy event. Three of my classmates in their zoot-suits and turbans reading their letters. Anne Noggle is in the center. September 1943.

while Mr. Gilligan talked about converting arc to time and mean civil time and sunset charts! My bay mates drooled and looked wide-eyed because they knew they would get some too. Where did Eloise get the chocolate for the tollhouse cookies? Gee, they are wonderful, but they are half gone already. Everyone thinks I have a pretty swell sis.

I read Mother's swell letters during navigation too. You tell so many interesting things, Mother. Always just the things I want to hear. It sounds as though you have a new [hired] man, though you didn't come right out and say so. I am very glad and hope you can get rested now.

How about coming to see me? One girl's mother is here to spend a week. She stays in town, of course. I would like nothing better than to have you both pop in.

I am glad you sent Eloise's letters because she doesn't write too often (neither do I!).

Mr. Wilfred Hottman, my BT-13 instructor. October 1943.

I am standing next to the left wing of the Vultee BT-13, our Basic Trainer. October 1943.

Me at the tail of a BT-13. October 1943.

Everyone is asleep so I shall take advantage of the opportunity and snooze too. Bye.

Lots of love from your flying daughter,
Marie

Oh, may I see the article? What on earth did I say in it?

Comments

June Braun (Bent), from Des Moines, was a member of WASP Class 44-3. She contacted my parents asking questions about the WASP before she went to Sweetwater. Uncle Elmer was the president of an insurance company in Des Moines and gave me advice on insurance policies.

Diary

September 28, 1943

Finished up 55 hours and 17 minutes of PT today by sitting in the backseat and giving Mr. Harper a lesson. Went up above fleecy clouds—9,500 feet indicated. Beautiful. Ground looked like bottom of the ocean under the white-cap clouds. Gave Mr. Harper a pink slip!

Diary

October 2, 1943

We were finally given the open post for the weekend at noon today. We drive to San Angelo through rain and beautiful barren rough country.

Diary

October 3, 1943

Had a nice good sleep on Beauty Rest mattresses and breakfast in bed. Dinner at Cogburn's. A look at the basic school and back to Sweetwater at 6:30. Had a swell time with Wanda and Kay. Met June Braun at Blue Bonnet.

Diary

October 4, 1943

Report to BT flight line! Mr. Hottman will be a wonderful instructor. Either do or die with him, I am sure. Doc Ives is our flight commander.

Diary

October 5, 1943

First ride in a BT! I love it.

Letter 20
EMM
Sweetwater, Texas

October 10, 1943
Sunday afternoon

Dear Mother and Daddy:

This is the end of our first week on BTs (basic trainers) which is the second of the 3 phases in our training—primary, basic, and advanced—and, boy, if I ever thought I was a hot pilot it is certainly being taken out of me now! I am perfectly terrible. But I remember I felt that way at the first of PTs too. So that is keeping up my poor bedrag-

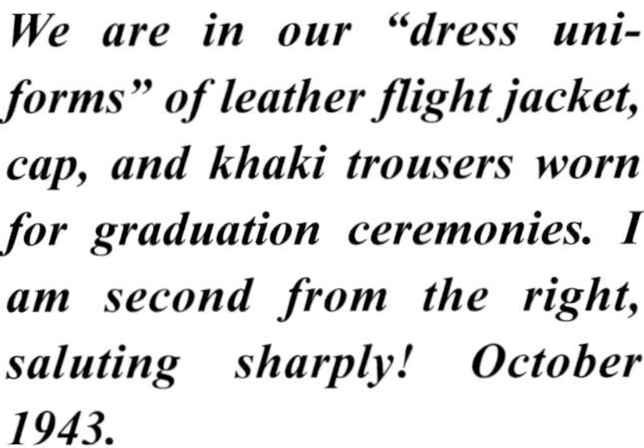

We are in our "dress uniforms" of leather flight jacket, cap, and khaki trousers worn for graduation ceremonies. I am second from the right, saluting sharply! October 1943.

Mr. Harper and four of his PT students at the graduation of class 44-W-6. L-R: Me, Wanda Mustain, Mr. Harper, Edie Keene, and Kay Murphy. October 1943.

gled hopes. But, oh, I love BTs. Gee, they are wonderful. If I could only fly them! We flew this morning and Madelon's flight flew this afternoon. I had my first instruction in a link trainer this morning—1 hour and 15 minutes. Those are the cockpits that sit on a bellows and you fly them (on the ground) by instruments. You are all closed in with a hood over the cockpit. It is supposed to simulate instrument flying. It was certainly fun.

Yesterday was another graduation. This class was 43-W-6 [1943-women-6th class to graduate in 1943]. There are just two more classes, 43-W-7 and 43-W-8, before our class! We just got here and already we are the middle class. *We get so thrilled at each graduation, to think of the training we are all getting. I nearly burst with pride. It is a very great honor to graduate.*

My new instructor is perfectly wonderful. He hollers at me; then at just the right moment when I am beginning to tense up or try too hard he eases the situation by saying, "It will take lots of time and practice. You're not supposed to do it perfectly now," or something just as appropriate. He seems to know just what I am feeling or thinking. It is uncanny. He knows just what to do about it, too. We shall either be wonderful pilots when he is through with us or we shall have to get out. In this class which

In front of a BT-13. L-R: Rosie Lewis, Myra Stockton, me, and Mr. Wilfred Hottman, our BT instructor. Edie Keene is in the cockpit. October 1943.

just graduated, one of the girls he had in basic received special assignment. The best students are given special assignment when they graduate which is one of several things—most of them still military secrets. The student is to fly B-26s, which are much, much larger than most girls are flying.

We feel very, very lucky to have Mr. [Wilfred] Hottman. He used to be a grade school principal. The other girls don't know that. We have been lucky with instructors all the way through. There are all kinds here.

Last evening Wanda and Carol and I went for a drive south through the hills over some different, strange, unmarked roads. It is beautiful and there are some colored leaves in a few places on the low shrubby growth. The trees must be beautiful at home. We came back before dark so

we wouldn't get lost. Then we had sandwiches at Starr's and bought some film at the drugstore and had to be in at 9:45 since we flew today. Yesterday at graduation when we were all standing at parade rest on the ramp in front of hangar No. 1, Jacqueline Cochran mentioned hedgehopping and how she hoped we would never, never! Mr. Harper looked at us kids from the audience and laughed. There isn't a girl here who hasn't hedgehopped some time; of course, we are usually working too hard to play.

The pictures we took still aren't back from Willis! We shall take some of the BTs now for you. They have somewhere between 400 and 440 H.P.—Wright Whirlwind engine and a two-position propeller.

You both write such swell, newsy letters. It sounds as though you are busy and having loads of fun. I am glad you are taking care of your appearance, Mother. Your clothes and hair worried me. Tell me all about the new clothes. Is the permanent nice?

I am glad some arrangement was made for the milk business. It should be good now with all the shortages of milk.

You made a swell master of ceremonies, I know, Daddy, because you always do make such a swell one. Bye.

Love,
Marie

My BT flight in front of the BT-13. L-R: Myra Stockton, Rosie Lewis, Edie Keene, and me. October 1943.

October 10, 1943
Sunday evening

Here I am again. I haven't been off the post today and tonight I practiced 2 hours in our bay. It was swell. The kids are so sweet. They insist that I practice and that they would love to hear it. I try not to wear out the welcome so I seldom practice here and never when there are more than 1 or 2 here.

Would you mind sending some things? My hands freeze when we fly in the mornings. Those brown wool-lined gloves are in the top drawer of my chest. I'd like my beige suit, that brown hat with the veil and the two green ribbons on top, the better pair of brown tie shoes, the beige pigskin gloves in the buffet drawer. I could use sweaters too—that purple thing—it can be washed but don't stretch it except in the sleeves, and that navy one that buttons up

the front (send it to the cleaners if it needs it)—also the blue silk blouse—pretty please! Do you think my phonograph and records could be shipped to me? I'd just die for good music. Some of the girls want so much to hear those things. This is a lot of trouble, I know. But I would love to have them. This is the psychological time to say that you are a very sweet family, isn't it. But you really are. You may keep all those cheap popular records at home. Can you tell which ones they are? They are all 10-inch records.

Almost time for taps! Sleep tight and sweet dreams!

Oodles of love,
Me

Comment

As is evident, my loving parents were very cooperative and helpful in meeting my every need! All the clothing and personal items were sent to me promptly.

October 11, 1943
Monday morning
[This note was slipped into the envelope with my October 10 letter.]

Good morning! Literature from Aetna Life Insurance Company came—upon Uncle Elmer's suggestion, they say—which seems to be accident insurance. Ask Uncle Elmer if the government policy, which we shall have eventually, is <u>disability</u> also, please. I would like to know just what government insurance does cover. Perhaps it doesn't cover disability and is the reason he had this sent.

We got out of PT this morning to get winter flying suits. Then we were informed that there weren't enough to go around, so here we are with some free time! There is no flying this morning. The ceiling and visibility were practically 0. Hope it clears up for our flying this afternoon.

Bye,
Me

Diary

October 12, 1943
Finally! Have the feel of a BT. It took about 5 hours to do it. After a successful dual period, took a pre-solo check from Mr. Ives and flew better than I ever had on a BT. It is a wonderful feeling.

Letter 21
EMM
Sweetwater, Texas

October 14, 1943
Thursday morning

Dear Mother and Daddy:
We just came from PT and it will soon be time for lunch. We were all very sore Fifinellas from yesterday's strenuous PT exercises, so when we bent over to touch our toes, there was a groan on each bend—an unanimous groan which might remind you of booming waves of Lake Superior! The drill corporal, after a while, said that we would keep up the exercises until we were all comfortable. The groans ceased, needless to say.

Several important things happened Tuesday. First of all we got our winter flying suits, so we all tried them on and took pictures. We have leather fur-lined jackets, leather fleece-lined trousers (with 7 zippers in them!), and heavy fleece-lined boots. We looked just as though we belonged with Admiral Byrd.

The same day I was excused from code class permanently—the first in the class to be excused. As soon as we can take 8 words a minute (both letters and numbers) for 2 minutes perfectly, they haven't room for us any longer. I have been taking it at that speed right along, but we just finished up the rest of the numbers. Madelon did the same thing the same day—the first in her class too.

Also Tuesday I took a pre-solo check on BTs. Passed it, too! Doc [Erwin E.] Ives from Ottumwa, our flight commander, gave it to me (we have 3 check pilots for our flight class). In the last two afternoons he has given 9 checks (pre-solo) and had flunked 4, so I feel very lucky. Tuesday happened to be the first day I really had the feel of a BT. In the dual period it had suddenly improved and in the check immediately following, I flew even better. I even felt very sure of myself. Along with the flight test, we had a blindfold cockpit test on all the gadgets and instruments. Not only do we have to accustom ourselves to flying a 2 ¼ ton plane but we have so many controls to learn to use. Besides several new instruments to watch. We have a propeller pitch control, a self starter to learn to use, a radio to use (all BTs and ATs are controlled by the control tower by radio). We wear earphones constantly and talk into a microphone. The radio can be switched to interphone so that the instructor and students can talk back and forth.

It is very amusing to hear another student give her whole cockpit procedure on

I am modeling the fleece-lined flight jacket, trousers, and boots to keep us warm in the cold Texas skies. October 1943.

the radio and then hear the control tower, when she has finished her lengthy spiel, say, "Say your cockpit procedure on interphone, please!" I called the tower 4 times one day and wondered why they didn't answer. It was turned on interphone! Thank goodness, I haven't talked to my instructor on radio—yet! It would be embarrassing to have all the other planes and the tower hear you. In another hour, I should solo. That big event happens after 8 hours of dual. I have 7 hours and 10 minutes so far. It is so wonderful—especially since I've learned to lead with rudder and follow with stick in the turns. My instructor must be one of the best on the field. He hollers and cusses and scolds constantly in the air, but somehow he leaves me determined to lick the old BT. He has the repu-

tation for turning out good students; perhaps that is how he does it. He certainly keeps one on the ball every second. I am very lucky.

Eloise sent some more luscious chocolate chip cookies. They are gone already. They certainly hit the spot during a long morning or afternoon. Isn't she a sweet little sis? Wish she had time to write a little oftener—but who am I to ask that? It seems like ages since I have heard from you. Are you please resting and taking care of yourselves? How is the new plan working out? How are Aunt Maple and Uncle Elmer and George and Jean and Mary Lea? I would love it if Aunt Maple would write all the cute things Mary Lea does. You can't imagine how I would love to see the two little girls in the family.

Dinner formation! Bye until later.

We're on the flight line now, and it is almost time for me so we shall get this off.

Mornings are very cold but afternoons are quite warm, not quite too warm, but almost in the warm Texas sun.

Please write.
Love,
Me

Girls all around are saying cockpit procedures over and over. 5:15 PM. I just soloed—bye again. Off to Link now.

Comment

As almost an afterthought I told my parents that I had just soloed the BT-13!

With this aircraft we were introduced to the use of radio for communication with the control tower, which regulated all flying traffic at the field. Most students soon learned (to their embarrassment) that whatever they said into the microphone would be broadcast to every other aircraft in the area if the sending control in the cockpit was set on "radio" instead of "intercom."

Diary

October 14, 1943

Soloed today at exactly 8 hours at auxiliary no. 1. Made just one landing—10 minutes.

Diary

October 15, 1943

Soloed 10 minutes again today. Very foolishly took off without flaps.

Diary

October 17, 1943

Wanda and I went to church and in the afternoon took a nice long drive through rough Texas north of Sweetwater.

Diary

October 20, 1943

Didn't get to fly today. Transition was cut to 15 hours and I already had 15:05. Very sad I was.

Letter 22
E.M.M
Sweetwater, Texas

October 21, 1943
Thursday, 9:30 PM

Dear Mother and Daddy:

Things certainly happen fast around here. Our course of training is suddenly changing. Wednesday we planned our cross-country to Mineral Wells for Wednesday. Wednesday morning came and our cross-countries were cancelled and we were to finish 15 hours of BT dual and then what, we didn't know. Well, I already had 15 hours so I didn't get to fly at all Thursday. Rumors floated thick and fast. 25 hours is the usual amount of transition on BTs, then x-country, night flying, and then instrument. Well, this morning we started 35 hours of instrument, then we go next to AT-6s (advanced trainers). Our training program is certainly being shaken up. They don't tell us much yet.

Instrument training is going to be wonderful. We sit in the back cockpit instead of front and pull a hood over us and fly by instruments alone. It is marvelous training. Our instructor sits in the front cockpit as safety pilot.

Tonight we heard that tomorrow we shall all have 15 hour checks. But I believe I can pass it. I heard through very good sources that my pre-solo check was good.

Bob Newman, one of the instructors with Greg at home, came down and passed a check and has been taking instructor's refresher so he can teach here. Today he passed an Army ride so he gets to start teaching tomorrow on PTs. He was very happy today when he told me he passed. He will earn more than $100 a month now. He said Greg was furious when he was told that Bob was down here. But now, after thinking it over, Greg wants Bob to write all the particulars. Greg has never been too much in favor of girls flying. But this is a nice setup here and all the instructors like it.

June [Braun] was over awhile tonight. She soloed today and was feeling very happy. I hadn't seen her for several days.

Thank you so much for sending my clothes and magazines. There will be a bond enclosed. Must get to bed. Goodnight.

All the love in the world,
Marie

Diary
October 21, 1943
Had first instrument ride today. It was fun. Am looking forward to instrument training.

Diary
October 22, 1943
Today we all were given 15 hour checks. Mine from Mr. Ives. Didn't do such a hot job. But I passed!

Many Us [unsatisfactory] and Fs [failure] were given, all of which were to be given E [elimination] rides tomorrow.

Had another civilian check with Doc Ives

and passed. A lot of Us and Fs were given. E rides for them tomorrow. Cleaned tonight for inspection.

Diary

October 23, 1943

Low clouds made it necessary to call off the E rides. Then it was announced that 5 additional hours would be given everyone! Link went much better. Became ill in PM and spent all Saturday evening in bed. Mr. Hottman says my coordination is good. From him!

E rides were called off partly because of weather and because it was decided, through Mr. Ives' interference, that we would all receive 5 more hours transition. Goody, goody!

Letter 23
EMM
Sweetwater, Texas

October 24, 1943
Sunday evening

Dear Mother and Daddy:

This has been such a beautiful Sunday. Wanda and I went to church this morning. This afternoon I went all by myself for a ride listening to the concert from 2:00 to 3:30—New York Philharmonic—on the radio. The music was beautiful, the scenery was beautiful, the day was beautiful, and the car sang. I rode on the side roads and north and east of the field in our BT practice area and I wondered where we find our fields for simulated forced landings.

This week has been quite eventful as far as flying is concerned. The course is being changed and our class happens to be the goat. I told you, didn't I, that transition on

Wanda Mustain on the wing and me in the cockpit of a BT-13. October 1943.

BTs was suddenly cut down and I had the required time and couldn't fly Wednesday. Thursday, I had my first instrument ride. Gee, it was fun.

On Friday we were all checked and I passed, but many flunked. So Saturday was to be elimination checks by the Army of all the girls who flunked Friday. But the weather closed in and the checks were called off and they then decided to give us all 5 more hours transition which made everyone happy. Madelon passed her check ride Friday, too.

Gee, you sound busy. The packages all came and the sweater too. Yes, we all enjoyed the shoetree. That little bit of candy didn't hurt me. No, I don't eat much candy. In fact, I did one day eat a lot of Wanda's chocolates and made myself sick. I have gained 10 pounds. I didn't believe it, but my skirts fasten with difficulty, and the kids say my thighs go together! And my shoulders aren't so bony. Isn't it wonderful? Lieutenant Monserud told me to drink 2 glasses of milk every meal, eat bread and butter, lots of meat and potatoes, drink only one cup of coffee each day, and to quit smoking! [I never smoked in my life!] I gained 3 pounds week before last.

Aunt Clara wrote me this week. It was fun to hear. I am glad you sent all those letters, clippings, and magazines. We have some pictures now. I shall send the copies I have and have more printed for my scrapbook-to-be.

This evening I dug out last March's Reader's Digest *from the rec hall to read* "On Being a Real Person" by Harry Emerson Fosdick. I shall read it now. Bye.

Love and love and love,
Marie

All the pictures I am sending this time were taken by [next to] a PT.

I am so sorry you didn't get to make your trip. You must have been disappointed. You haven't been away for so long.

Diary

October 24, 1943
Wanda and I went to church. Then I went riding by myself through the hills and listened to the [New York] Philharmonic. Nice.

Diary

October 25, 1943
Mr. Hottman was in such good humor today, so I gave him a fairly good ride. It

A roadside picnic with classmates on a trip to San Angelo, Texas, during a break between Basic and Advanced Flight Training. November 1943.

was fun. Did turns in link not too badly. Link is becoming a little more fun. But, gee, flying is wonderful! Took "Hanging Teeth's" test on link tonight. Nearly died laughing at the questions.

Diary

October 26, 1943

Had a general meeting with Mrs. Deaton. She is marvelous in building up morale and allaying fears. The girls hang on every word she says.

Diary

October 27, 1943

Mr. Hottman said today that I have received no pink slips in BTs. Biggest surprise of my life. He is so swell. He practically promised an Army check! Sweet of him, isn't it? Wanda flunked a civilian check today. My favorite, too. I hope more than anything else that she passes the Army tomorrow.

Diary

October 28, 1943

Finished BT transition today with some acrobatics, both solo and dual. Won a bet from Mr. Hottman that I couldn't make a good landing. Really slicked it on. Wanda Mustain flunked her E ride today and so did Jean Sidwell. Jean is the first one from Des Moines to wash. Just 3 of original B-4 [bay] left.

Diary

October 29, 1943

We moved today from B-4 to A-7. And we left for our 2nd weekend off! Went to Carlsbad—driving on borrowed gas tickets—starting at 8:30 PM and arrived there about 1 or 1:30 AM. One can certainly roll off the miles in Texas. Found one double bed for 3. Kay Murphy slept on the lovely soft floor, while Dolores Meurer and I slept in the bed. Selfish, weren't we?

Diary

October 30, 1943

The drive out 25 miles to the caverns was beautiful. Very rough and winding—almost as thrilling as we later found the caverns. The caverns were a fairyland. Now, the memory seems like a fantastic dream. Lovely was the scene in a large room where we all sat up high. Lights were turned out. The room was in complete blackness. Then while "Rock of Ages" was played (recording) lights gradually came on in the far distance and gradually moved toward us until it was again completely lighted. Very thrilling. We ate lunch in the cafeteria in a mammoth stone room deep underground.

In the evening we went to the air base to a party at the officers' club. A hula dance by a major was the highlight. In the orchestra were Bob Bagley, Gordon Bird, and Leland Anderson. Such a surprise! Had a lovely time.

Comment

Bob Bagley was the band and orchestra director at Roosevelt High School in Des Moines and was the dance bandleader at

My instrument instructor, Mr. O. A. Martin and his students. L-R: Harriet Kenyon, Mr. Martin, me, and Myra Stockton. October 1943.

Carlsbad AAB. Gordon Bird was the band director at Drake University, and Leland Anderson, a baritone, was a voice student at Drake when I was there. They were serving in the USAF band on the base.

Diary

October 31, 1943

Slept beautifully in a lovely soft bed until 11:00 or 12 o'clock. Gee, it was wonderful! Jack Dwyer [an officer at the Carlsbad AAB] took us all to dinner at the Crawford Hotel coffee shop. There were beautiful, large trees with yellow leaves lining all the streets. We started home at 4:20 PM and rolled off the miles to Big Spring where we ate dinner and arrived home [Avenger Field] at 9:45. It was a wonderful weekend.

Diary

November 1, 1943

We are glad to be home at Avenger again. All the BTs are grounded because someone elsewhere snapped off a tail, but we met our new instrument instructors. Luck of all luck! I have Martin! I have been so lucky with instructors and this was just too good to be true. The very one I wanted! Instrument will be more fun

Got frisky today and jumped over a box about 12 inches high and sprained the right ankle. Lieutenant Monserud, the surgeon we are crazy about and who used to play the flute, x-rayed it and bandaged it up. The girls made me walk to dinner by myself. It was a little difficult.

Comment

This is the last of my Diary entries. After this date I was probably too tired or too busy, or both, with flying and ground school to continue writing in my diary.

Letter 24
EMM
Sweetwater, Texas

November 2, 1943

Dear Mother and Daddy:

Were you surprised to hear from Carlsbad? It was suddenly announced to our class Thursday night that beginning Friday night we could have the weekend off, since BT transition had been complet-

ed. We had used most of our gas tickets, so we borrowed several from Mr. Hottman and several more from Mr. Ives. It is 250 or 260 miles to Carlsbad. We started about 8:20 PM from Sweetwater and arrived in Carlsbad about 1:00 or 1:30 in the morning. We stopped in Big Spring about 65 miles from here for about 30 minutes. From Big Spring to Carlsbad—about 200 miles—there are only 3 towns and we really rolled off the miles. The roads were straight as arrows. Between Hobbs and Carlsbad—70 miles—we noticed that the gas tank was about empty so we watched and hoped and prayed. We rolled into the first filling station in Carlsbad and filled up. Then the car wouldn't start for a bit! It was that low—down to the last drop. Weren't we lucky? We arrived home Sunday night with practically an empty tank and no more gas tickets until Nov. 21.

To get back to the story, we found one double bed at the Crawford for 3 of us— Kay Murphy, Dolores Meurer, and I. Kay slept on the floor. Saturday morning we drove out to the caverns—35 miles out. The drive was as beautiful as the caverns. The last several miles were a drive up a winding canyon—something like Spearfish Canyon—remember? The caverns were like a fairyland. Now the memory seems like a fantastic dream. But then, you have seen caverns. The temperature was 56° and we ate lunch underground in a mammoth cafeteria. The most thrilling thing was a scene in a mammoth room where we were all seated up high by the rock of ages. The lights were all turned out and in the total blackness a recording of "Rock of Ages" was played. Then the lights about a half mile in the distance were dimly seen and gradually were turned on up toward us until it was completely lighted again. It was the most thrilling beautiful thing.

Saturday night we went to a Halloween dance at the Officers' Club at an airbase just outside of Carlsbad—some fellows, whom some of the other Sweetwater girls knew, invited us. And whom should I see in the front row of the orchestra but Bob Bagley, Roosevelt band director, Gordon Bird, Drake band director, and Leland Anderson, a boy with a beautiful baritone voice who was in Drake when I was. I knew that Bob and Gordy were stationed in New Mexico but I didn't know where. Bob was in D.M. about 3 weeks ago. I talked to them a little while, but, of course, they were busy playing and besides, they were "non-coms." [Non-commissioned officers with whom we were not supposed to fraternize. This made little difference to me, of course.] We had fun at the dance. The highlight was a hula-hula by a major in the appropriate grass skirt and bra-top and kerchief on his head. He was a scream the whole evening.

Saturday night we stayed at the Stevens Motel—tourist cottages. They were lovely and so inexpensive—$4.50 for the 3 of us and 2 double beds. Kay and Dolores went to church—they are Catholics, but I was sleeping too well and we don't often have a chance at soft beds. Lieutenant Dwyer took us to dinner and we started home at 4:20. We arrived home at 9:45 after an hour's stop at Big Spring for a steak. There are trees in Carlsbad! With yellow leaves! They were <u>big</u> trees that meet over the street like Grand Avenue. Cottonwoods, I think.

We were glad to get home and more enthusiastic than ever to get back to flying. It does wonders to one to get away just for a couple of days.

Wanda washed out last Thursday—my favorite. Jean Sidwell washed on Friday. Too bad, but it has to happen to many of us before we leave. 58% of our class is left.

We were to have started on instrument flying training yesterday, but the BTs are all grounded until after inspection because someone snapped a tail off somewhere Saturday in a snap roll. But we met our new instructors. Wonder of wonders! I got Martin. The very one I wanted! Gee, it is just too good to be true. I have been so lucky with instructors and that is half the battle. Mr. Martin was an instructor—refresher instrument instructor—before he took us. Bye. Have to go to Link.

We moved last Friday. We are living in A-7 instead of B-4. The whole class was pushed up in A barracks and 2 bays of B barracks. We are so much smaller. Dolores and I are still together with 4 other girls, but Kay is in A-8. We 3 are the only ones left of the original bay. Carol [Woods] who lived with us for a while is back in alphabetical order now so she is in B-2. So my address is: 44-W-1, A-7318*th* AAFFTD,

Sweetwater, Texas.

Madelon and I are evidently doing alright. We are both still here. That is all any of us can say. I haven't heard how her flying is officially, but I am sure it is O.K. What we will be assigned to heaven only knows. Some special assignments are still military secrets.

We are not in the Army yet. Did you ask Uncle Elmer what kind of insurance we shall receive in the Army, because that will affect what type I would want from Aetna. We were interviewed last week to see if we would become WACs [Women's Army Corps] but everyone said no very emphatically. We want to be in the Air Corps. Time will tell.

I do hope you can make the trip you are planning now. You need a change so much. Just look what one weekend does to us once a month.

Would you call King's for some more of no. 171473 and Wiess (4-7211) for 1 dozen tablets of 56328 and just ask each place to mail them to me right away please. And I would love to have my chenille housecoat. Must go to lunch. Bye.

Lots of love,
Marie

Letter 25
EMM
Sweetwater, Texas

Saturday, November 13, 1943

Dear Mother and Daddy:

I know I have been a very bad girl, but it seems as though there is always something to do. I am so glad you aren't so lax in writing to me. You both write such sweet letters. I liked Daddy's analogy of a symphony and life. I hear the [New York] Philharmonic usually too on Sundays.

Suzie's picture came a few days ago and all the girls think she is so cute. She sits on top of my locker. Dolores always talks about Suzie's fun little teeth. Gee, I would like to squeeze her.

W-7 graduated today and now there is just one class ahead of us. We had the usual ceremonies including the review, in which we all marched on the ramp in front of hangar 1. Our new gym is just about completed, though, and the weather will probably make it necessary to have graduation in there. Our graduation is supposed to be February 12—for those of us who are left! We have completed 14 weeks of training and 13 to go. The last two weeks have been on instruments. This last week we started buddy riding, so every day we have one dual period under the hood, a buddy ride under the hood, and another period as safety pilot while another girl is under the hood. We even take off under the hood (on instruments alone) during the dual period,

but on the buddy rides the safety pilot takes off and lands and watches other airplanes. This is all done in BTs. We pull the hood over us (over the whole rear cockpit) so that we cannot see out and we fly by the gyro compass, artificial horizon, altimeter, airspeed indicator, turn and bank indicator (needle and ball), vertical speed indicator, magnetic compass, tachometer, and clock. Yes, those are all the instruments we have to watch constantly! You look at one instrument and off go the other instruments. Then you check another and the others all go off. You look at the horizon to see the altitude of the plane and the altitude and the airspeed go haywire. You look at the turn and bank and you go into a dive. You try to keep it on the heading by watching the gyro compass and you start climbing. The horizon is the number 1 instrument, but sometimes we cage the horizon and the gyro compass and fly by the so-called rate instruments, needle ball, and airspeed. That is when things go really haywire with no horizon to watch for altitude. When the airspeed goes up and the altimeter goes down the vertical speed indicator shows a descent and you know you are diving. So you pull the nose up and the airspeed goes too low and the altimeter goes way up and the vertical speed shows a climb. You climb and you dive. It certainly simplifies matters to have the artificial horizon to keep the nose on. At the same time you try to keep the wings level by keeping the ball centered (without the horizon) and you have to keep the ship from turning by keeping the needle centered, without that gyro compass. Of course, all that is flying straight and level. We make standard rate turns (3 degrees per second) to certain headings, do descents and climbs, and try to put them all together in certain patterns. We all expect to be in straightjackets when we finish 35 hours of instrument—but we love it. I have the finest instructor on the field. He previously taught two classes of instructors in instruments.

We were all given shots for typhoid, tetanus, and vaccinated for smallpox Tuesday. The smallpox is taken for the first time in my life. In the other classes people fainted like flies and whole classes didn't fly and some didn't even go to ground school, but our flight lost no flying time at all. Madelon's flight all cancelled flying one day but 7 or 8 people. Madelon was one of the 7 or 8.

Did I tell you that Wanda washed two weeks ago? Dolores and I are going to the recording room at the U.S.O. this afternoon to hear good records. We spent 3 evenings this week in another bay listening to wonderful recordings that a girl had borrowed.

Did you ask Uncle Elmer about government insurance?

Love,

Marie

How is Duke?

Comment

"Buddy" riding is a flight in which two student pilots fly together. In our case, we flew the BT. The one in the front cockpit is called the safety pilot while the other in the rear cockpit flies with a hood pulled across the cockpit canopy such that she can see only the instruments. Under these conditions she flies the aircraft only with reference to the flight instruments, as one would do under actual flying in clouds, night, and weather. Flying without reference to the gyro-stabilized instruments is known as using "partial panel"—or flying with input from only "needle-ball-airspeed"—with secondary reference to the altimeter and rate-of-climb instruments. An experienced instrument pilot must have mastery of "partial panel" techniques as well as capability of flying using all the instruments, known as "full panel." Many inexperienced private pilots find themselves in serious difficulty when they lose their reference to the horizon. This can happen when flying at night over an unlighted land mass or toward an open ocean. Without the ability to use at least the "needle-ball-airspeed" instruments, a pilot risks entering what is called the "death spiral," a constantly increasing bank and turn and loss of flight control. This usually ends in a crash. It is likely that this was the cause of the deaths of John F. Kennedy, Jr., his wife, and her sister.

"Duke" is the much-loved family dog.

Letter 26
ЄΜΜ
Sweetwater, Texas

November 16, 1943
Tuesday evening

Dear Mother and Daddy:

We have had another typhoid shot and everyone feels terrible, but we love it still. Our arms are extremely sore and we have fevers and we ache all over and it is so much fun to keep up our usual routine. Like fun! Dolores is very ill in bed. All last night she had chills and her fever has been very high, but she looks a little brighter tonight.

Off to link! Back again! I am doing radio in link now and it is fun. I have been bracketing radio beams by different methods. We were to have started this in the plane today, but the ceiling was too low. We are on one of the Abilene beams here so we shall bracket the right side to Abilene and the other side back again.

Yesterday the sky was pretty well covered with cumulus clouds at 5000 feet. We flew above them going up and down through holes. I couldn't enjoy them under the hood the two periods, but when I was safety pilot it was wonderful. We were at 7000 feet which was just about even with the tops of the highest towers. We floated around among the tufts and I wanted so much to go through one but miraculously Myra, who was in back under the hood, always just happened to turn in time (much to my disappointment). Of course, we are not supposed to go through them. The clouds look like mashed potatoes or white candy floss. I can't wait until I can take you up to see them.

Yes, I was flying the bomber over—the low one with the 4 motors. Didn't you see me wave and shake the wings? I do hope Eloise and Johnny and Suzie get to see you next weekend. Suzie is watching me write a letter to her grandmother and grandfather.

The number in our class is a military secret, but I shall tell you very quietly when I go home. The girls when they wash seem to be fish out of water. It must be a terrible blow. Most seem to travel awhile. Some are still in town. Ruth Meyerpeter is working as a dispatcher on the field and lives in town.

About the insurance—I shall send you this information and let you decide. I want both life and accident and <u>plenty</u> of it and hospital too. Will you take care of it please? I can get the physical here at the hospital for nothing. I think that $5 per concert rent for the piccolo would be right, don't you?

I had planned to send Aunt Maple a picture. Aren't those developments terrible? So scratchy! I am going to send them home after this.

I was glad for the pictures. The hat looks as though it might be kind of cute. I shall put the picture in my mirror frame. How about those pictures of the family that you promised to take?

I haven't had very much time to read Triumphant Living *for a little while, but I liked it so much what I have read. It sort of takes the place of my poppy and mommy since I can't have them. I must make a desperate effort to read it every day.*

I would love my flannel nightgown—the cute one you made, Mother. How about my phonograph and records. I would love to have them. Taps!

Goodnight and loads of love,
Marie

Comment

The "Abilene beam" refers to the arm of the Abilene, Texas radio range that projects toward Sweetwater. When on the arm of the beam, a constant tone is heard in the radio headset. On one side of the beam the tone is a Morse Code "A" and on the other side the tone is an "N." Thus, by listening to the tone it is possible for a pilot to know which side of the beam he is on.

Letter 27
EMM
Sweetwater, Texas

November 25, 1943
Thanksgiving evening, 5:45 PM

Dear Mother and Daddy:

What are you doing today? Are you having turkey and stuffing with Aunt Maple and Uncle Elmer? I'll bet you are. We are having our usual routine today which is just swell with me. But we had a wonderful dinner this noon with turkey and all the fix-ings, dressing, cranberries, mashed potatoes, sweet candied potatoes, peas, asparagus, cabbage and apple salad, pumpkin meringue pie, Vienna bread. It was wonderful.

Tonight we are having a program in our new gymnasium-auditorium, which opened just this week. It is the same program which we put on at the American Legion banquet in their clubhouse out near the park Tuesday night. It was a lovely program. One of the trainees spoke on her experiences of 6 years with her family in China. Her father was General Chiang Kai-Chek's personal pilot. A trio sang several Avenger Field songs. Then a trainee who was in the English ferry command and who had just come here spoke beautifully. Then I played, and then Mrs. Deaton, our chief establishment officer, spoke about the WASPs [us]. Tonight, instead of Mrs. Deaton's talk, the Presbyterian minister is going to talk about something appropriate to Thanksgiving. Mr. Morrison of the ground school staff always plays for me. He is very good. I have spent a lot of time practicing the last week.

The cookies were swell, Mother. The kids all said, "Your mother makes the swellest cookies!" My favorite kinds, too. They really hit the spot between meals. We are out of food now. Dolores expects a promised box of cookies everyday but they haven't come yet. My housecoat came too. Thank you so much.

Why don't you take my phonograph and records and let them pack them somewhere

where records are sold, either Yonkers or Des Moines Music House.

I am having so much fun flying the radio beam under the hood and in the link. It is by far the most interesting part of instruments. I have found a wonderful little link instructor so I ask for him every time. Perhaps I like him because he says I am good. 'Spose? I hit the field right on the nose of the link yesterday. Oh, I must tell you. Yesterday in link the instructor turned on the rough air and it is the craziest feeling. In a real airplane in rough air, the plane is stable and will go back to the original altitude after it has been knocked out of position. But the link is not stable and you fight the controls constantly. I thought someone was playing with it and I lifted the hood to see, but my little instructor said, "Put the hood back down. Haven't you ever flown in rough air?"

Yesterday I had a propeller mechanics lesson. I watched the mechanic take a prop off and he explained everything. I wish we could get some mechanics.

Last Sunday 4 of us girls drove out south of town in the hills and took a lunch. We climbed up on top of one of the hills where we could see a long way and ate and picked mistletoe. We are going to do that again.

Dinner formation! Must go. Bye.

Loads and loads of love,
Marie

Friday morning

It is foggy and drizzly this morning. Our meteorology instructor left us today to go to Randolph Field for more training. We hate to lose him. I have a 99 average in meteorology. I don't know what it is in navigation—somewhere around 98 or 99. Did I tell you that we had to go back to code because the Army set the requirements higher. Miss Howell said I am her star pupil. Our new requirement is 10 words a minute and I am taking it perfectly sometimes at 12 words a minute.

I must tell you about the terrible thing that happened to me last Monday—but it all came out all right. The instructors gave one another's students check rides—and your precious little daughter received a U [unsatisfactory]. It spread around the field like wildfire. And was I miserable! It was terrible. It would go on record and affect my assignment upon graduation and I had let my instructor down worst of all. He had bragged so much about his 3 students. It was certainly an off day and I wasn't proud of the ride, but it wasn't as bad as the check pilot had said. He said I missed the first turn 30° but I didn't miss any more than 5° and we are allowed an error of 10°. Well, I expected to be washed out right away. But Tuesday Mr. Martin said, "Don't worry about it. You won't have to take another check. You just had an off day." Yesterday when I insisted on some basic instrument work instead of radio, he told me that that unsatisfactory was changed to a satisfacto-

ry Tuesday morning and that the check pilot had admitted that I flew better than his own students!

Now I have all my confidence back. It was certainly shot for a few days. The kids thought there might have been some ill feeling between instructors because Mr. Martin doesn't hesitate to let everyone know how good his students are. Mr. Hottman suggested (remember him, my BT instructor—the one just before Mr. Martin on instruments) that that may have been just what I needed since I have been slipping through everything so easily. All my instructors are so swell.

I wonder often just what you think of your wandering daughter's being in flight training. Are you sort of proud or ashamed. Please be proud because it is such an honor to be able to successfully complete the training and the training is the most wonderful there could possibly be. You couldn't buy it for any price. It is the same flight training that cadets receive and our cadet training is the best in the world. The only exception is gunnery which the WASPs don't receive.

And I love to fly as you know. There is music and rhythm in the sound of the motor in front of you as it guides you sailing through the sky. Such big powerful motors they seem to us! They sound so solid, Dolores says. And there is such music and rhythm in winging your way through the air maneuvering smoothly here and there. Mr. Martin and Mr. Hottman both talk about what a smooth flyer I am. Gee, flying

is wonderfully thrilling.

Guess I had better quit swooning and get some radio studied. Oh yes, the pictures. They are just perfect and I won't be satisfied with just one. I want every one of them and I shall pay for them. Pretty please!

Love,
Me

I have just sent my summer clothes home and some anklets which need darning. Pretty please.

Letter 28
EMM
Sweetwater, Texas

December 5, 1943

Dear Mother and Daddy:
I had a big notion to call you today, but I didn't. I am broke and it costs more to reverse charges, doesn't it? I wanted to tell you that I have passed the biggest stepping stone in our training—instrument training. This is the most complete instrument course any class had yet received and our checks were for an Army instrument rating! Captain Hunt, the head check pilot on the field, gave mine to me Friday morning and I passed! The orientation problem and radio range work I did for him was the best I have ever done and I feel so proud. A check from Captain Hunt is something to have on one's record. Dolores passed her ride from Mr.

Lowery. We had two Army and two civilian check pilots for our class. Ted Merchant had promised to check all of Mr. Martin's students personally, but they decided to send the best students up with the Army! To make a good impression with the Army! Dolores was unfortunate in having a very poor instructor. Poor kid! She said it was the closest shave she has ever had. She is one of the best in the class ordinarily.

The letter of Thanksgiving Day was so much fun to read. You must have had a lovely day. I was so happy to hear about Eloise and Johnny and Suzie being there. You must watch Suzie being there. You must watch Suzie grow up as long as you can. She does such cute things.

I don't know what to do about Christmas. Every time I look in the shops I think how much nicer those things I see are at home. Do you think it would be terrible if I sent money and asked you each to get something nice you want very much and maybe wouldn't get otherwise.

That takes all the fun of surprise out of it though. What shall I do? If I did that would you promise to buy it now before stocks are gone? We receive checks [money] *tomorrow.*

You asked what I want for Christmas. I can't think of much but here it is—a fuller brush for my face, long underwear either two piece or with a drop seat, some recordings (Tchaikovsky's 6th Symphony and Brahms' 1st Symphony), some Chantilly cologne, oh yes, a radio and a watch! Instead of a plain watch a chronograph

would be nice but I want a good standard make which is impossible to buy now. The $150 is thrown away, I think, if it wasn't a Hamilton or Elgin or something else good. Some white shirts I need, but we may need a different type with our new uniforms so the shirts I have will do until then.

Now, I know I shall not be home for Christmas because nothing can stop me now. You bet I shall be home on my furlough just as fast as I can get there. I have been looking forward to that ever since I left. I would like to come home now for a few days but I would want to come back to flying again. I sort of like it here. I have never been homesick. But I shall see you on February 13 when you come for graduation.

When you take care of yourselves I am perfectly happy, so just go ahead, Mother, and keep your hair pretty and wear pretty clothes for Daddy, and Daddy, you keep yourself spruced up for Mother. Please have Christmas as usual with Aunt Clara. This idea of not doing things because someone is absent is nuts. Those away are much happier if they can think of things going on as usual. Then you have a good time, I am having a good time with you. Please go to Aunt Clara's—if you get an invitation, of course. That is, if that is what you want to do. Have a big family dinner anyway.

The church sounds as though it is thriving. That is swell. I dream (daydream) of going home and going to church. It is swell you have made such a swell choice of preachers. I shall hear him someday.

Yes, the cotton was the parachute episode souvenir. I do need the anklets as soon as you have a little spare time, Mother. It isn't cold enough for a winter coat yet. Mornings are cold but the days warm up usually. It was up pretty close to 70 degrees today. I don't know whether letters arrive earlier by airmail. I doubt it. I just have never noticed.

The last letter from you, Mother, was so swell. I just loved it. I liked your quotation at the end especially. The Thanksgiving letter was so much fun. I liked Johnny's letter especially. I think it is the first one he ever wrote to me. He is such a swell little brother-in-law.

You asked if I ever got nervous or worried. I have never in my life been so relaxed before as now. I go right to sleep at night and sleep soundly. Many of the kids have become very nervous from the instruments. Poor kids. But I have loved it. I glow with pleasure all day.

This was a beautiful day. We awakened and heard it raining steadily outside. We walked to breakfast in the rain about 10:00, but after breakfast it had stopped. So Edie Keene and I went for a walk all over the post in the damp, still air. It smelled just like a rainy day in Minnesota—all piney and stuff. Then it cleared quickly and a strong wind came up and made the sunlight dance in the puddles.

This was the first day we have missed church except when we have flown on Sundays or have been on weekend leave.

Dolores and Ruth and I went out into the wind and sun and took pictures and then played ping-pong this afternoon.

Yesterday we flew and I practiced with Mr. Morrison for an hour and a half and a bunch went to the show at night. Mr. Morrison becomes our meteorology instructor tomorrow.

Guess maybe this makes up for a week and a half of absence!

Love,
Marie

P.S. Yesterday I still had about 2 and ½ hours of instruments to finish up so Harriet Kenyon went along as safety pilot and I flew under the hood on the beam to Big Spring. I hit the cone of silence over the station right in the middle and we were headed right down the runway when I shook the stick to let Harriet know that, according to my calculations, we should have arrived at Big Spring field (it is a bombardier school). She said, "Come out from under the hood and see where you are." She had to turn the plane on the side so I could see the runway beneath us! Isn't that swell? Of course, we were 5000 feet up. We had so much fun on my last ride in BTs.

Bye,
Me

Suzie's lock is so cute.

Christmas Card—Avenger Field.

Letter 29
EMM
Sweetwater, Texas

December 9, 1943

Dear Mother and Daddy:
It is misty outdoors this morning and very warm. The air smells wonderful. Dolores and I played ping-pong during PT and I am getting worse every day it seems. I did win one game. Dolores is teaching me how to play. Ruth Meyerpeter is finally going home today. She has worked on the field as dispatcher most recently. I should think it would be a relief to Dolores, because she has monopolized all of Dolores's time every weekend.
We have flown Stearmans [PT-17, a bi-plane Primary Trainer having 225 HP] the

last two days and it is more fun—just like flying a toy airplane! Mr. Martin calls them "flying machines" because they look like World War I airplanes. But they do wonderful acrobatics. Mr. Martin is helping finish up the kids on instruments, so I am having to ride with another instructor for a few days. I can hardly wait until Mr. Martin is finished with them.
Here is your Christmas money and please buy something nice for yourselves with it—something you would like very much.
All my Christmas cards are like this and I am going to send the snapshot of me and the BT tail to all the kids.

Love,
Marie

Would you please pay my bills at Wiess's and King's pharmacies?

Letter 30
EMM
Sweetwater, Texas

December 12, 1943

Dear Mother and Daddy:
Almost time for taps! We decorated our Christmas tree tonight. Dolores and I bought it last night and some decorations, and found out later our bay mates had also bought decorations. We have balls, icicles [tinsel], snow drifts, and a white fluffy cord strung around it. On top is a red and silver

bow which was our own idea and making. The tree is sitting on a desk and reaches to the ceiling. There is cotton at the base and our Christmas packages are under the tree. It is very Christmasy in here now. On our door we tied a red ribbon bow and put a medium sized paper bell below it and a lot of little tiny metal bells tingle below the big bell. We have drawn names in our bay.

2 suits of underwear should be plenty— long, heavy underwear. The size is hard to say—34 or 36—it must be long. Something else I would love is a box of fruit—oranges and apples—and some of Aunt Maple's brownies. Do you suppose she would mind? You might send my ¾ navy wool socks in a Christmas box.

I soloed a PT today. We were required to have 3 hours dual first, but I soloed at 2:49. I think he got tired of riding with me. I had a whole period of solo, in fact, practicing chandelles, lazy 8s, and slow rolls. It was fun. We have had several days of unflyable weather. So half of our flight still hasn't had instrument checks and only two of Madelon's flights have been checked—she was one and passed. I had my check over a week ago so I have been as free as a breeze. I felt so sorry for the other kids because they have been nearly crazy with "checkitis." 4 were checked today though and 3 passed.

I talked with Mr. Harper (my dear former PT instructor) today in hangar 3. He seemed so glad to see me. We talked quite awhile. He explained all the acrobatics to me—they are quite different on these PTs

than any other ship I have flown. He is still the favorite of all the instructors I have had.

Monday evening

It is 6:45 and we just got out of ground school. In one of my solo periods today I stopped at auxiliary field n. 1 (prearranged) for Mr. Harper and he rode with me for an hour doing acrobatics. Gee, it was swell. We just heard that we are to stop Stearmans and go to AT-6s immediately!!! Tomorrow! Boy, those Stearmans were cold today. It was 43° or 44° and our faces froze. Up above it was warm though.

Here it is Tuesday afternoon. We just finished PT and we shall go to ground school at 4:30—4:30 to 7:00. We did calisthenics and then tumbling in PT. It was fun, but, goodness, I am awkward at tumbling.

We flew AT-6's this morning for the first time. AT-6's were the ship that really made up my mind to come down here. They are wonderful! 650 HP! Controllable pitch propeller, hydraulic flaps, retractable landing gear and everything. It is the ship used for training combat pilots before flying pursuit ships. My instructor is the only woman AT [Advanced Training] instructor on the field and one of very few on either PT or AT [there were none on BT and 3 or 4 on PT]. She is swell and she would really have to be, following Mr. Martin.

This afternoon it has clouded over completely, the wind is blowing hard, and the temperature is down to 35°. It looks as though it could snow maybe. I am glad we

I am sitting on the front wing of an AT-6 with two of my classmates. December 1943.

On the wing of an AT-6 with two classmates. December 1943.

flew this morning when it was pretty and clear. Are we ever glad to get into a closed plane!

Could you please right away send me addresses of Dr. Woods and Mr. Noyes? I would like to send them Christmas cards. I am sending out 100 cards. Pictures of me standing by the BT tail are going to all the kids. Maybe I am flattering myself, but I thought they might like it. All the cards are out except most of the kids' and I must do those right away. I have written letters and notes on all of them. Is it ever a job!

I got an invitation to a buffet supper at the Presbyterian Church-to-be for the first Sunday that we don't fly for the girls at the field who attend church there. I am to play for it. I am so glad our church is doing so well *and that everyone likes the new minister so well. I would like to hear him. It must be swell, new church, swell minister, and large congregation.*

We are in navigation class now—then meteorology with Mr. Morrison. Some of the kids still have to go to code from 6:30 to 7:00.

Mr. Gilligan [a friend of Mr. Harper] *is here now, so bye.*

Lots and lots of love,
Me, your WASP

Oh yes, what is Dotty and Leo's address? [Dotty was my cousin and Leo her first husband.] *We thought we saw a snowflake as we marched over.*

Comment

Having a female instructor for Advanced Flight Training was very unusual. As I recall, her name was Helen Duffy. After one flight with her I never saw her again. We were never told the reason why she left.

Letter 31
EMM
Sweetwater, Texas

December 17, 1943
10:30 AM

Dear Mother and Daddy:

I fly last period this morning so I have just finished up the last of my Christmas cards. Whew! What a relief! 95 of them. S'pose I should have sent more, but I am tired of writing notes—notes on every one of them.

The colored pictures are all lined up on my locker where I can see them. They are such good pictures and thank you so much for them. I would like to have two books from home, The Story of Philosophy *and* The Woman You Want to Be. *Please!*

Would you pay the insurance please? I forgot to tell you that. I signed that paper. If they want a physical report, I can get one gratis here.

Another thing before I forget. Don't publish any of my letters or information from them without an O.K. from here, unless it is entirely personal. The intelligence officer just got through having a fit concerning some that were printed because some of the information contained was restricted and some was very inaccurate. The one about the parachute drop was O.K. though, because that was purely personal.

We are to be off from Friday noon until Sunday night for Christmas and the girls who live near enough may go home. We shall be right here! Would Eloise and Johnny be there by 6:00 or 6:30 Christmas Eve? It might be possible to get a call through then, but any later in the evening I am quite sure would be impossible. I shall call you because we probably get better priorities. May I reverse the charges? It will be fun talking to you.

Did I tell you that they suddenly took us off Stearmans after 3 or 4 days on them and said we were wasting our time as accomplished instrument pilots flying those? We have been on North American AT- 6s since Tuesday. They have 650 horse-power and are smooth and beautiful to fly. Gee, they are wonderful. They have retractable landing gear and controllable pitch propellers and hydraulic flaps. The picture of Mr. Rowe and me is taken beside one. [This photo is shown on page 34.]

I often think of the house and how it looks. Is it finished—painting, new linoleum in both kitchen and breakfast room—new curtains out there, etc.? I wish you would get Daddy a new chair. Mother, won't you please take him downtown and just <u>make</u> him sit in chairs? I still would love to have a new suite in Eloise's room, and new curtains. Pretty please.

Guess I had better get to the flight line. Bye now.

Oh, it was 18° here Wednesday morning, but it was up to 58° yesterday again. Funny Texas, but I love it.

Yes, the pictures are taken with our Kodak, all but 4. We aren't finished with the negatives yet, but I shall send them home when we are. I sent one of those picture booklets to Uncle Fred. They cost a dollar apiece.

I'd like a T-bone steak for Christmas dinner. How about it? Did you have any meat for a month after my last lunch at home? I've never forgotten all the good things we had to eat that last dinner (lunch). *It was swell.*

Bye again,
Me

Letter 32
EMM
Sweetwater, Texas

December 20, 1943
Monday evening

Dear Mother and Daddy:

Today I soloed the AT-6! Whee-e-e-e-e!!! We are supposed to have 5 hours before soloing, but Mr. Martin turned me loose at 4:42. S'pose he was too scared to ride anymore with me? We have to have 3 supervised solos—one each day—before we are allowed to go out into the practice area. For 3 days we ride dual then finish up the

period with solo for 1 or more landings, not leaving the traffic pattern right around the field at all. Those are the 3 supervised solos. Then we can break traffic and go out into the practice area for a whole period. Let's see, I shall have a second supervised solo tomorrow and a third on Wednesday, then later Wednesday I can take a plane and go out all by my little self in a big AT in a great big sky.

We had our last shot today—tetanus. We are glad. Tetanus affects you right at the time—your arm aches terrifically for a few minutes and then it is just a bit sore, but we don't notice it.

Yesterday we had such a nice time. Madelon and one of her bay mates and Dolores and I went out south of town and explored a canyon that looked very enticing from the road. It was bright red and a ways back it became white and finally ran into a hillside sort of like the badlands. Then we climbed to the top of the hill. We could see Sweetwater Lake in the valley several miles away and the town, and then way over to one side was our field up on a hill. We hadn't realized before what a hill we really are situated on. We took coffee in thermos bottles from the mess hall and barbecued beef sandwiches and potato chips from Starr's and sat on the red rocks to eat. It was so quiet, a novelty to us.

I went to the Presbyterian Church yesterday and heard a very nice Christmas program (service, I mean). The church was very pretty in white and green. The choir sang a whole service of Christmas carols.

The choir is very good. All the Catholic girls wished they had gone with me instead of to their own church. Madelon wanted to go with me in the evening but I wasn't in the mood.

Dolores and I stayed home Saturday afternoon (I slept all afternoon—we had a strenuous night preceding) then we went into town right after supper and did a little Christmas shopping and then went to a show—Aerial Gunner. The only good thing in it was the AT-6s which they flew.

The excitement Friday night was this. 43-W-8 graduated at 8 o'clock in our new gym. Then they had a party at the Avengerettes Club in town. While they were gone some of the girls in our class messed up their (W-8s) bays (after taps and bed check). Then when they arrived home in the middle of the night they tried to break into our bays (we hooked the screen door and window screens). In the wee hours here came a leg and an arm through the open upper quarter of one of our windows. We all jumped up at Rosie's screaming and tried to push her out again, but in she came—with outside help. I grabbed her and sat down on the edge of Rosie's bed; then she gave a lunge and we both went on the floor. We didn't know what to do with her because if we let go she would unlock the door and let the others in and if we put her out she would still let the others in. We had visions of wrestling all night long. But—the one establishment officer whom we do not like, Miss Bristol, walked in after knocking to be let in and were we ever glad

Two AT-6s parked on the ramp at Avenger Field. December 1943.

to see her! We are no longer threatening to duck her in the wishing well when we leave. Everyone wished they had seen me— of all people!—doing that wrestling act in my nightgown on the floor. Miss Bristol even laughed about it and called me "Miss Wrestler" today.

Another letter came from Daddy today, and Saturday one came from Aunt Maple. I was so glad. I have lots of Christmas cards all standing on top of my locker and some packages, too. I believe the underwear can be a size larger yet, if you can get it. Thank you so much for sending it and the socks too and the apples. I crave apples and they are so expensive to buy.

Would you please write the address on Marjorie's envelope. It is in the directory. Have a wonderful Christmas.

Love,
Marie

I sent the Burchams a card with a note and they sent back a card with a sweet little note on it and a hankie.

P.S. We are now the top class! We shall be the next to graduate on February 12. Just 8 weeks to go including this! Friday night (afternoon), after physical training, we got the Squadron A flag (which always belongs to the top class) and paraded all around the flight line in front of all the hangars and sang, "W-1 is the upper class, parlez vous" and "W-1 is squadron A, parlez vous." Everyone cheered us. It was very impromptu. It was a riot for us. Everyone says ours is the screwiest class on the field as well as the class with the best pilots (they have said that all the way through)!!! Brag!

Just Me
Merry Christmas!

Letter 33

December 26, 1943
Sunday evening

Dear Mother and Daddy:
This has been a wonderful Christmas. I knew that you were having a good time at home with Eloise and Johnny and Suzie and the Wrights and everybody and I had a swell time here. I did the very thing I had hoped to do. Mr. and Mrs. Harper invited me to eat Christmas dinner with them. (That is off the record because we are not allowed to be entertained by instructors and another reason is that I was the only girl invited so no one here but Dolores knows it.) Mr. and Mrs. Harper are just swell. He will always be my favorite instructor. Whenever his former students have a problem, they cry on his shoulder, and when something nice happens, such as passing a check ride, etc., they tell him. We tell him everything. Another instructor and his wife were there and an instructor from an Army flying field at Coleman, a friend of the Harpers! And darn! He caught me under the mistletoe! Otherwise, we had a wonderful dinner, a ride, a show, a supper and everything and I stayed until midnight. Some <u>dinner</u> guest I am!
Friday night we had a party and dance in the new gym. We entertained soldiers from

Christmas Card from Avenger Field, 1943.

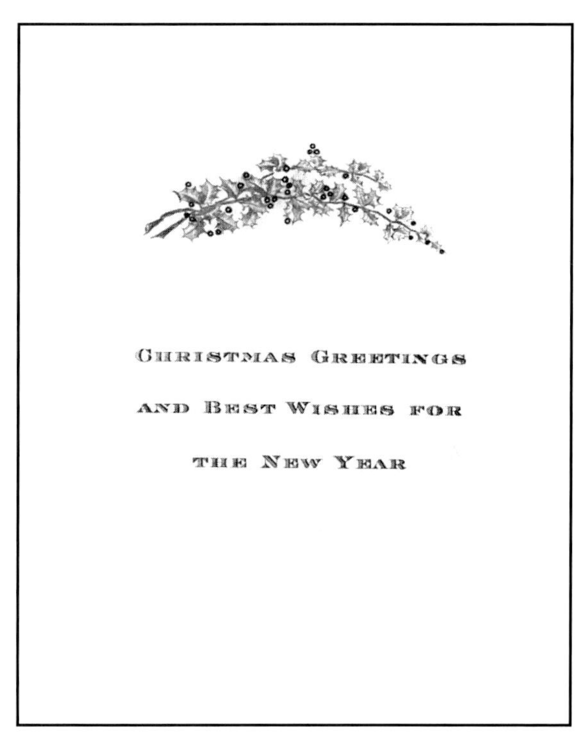

the bombardier school at Big Spring and officers from Camp Barclay at Abilene. It was a huge success. I was to have played my flute in a carol group by the glee club (a solo in the midst of their group), but intermission, when it was to be, hadn't arrived yet when it was time to go to midnight mass at the Catholic Church with Madelon and Dolores, so I <u>didn't have to play</u>! Was I tickled, because it would have been a very hard time to play. People just wouldn't have been in the mood for carols during <u>dancing</u> intermission. There were skits by each flight (10 in all) and a prize was awarded the best (prize is open post

for that flight). They were a scream and started the party off in <u>high pitch</u>.

After bed check Christmas Eve we opened a few of our packages by candlelight, but we saved most for Friday morning to satisfy everyone. It didn't matter to me.

After the invitation to the Harpers' came, one of the girls in Flight 1, Rosemary Hall, about the sweetest and loveliest girl in the class, asked me to go with her on Christmas Day to Abilene where she was being entertained in the home of the commanding officer of Camp Barclay. She had a wonderful time. She said the atmosphere of the day was beautiful. There were 25 very nice fellows from the post and about 15 girls. They had a lovely dinner and sang carols and just had a swell time. That would have been nice, wouldn't it? Rosemary spent the weekend there on our last weekend leave (when we went to Carlsbad). She is a musician, too.

This has been a perfect evening. I have been here all by myself. I am writing letters on new Christmas stationery from Dolores (we drew names in the bay) which I had asked for, I am wearing the new Chantilly cologne, and best of all, Tchaikovsky's 6th [Symphony] has been going over and over. Oh, it is wonderful. The second movement is exactly how Dolores and I feel when we fly so we have played it many times. It was fun to get just the things I wanted, the records, cologne, face brush, photograph album—and underwear! The packages were so cute with bells on them. And that photograph album from Aunt Maple and Uncle Elmer! All the kids who have seen it want one just like it. We have never seen anything like it before. It is just perfect. All the pictures are in it including your colored pictures and the snap of Mother and the sweet little gift card which was with the album (all these last things are first with Mary Lea). It seems as though Aunt Maple and Uncle Elmer always give things just a little bit "super," something different from what anyone else could think of. The gift card was different and so sweet as well as the photograph album. Thank you so much for all the swell things. Eloise and Johnny sent the book On Being a Real Person,

which I wanted above all other books. Gee, it was a thrill to open each package.

Please tell me what you received. Oh, yes, Bertha sent two very pretty hankies and a rose sachet which smells very pretty. Tell me all about Christmas. We had wild ideas of coming home, but Major Urban put an end to that. We were going to start when the girls were released Friday noon and get home Saturday noon and start back Saturday night to arrive here Sunday night. We even had the gas all borrowed. Dolores and Madelon and I (Dolores was going to St. Louis from Kansas City). Wasn't it wild? But it was worth it, we thought—just for a few hours. Major Urban said the weather could change too quickly. He was right. Friday everything was covered with freezing rain. Ice was from ¼ to ½ of an inch thick all over the poor little car. The sun came out yesterday afternoon and was out today.

Goodness, it has taken a long time to finish this. The kids came home at 9:00 and there have been many distractions. We have a lot of fun together.

Must get to bed. Goodnight! Sweet dreams!

Love,
Marie

Monday morning
It rained most of the night and the field is too soft to fly. I forgot to tell you that it really snowed the day before Christmas—our first (we were disappointed once before). But the ground didn't even get white.

I went to church yesterday—Ann Hopkins and I—to the Presbyterian. I feel at home there. Yesterday a buffet supper was given by the Presbyterian ladies for girls from the field who attend there. I played. The table was just beautiful—and the food! I stuffed myself. Mrs. Monserud, wife of Lieutenant Monserud, our favorite doctor, played for me. She is wonderful. They can't entertain us, but she said to have a "flat tire" in front of their house someday soon. They have a lovely big home. Bye now. Dolores is waiting for me to go to the post office.

Me

Letter 34

First Presbyterian Church
CLIFFORD W. WILLIAMS, PASTOR
Sweetwater, Texas
December 28, 1943

Dear friend,

We considered it a genuine pleasure and privilege to have your daughter in our congregation last Sunday. We felt that you would want to know that she has made many friends in our church.

In the case of the absence of your loved one, your loss is our gain, and we will endeavor to do our utmost to make her feel at home here every time she returns.

We do not have a large impressive looking church, but wish to be known as a friendly group of people who love the Lore Jesus Christ and who seek to do His will on earth.

The entire congregation joins me in extending to you our hearty congratulations for having such a daughter who is so well fitted to carry on the high standard of Christian leadership in the service of our country.

May the Lord bless and keep you both now and evermore.

Sincerely your friend,

Clifford W. Williams

Clifford W. Williams,
pastor

CWW/es

P.S. We surely did appreciate Marie's sharing her marvelous talent in playing for us at our buffet supper last Sunday. She plays beautifully. Mary Agnes (Mrs. C.W.) Williams

Letter 35

Avenger Field
SWEETWATER, TEXAS

December 30, 1943
9:30 pm

Dear Mother and Daddy:

It was swell to hear you talk Tuesday night. Your voices sounded so bright and happy. We should do that more often, especially if I can reverse the charges (hah!). I am always broke a week after payday and I spend very little too, it seems. The car, of course, takes quite a little. But we would go nuts without it.

Your letters were so sweet and they sounded so happy, too—kind of super-special happy. You must have had a <u>very</u> nice Christmas. That makes my Christmas nicer than ever. The coffee table sounds like a snitzy idea, Mother, and I am glad you are finally getting the books you want, Daddy.

Everything is in a dither tonight for everyone but Dolores and me. People are being pushed up in the bays, and our 3 bay mates are moving to A-6 and the 4 girls from A-8 are moving in with us. So we just sit and gloat and look satisfied with ourselves.

Mrs. Deaton called all of W-1 in tonight to tell us about our uniforms. We probably will have slacks and battle jackets by graduation. Then she went ahead to tell us about all of the uniform. Everything but a few accessories are to be issued to us. We

are so happy about it. We flew this morning after a seven-day layoff. The field was still wet but we used the north-south runway and a strip on one side of it. There was a stiff crosswind from the west and one of the very last planes to come in at 1:15 ground-looped, so that flying for the other flight this afternoon was called off. It was dual only this morning. The plane felt solid under us today. It had been so long and we were so eager to get back. The long vacation gave us a new feeling for it. It was wonderful. Just taxiing out gave me a thrill. Our grade charts are in the dispatcher's office, but they are hanging on the wall opposite the window through which we talk to her. We look them over carefully whenever the opportunity arises. One of the other girls with my instructor and I have the two highest records in the class. Are you as thrilled as I? We have just two check rides to go!

You would have been quite pleased to hear the conversation which occurred in our bay Sunday night. One of the girls seems to be practically an atheist although she belongs to the Mormon Church. I hadn't realized it before, but Dolores is quite a devoted Catholic. I knew that she was very conscientious about going to church, but I didn't know before that her religion was so personal to her. She really lives it. She has such a cute little face and has so much fun that you wouldn't think there was a serious thought in her head. (Religion has become much more personal to me down here.) Isn't it strange? Remember I told you,

Mother, that I used to worry about me and my religion? Well, it seems that all that was needed was for me to be out on my own to realize that I was not complete in myself. Something bigger than I was taking care of me. It gives one new strength, doesn't it? Do you know what I mean?

Taps!

Love,
Marie

Comment

I now realize that my observations regarding my personal faith and religion were the beginning of a deeper understanding of the role of the Divine in my life. I learned that God asks us to open our hearts to His presence and He will enter. As is often the case, this opening of our hearts comes at times of great need. I think I first became aware of the power of God and His Truth at Sweetwater, and it has sustained me in the years since. Fortunately, I married a man who shared this Belief. His was honed in the skies over Germany, during brutal aerial warfare in 1944–45.

Letter 36

January 3, 1944
8:15 PM

Dear Mother and Daddy:

Your hotel reservations are made for February 4, 5, and 6, and 11, 12, and 13. The 12th and 13th are just in case we have to stay over to fly. You will stay at the Blue Bonnet Hotel. Gee, I am so thrilled about you coming and for a nice length of time too. Gee, I can hardly wait. I want you to see the field so much and to watch us fly. Please don't let anything happen to spoil plans.

The packages came today. It was just like unwrapping a Christmas box. It was fun. It was so sweet of you to send the cookies and candy and nuts. They came just as our other Christmas food had disappeared down human gullets. Your timing was perfect. Thanks for everything—the underwear, too. Everyone knew that I was receiving it because the box was completely torn open and the underwear was lying out in the open with a string around it. We all just laughed and laughed.

Today the field was wet still from a hard rain Friday night and Saturday morning, so we could use only the runway and a strip just west of the runway for landing (we couldn't fly at all Saturday and Sunday) so we went on cross-country to

San Angelo and to Brownwood and back to Sweetwater—264 miles in all in 1 hour and 44 minutes. It was fun.

Saturday Dolores and I took our turn at being hostess at our club in town. We had fun. We opened it Saturday afternoon and set up the chairs and tables and arranged the furniture and served cakes and ice and greeted people at the door and kept out undesirables. And we gathered up empty bottles and glasses and danced once in a while. We went to mass at 8:30 PM and to the club again afterward. Sunday we went to the Presbyterian and Dolores and I went for a ride and listened to the symphony program (we drove very slowly to conserve gas). Then to a show in the evening. I am sleepy. Goodnight.

Love,
Marie

O, Mother, one should always have one good black dress, don't you think?

Letter 37

Avenger Field
SWEETWATER, TEXAS

January 5, 1944
9:03 PM

Dear Mother and Daddy:

I am so sleepy tonight—my eyes are at half-mast—but, gee, am I feeling good otherwise! I passed a check ride today! 4 of us were checked—the first ones. That seems to happen to me every time, doesn't it? Getting the check over early, I mean. Mr. Stolz, our flight commander, does the checking, but Mr. Elmer Riley, director of all flying, told me a week or two ago that he wanted to ride with me, so he came down today when he saw that I was up for a check.

Mr. Morrison took me into our new weather bureau today so I could see the weather map. It was fun because I love meteorology. One can learn so much more about it when one can see just what is happening outside on the weather map. More practical learning.

Oh, I forgot to tell you we have only one more check ride to go—that will be an Army ride. Did I tell you that we went cross-country to San Angelo and Brownwood and back—oh yes, I remember telling you. Tomorrow we shall go to Lubbock and Big Spring.

We are listening to the Tchaikovsky 6th [Symphony]. It is wonderful. I believe I shall buy a record with Uncle Elmer's gift. The Christmas card is so lovely. It is the only one still up. I love to look at the scene.

Would you mind calling Miss Shinn or Miss Lorenzen to see if they received my letter requesting cleansing cream and night cream please? Add to that some more shampoo. Thank you so much.

Can't hold the eyelids open any longer.
Love,
Marie

Letter 38

Avenger Field
SWEETWATER, TEXAS

January 7, 1944
11:30 PM

Dear Mother and Daddy:

We are having a lovely blizzard tonight—real snow—heavy—and lots of really strong wind. Everyone was so excited—me, too. So all formations have been called off for tomorrow and we may have breakfast between 8:30 and 9:30.

After bed check tonight at 10:15, I went to the laundry room and practiced until my lip wouldn't take anymore. When I came back, two of my bay mates and two from next door were playing cards and Kay was visiting elsewhere. While I practiced, a bunch of kids were out-of-doors playing in the snow. Aren't we wicked?

I am practicing "Meditation" from Thaïs to play at church Sunday morning. It was a thrill playing it tonight. Goodnight!

Sunday evening, 6:15
Hello again!

Yesterday the wind had gone down and all the girls were outdoors playing in their winter flying suits in the snow. There was a really fancy snow lady too.

Today the temperature was up nearly to 60°. The field was very wet but we used the runway and went cross-country to Lubbock(!) and Big Spring and back. It was a beautiful day for it—the sky was perfectly clear and visibility was very good. The land just this side of Lubbock and north as far as we could see was perfectly flat. There are tiny little dry lake beds all over it where the water stands when it rains. Just south of this flat land is a table land and from the table land to the flat land is a very sudden drop and then here and there flat topped mountains just the height of the table land. Mr. Korges, flight commander of Flight 1, who rode with me, said that in the process of the Earth's formation the soft land settled and the part still high had rocky foundation. You could see the rocky edge protruding just beneath the surface soil.

Section lines in Texas are certainly screwy. They will be straight for a while then they make a 30° bend and are 30° off for a great territory. One certainly cannot navigate by section lines as in Iowa.

Mother, how about a suit with a plain colored jacket, but with a plaid skirt? But be sure the plaid is of soft colors and not rowdy reds, etc. for quiet little you. You need a black dress, too, don't you? Both of you bring only winter clothes. After our blizzard you will think this is the Arctic Circle, won't you, Daddy? I don't believe it will be necessary though to bring your fur coats and "longies," just whatever you wear for dress in the winter at home.

You have both written just swell letters this week. Mr. Williams said he received a very nice letter from you, Daddy. He was very much pleased. Mrs. Monserud and I practiced at Williams's last night and then we went back to Monseruds's (Lieutenant Monserud is our favorite doctor in the post hospital, no doubt I have already told you) and listened to records and ate. I had been invited for the whole evening, but we had to be in at 9:45 for flying today. They are wonderful people. They want to entertain you too. They have a darling little new brick home which they rent furnished. They insist that I come often and bring a friend along. Lieutenant Monserud used to play the flute beautifully.

What do you suppose Texas would do in Iowa weather? Hibernate, I think.

Yesterday after much deliberation the girls were given open post only until 6:30 because the powers-that-be were afraid of ice. I was on a special pass last night authorized by Mrs. Deaton. I saw only one other special pass go out in spite of many applications. (Note: the roads were perfectly clear!) Dolores and I saw The Constant Nymph yesterday about a composer. It was wonderful. We want to see it again. Do see it if it ever comes back. It was at home before I left. I am hungry.

Love,
Marie

ÆTNA LIFE INSURANCE COMPANY
HARTFORD, CONNECTICUT

E. H. SNOW, GENERAL AGENT
LIFE, ACCIDENT AND GROUP DEPARTMENTS
3RD FLOOR, HUBBELL BUILDING
DELIVERY UNIT NO. 7

DES MOINES, IOWA

January 10, 1944

Miss Ethel Marie Mountain
44-W-1-, A-7
318 AAFFTD
Sweetwater, Texas

Dear Miss Mountain:

You will please note I am enclosing rider forms for your signature on the lines designated with the letter "X". This rider is for exclusion of protection for injuries sustained while on or falling from aircrafts other than those pertaining to passenger aircrafts on a regular passenger route.

Your mother tells me that you will soon complete your course. Congratulations! Also congratulations to you on your return to earth via parachute. What an experience! What a dull prosaic life we home folks are leading these days – and again congratulations to you for taking advantage of opportunity when it appeared.

Will you kindly return the signed forms to me in the addressed envelope and we will send one of them to our Home Office, retain one for the files of this branch office, and attach one to your policy which I delivered to your parents and is now in their possession.

Thanking you, and best wishes for continued success, I am,

Sincerely,

EEK:mg

Letter 39

Letter 40

January 12, 1944
Wednesday evening

Dear Mother and Daddy:

It is not long until taps, but you will get a few lines tonight anyway. The ceiling was low this morning so I didn't get an Army check (Lieutenant Armstrong from Des Moines is to check me) and this afternoon there were a few snowflakes in the air, but the kids say it is snowing hard now. We are days and days behind schedule now.

Today the upper class (us!) could get special passes to leave the post from 2:30 to 7:00, so Dolores and I went in just a little while, long enough to buy some records (I bought "Valse Triste" by Sibelius with the dollar from Uncle Elmer—I have been wanting it) and some film and to order prints from some negatives. I am trying to get some film stored up for you. The stores give us priorities on them. They all laugh when I ask for Kodachrome!

The tires are O.K. for the trip. Another was vulcanized since we came down here. Perhaps I can get gas for you. Mr. Martin asked just today if I needed any. It will be so swell for you to be here. I can hardly wait. Pastor Williams has asked me to play at church again the Sunday, Feb. 6, when you will be here.

Yesterday we went cross-country to Stephenville and Mineral Wells (supposedly!). When we got to Stephenville we decided it was only 80 miles to Dallas (Mr. Martin's home)—why not go? We were there in no time at all—saw many airports around Fort Worth and Dallas. Mr. Martin buzzed the airport where he used to fly a lot and did acrobatics over it. Then he buzzed the middle of town and did a slow roll over a building in which I understood him to say over the interphones that his restaurant was located. That cross-country took us 3 hours (it should have taken only two) and we were almost out of gas in spite of our flying at 8000 feet to conserve gas. Of course, not a soul knows about this flight but Mr. Martin and me so keep mum!

The length of our furlough will depend upon where we are stationed. Ordinarily 10 days are given. If we have some flying to finish after graduation that will not come out of the length of our furlough. No, we have no idea of our assignments yet and will not know until the last minute most likely. What did you mean, Mother, "Will they be putting you at top of list as stated in enclosed clipping?"!! I read the clipping, but I still don't see what you are talking about.

Thursday PM

W-1 has open post again today but I am going to try to do some letter writing. We flew transition this morning. The weather was too uncertain for x-country. The field was snowy but we flew anyway, but left the landing gear down so snow would not get up into the mechanism.

Please hurry and come. And don't worry about the tires. Very, very little mileage has gone on them down here. The tread is still good. Even if they do wear out I don't have to have the car anyway.

So Eloise and Johnny are moving to St. Louis! That is Dolores's home, you know. I know they will like it there. I haven't heard from them since before Christmas. Johnny's mother wrote me a nice Christmas card.

I am enclosing a bond and a money order and the letter sent about the insurance. Bye.

Love,
Marie

P.S. If you hear anything about Jim's getting a furlough when I have mine, please let me know, but don't ask anyone about it. I don't want to be bothered. He mentioned getting one—maybe when I get mine. Of course, I don't know when mine will start because we are behind.

Comment

The "Jim" mentioned in the P.S. is Jim Nuzum, the son of the owner of the Minnis grocery store in West Des Moines, who regularly delivered groceries to our home before the war. At this time, Jim was serving in the US Army.

Letter 41

January 14, 1944

Dear Mother and Daddy:

Sit down in your chairs please. I have some news for you. Here goes! I have just passed my last check ride!!—with Lieutenant Pinkston instead of Lieutenant Armstrong. Isn't it wonderful? It looks as though I would graduate, doesn't it? You may plan definitely to come now, can't you? Gee, it is wonderful to have things work out according to plan. We are fortunate. Some classes have taken check rides up to the last day. Of course, just a few of us have taken the last one, but everyone should be checked in a week or two.

We graduate 4 weeks from tonight and I shall see you 3 weeks from tonight!

This morning I took my first solo x-country—to Vernon and back—258 miles—1 hour and 31 minutes. X-country seems to be a cinch so far. I hope it continues and I don't know why it shouldn't be.

Love,
Marie

Letter 42

(enclosed with letter 40)

January 15, 1944
6:00 PM

We had fun this morning. Mr. Martin and I were the control ship at Plainview. We went over a few minutes early before any of the others arrived and then we controlled the traffic from our ship as each arrived over the field and asked for landing instructions. Then we cleared them by radio to take off again. We were there all morning and arrived back at 1:40. Mr. Martin and another instructor, also a wonderful pilot, did dog fighting part of the way home, then I got to do acrobatics, the first I have done in Advanced Training. Mr. Martin flew under the hood, too, part way home.

This afternoon, after a very late lunch, Rosemary and I played ping pong until she had to go back to the flight line and Dolores and I have been dancing awhile. Leisurely Saturday, huh? We start night flying tomorrow night.

Bye now,
Me

Plainview is north of Lubbock. We could see Lubbock in the distance on the way.

Letter 43

January 25, 1944
Tuesday, 4:30 PM

Dear Mother and Daddy:

We are a group of birds with clipped wings "weathered-in" at Tyler, about 300 miles east of Sweetwater, in fact, it isn't far from Louisiana. We are in the first group to make the 2000 mile cross-country—5 from our flight and 6 girls from the other flight—with Mr. Hatcher, the Advanced Training Group Commander and Captain Miller, one of our check pilots, and Colonel Fowler from Randolph, who is a great backer of the WASP and who asked to go with the first group. Each girl has her own ship—an AT-6—and take-off time is spaced a few minutes between each ship so that each girl is completely on her own. We file our own flight plans and everything. It is a wonderful experience. Texas has had beautiful warm, clear weather for 2 or 3 weeks, but we are very glad for the bad weather to see if we really can navigate. We flew with a minimum ceiling and through very hard rains around Fort Worth and Dallas to our first stop at Tyler; in fact, only 5 girls arrived here. The other six are at Mineral Wells and Fort Worth. So we shall wait until the weather improves enough for them to catch up. There are to be 7 legs in the trip and this is only the end of the first leg.

Traffic is certainly well controlled. Before a pilot takes off, he files a flight plan with Airway Traffic Control or Army Flight Control, including all data concerning ship, pilot, point and time of takeoff, point and estimated time of arrival, and a clearance from the weather officer. This is telegraphed to all stations along the airway and at each radio range station we report our position and altitude by radio. If the pilot hasn't arrived within a reasonable time of his stated estimated time of arrival and within time of his stated fuel supply, the Army goes out looking.

This is our first opportunity to file our own flight plans. Always before, on our short cross-countries, we have all gone on a group flight plan. We have been all over northern Texas, several times to Lubbock and Amarillo and east as far as Forth Worth, Dallas, and Gainesville, a few times, and south to San Angelo and Brownwood. On this trip we shall be in 6 states.

We are to make a 1000 mile x-country in PT-19s too. In fact, a group was to have started that yesterday, but the Army wouldn't send them out in such doubtful weather because they have no radio. We could be called down any time by radio. We were required to keep tuned to the nearest radio range station.

It looks as though my flying will be finished next week. Last week we were very busy. We flew all afternoon from 1:00 to 6:30 and every night from 7:30 until the wee hours—3:00 AM sometimes, and slept all morning. It was my very first night flying and it was perfectly wonderful, but I still can't get the ship down by myself. I will soon though. All I have left is this cross-country, the PT-19 cross-country, and some more night flying.

Last night we saw a very good show with Bette Davis as leading actress, then we slept in our hotel "bay"—we all 5 slept in one room. This morning we walked around to see the town then this afternoon I spent almost 3 ½ hours in the library by myself reading more of On Being a Real Person. *I enjoyed getting away by myself. The others are all asleep and I am on the mezzanine now.*

Isn't this a strange letter? It just rambles about nothing. Are you all ready to come? I am getting eager to see you. Are Eloise and Suzie still there? I do wish they could be there when I go home. Do you suppose? You must be having a lovely time.

I am sleepy. Bye.

Love,
Me

Comment

One of my last assignments at Sweetwater was to complete a solo night cross-country flight in an AT-6. This flight was taken on a beautiful, clear and cloudless night under a full moon. It was a flight I shall always remember. The aircraft flew as smooth as silk, the air was calm and the gentle purring sound of the engine could have easily lulled one to sleep. In front of me in the dark cockpit the instruments appeared as circles with their numbers and symbols glowing with green luminescence from the florescence lighting. It was truly a peaceful setting, filled with transcendent meaning, giving me the feeling of a spiritual presence that nourished my soul—an airman's dream. Flying to my destination the moon was off my left wing, its soft light reflecting from the silvered surface, creating a beautiful golden path along its entire length, from wing tip to cockpit. When I reached my destination and turned back the same effect was produced along my right wing.

This was truly "a night to remember."

Letter 44

January 26, 1944
Wednesday evening

Dear Mother and Daddy:

We are still "weathered-in" in Tyler. Mr. Hatcher and the Army officers with us say that it happens to pilots often. All the bad weather seems to be right here now. It has cleared east where we want to go.

I am enjoying this immensely. As I told the girls, this is the first time I have been stranded and not worried about the million things I should be doing. I read in the library again today—more of On Being a Real Person *and* Wind, Sand, and Stars *which Eloise had long wanted me to read. I took the books out so I can read them in the room tonight.*

I took a long walk today in the warm misty air. It must be a wealthy town. There are many lovely, beautiful homes and nice cars and well-dressed people (we have seen only two pairs of slacks on the street besides our own). There are so many oaks here as in D.M. and magnolias, and cypress, and sycamore and many others. Some flowers are in bloom and the shrubs are green and there is real <u>green</u> grass and the magnolia trees are constantly green as well as the evergreens. The oaks are brown though and everywhere is the odor of moist, decaying leaves. It is wonderful.

Must get to reading. Graduation has been changed to Saturday morning, Feb.12. I am so glad.

Love,
Me

Comment

The date of our graduation was changed once more to February 11, 1944.

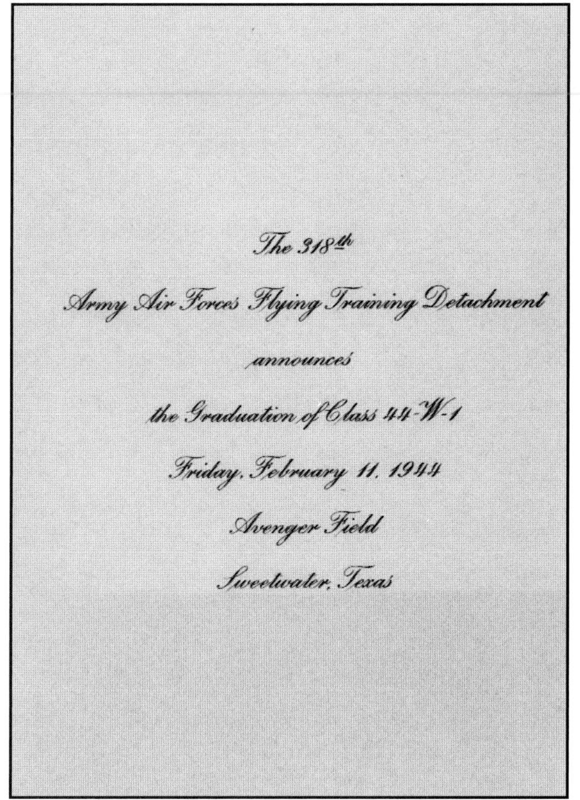

The official invitation to our graduation exercises and my personal card. February 1944.

Graduation of WASP
Class 44-W-1
February 11, 1944

The great day finally arrived and I had the pleasure of celebrating it with my parents present. They had arrived from Des Moines by train a few days before and stayed at the Blue Bonnet Hotel in Sweetwater. During the day they came out to Avenger Field to watch the flying training activities. One afternoon, while they sat below the control tower, I made a series of takeoffs and landings with a group of WASPs in AT-6s and waved to them each time I taxied past the control tower to take off again.

Madelon Burcham and me, on the left, in our new WASP uniforms. February 1944.

Classes 44-W-1 and 44-W-2 in formation in front of the administration building for flag raising before the graduation ceremonies. February 1944.

Class 44-W-1 lining up to march past the reviewing stand prior to the formal graduation ceremonies. I am fourth from the left. February 1944.

Our class was the first to wear the stylishly tailored, Santiago Blue WASP uniform, complete with a beret adorned with an officer's emblem, a skirt and slacks, shoes, gloves, a handbag, and a trench coat. Miss Cochran had personally designed the uniform and selected a Dallas, Texas clothier to produce it. The uniform harmonized the feminine personality with military orderliness and was personally fitted to each WASP. I have always been proud to wear it.

Our class entered training in August 1943 with ninety-nine students and graduated forty-nine, approximately a 50 percent washout rate. I believe this is a higher failure rate than that of male aviation cadets of this period. This may have been because the WASP program was the first of its type and margins of acceptance were narrower

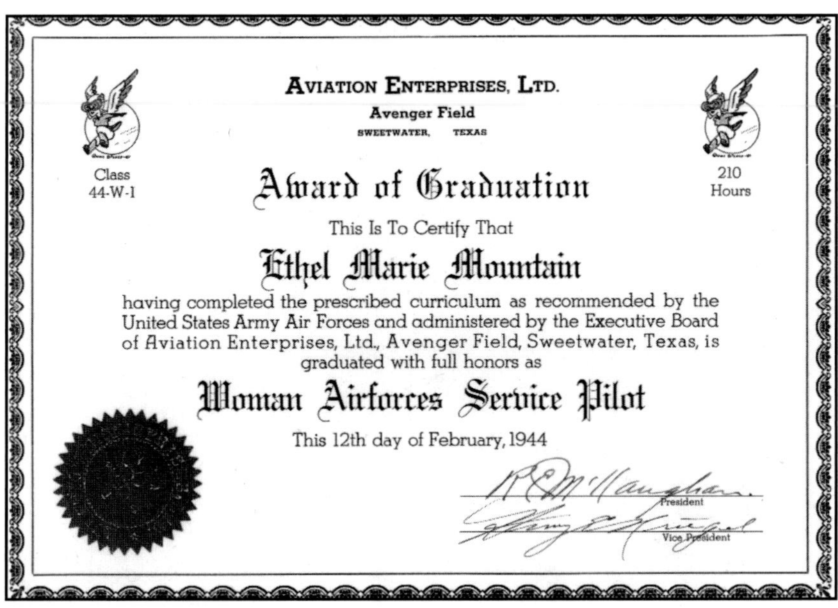

My graduation diploma certifying that I had completed the requirements to become an Air Force Pilot. February 1944.

I am standing in my new uniform in front of an AT-6 at Avenger Field after graduation. February 1944.

than for the established male program.

The graduation ceremonies began with Class 44-W-1 marching in full dress uniform past the reviewing stand to receive an official salute from the civilian and military officers and distinguished guests.

The graduation ceremony consisted of the usual speeches and presentations by dignitaries. These included Brigadier General J. C. Bartholf, the father of one of the 44-1 graduates, Anne Bartholf. Mrs. Ethel Sheehy, the Special Field Assistant to Miss Cochran, presented the graduates with their coveted silver WASP pilot

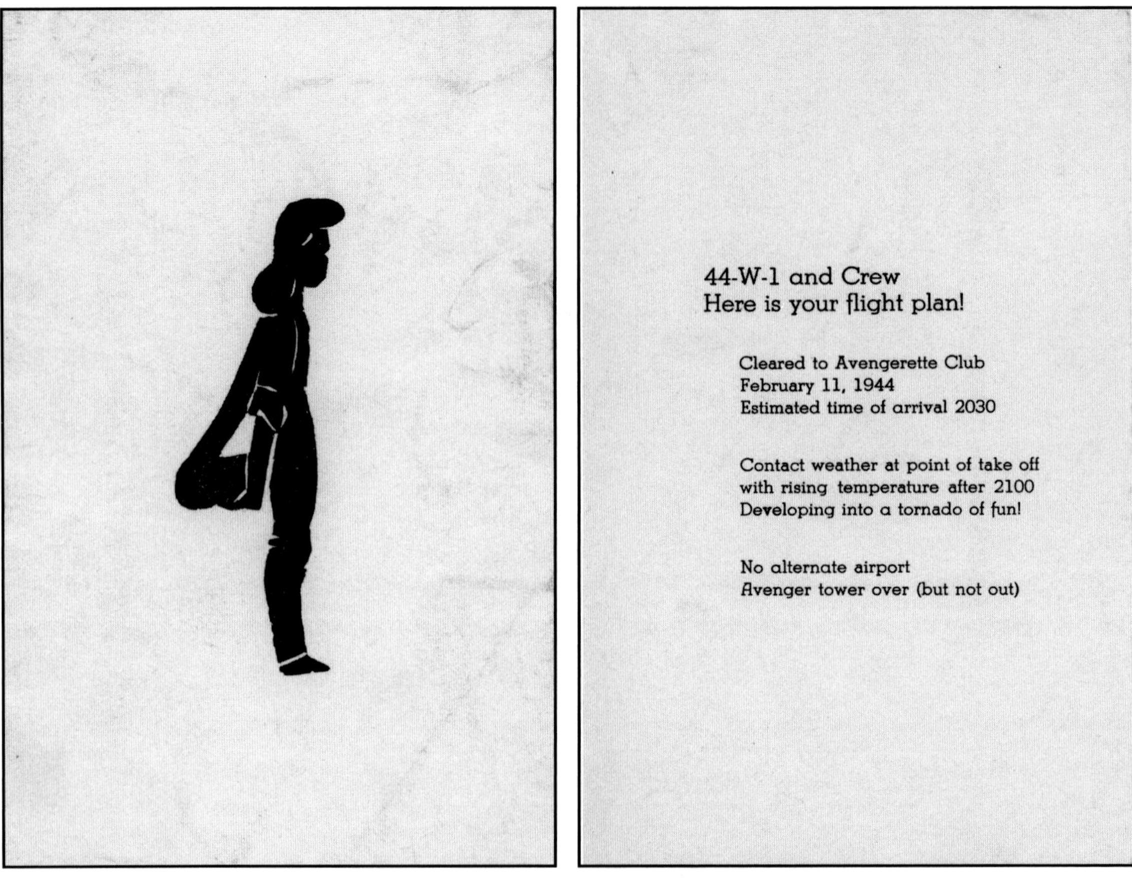

Silhouette of a WASP wearing a parachute, a symbol of the women pilots.

wings. I had interviewed with Mrs. Sheehy in Des Moines about a year earlier before being admitted to the WASP program. Mother pinned my wings on my blouse while Daddy stood by proudly.

We were all thrilled to have completed the rigorous six-month USAF flight training program to earn our wings and wear the beautiful WASP uniform. Although I have been fortunate to have had many personally fulfilling experiences in my life, I believe the satisfaction I felt in completing WASP flight training was one of the most gratifying. Mother and Daddy were very proud, too. I believe, however, they were also somewhat anxious about my future, as they rightly believed flying could be hazardous.

At the end of my Sweetwater flight training I had completed 315 total hours of flying, including eleven hours of night flying, forty-four hours of instrument flying, mostly under the hood, and thirty hours of simulated instrument flying in the Link Trainer.

My next assignment came immediately with orders to report to the Las Vegas Army Air Base in Las Vegas, Nevada, on February 21, 1944, to serve as an Air Force Pilot under the directions of the Base Commander.

Mother and Daddy at the Carlsbad Caverns, New Mexico. February 1944.

Sweetwater, Texas to Las Vegas, Nevada

Mother and me at the Saguaro National Forest, Arizona. February 1944.

I was given ten days leave and ordered to report to Las Vegas AAB, Las Vegas, Nevada. So the day following graduation, Mother and Daddy and I started for home in my car. However, by the time we reached Abilene, about forty miles east of Sweetwater, I suggested that we take an extended vacation trip west instead of going home to West Des Moines. Mother and Daddy had been considering a vacation, anyway, so this seemed like a good time to take one. We decided to go all the way to the west coast, do some sightseeing, and return east as far as Las Vegas to drop me off. They could then continue on home in my car, as I thought I would not need it in Las Vegas. As it turned out, I soon dis-covered that a car was a virtual necessity

Mother and Daddy in front of a Saguaro cactus at the Saguaro National Forest, Arizona. February 1944.

In Phoenix, Arizona, in my uniform, complete with handbag, gloves, shoes, and a new hairstyle. February 1944.

Mother and Daddy in front of the pool at the San Juan Capistrano Mission. February 1944.

on the air base, as it was far from town.

After reversing our direction at Abilene, we drove west as far as El Paso where we stayed overnight. On the way we stopped to see the Carlsbad Caverns in New Mexico. We also crossed the Rio Grande to be briefly in Juarez, Mexico. The next day we drove to Phoenix, Arizona, stopping briefly at the Saguaro National Forest near Tucson. We stayed at the Westward Ho Motel at Phoenix where a hairdresser suggested that I have a new hair arrangement to compliment my WASP beret. I gladly accepted her recommendation. It had been a long time since I had visited a hairdresser.

We continued our westward journey driving through the deserts of Southern California, ending up in San Diego. This was a very busy city filled with thousands of soldiers, sailors, and marines. In normal times San Diego is a navy and marine town, used to the presence of many soldiers and sailors. However, with wartime the number of military had expanded ten times. The situation was hectic. Mother and I were lucky to find cots to sleep on at the YWCA but Daddy could find nothing. He ended up sleeping in a chair in a hotel lobby. We had little desire to stay long.

The next day we drove north to the San Juan Capistrano Mission near Los Angeles, where we visited for a few hours.

The next stop on our trip was Pasadena for a visit with Mother's cousins, Mary Belle and Elizabeth Fogg and Mary Hall. We were there for a couple of days staying with Mary and her husband Barkley. Elizabeth gave some advice about military dress protocol, telling me that I should have a formal gown in my wardrobe. I never learned how she knew this, but we did go shopping in Pasadena for a gown.

Her advice turned out to be very good. I wore the gown several times at parties and dances at the Officers' Club in Las Vegas AAB and for many years after the war.

We left Pasadena and turned northeastward toward Las Vegas, following the highway through Barstow, Silver City, and across the barren stretches of desert south of Death Valley. I was later to fly over much of this region on missions out of Las Vegas, seeing it from quite a different perspective.

Mother and Daddy dropped me off at the air base in time to report as ordered, made sure that I was settled properly, and then drove home to West Des Moines in my car.

OFFICERS MESS
LAS VEGAS ARMY AIR FIELD
LAS VEGAS, NEVADA

Part II

Letters from Las Vegas
Army Air Base, Nevada

Part II contains the forty-nine letters I wrote to my parents in West Des Moines, Iowa, from my USAF duty station at the Las Vegas Army Air Base, Nevada. There are two others, one written to my mother by John, the other from the pastor of the church in Sweetwater that I attended and where I often played my flute. I reported to this base on February 21, 1944. I had requested an assignment in the southwest part of the United States after graduation from flight school. With this assignment, my position became more professional, my duties more responsible, and my status improved significantly, as I was given all the rights and privileges accorded an officer in the USAF. My pay also increased to about $250 per month.

An air base is essentially a community in which each individual is expected to conform to certain social and military customs. Although the WASPs—as civil service employees—were technically civilians, we were treated as officers. That included being subject to orders from commanding officers and obeying all US Army Air Force regulations. We also were subject to military court martial, although I never knew of any WASP experiencing that.

The military and social atmosphere in Las Vegas was disciplined but relaxed. I enjoyed my service there very much, as my letters show.

Letter 45

OFFICERS MESS
LAS VEGAS ARMY AIR FIELD
LAS VEGAS, NEVADA

February 29, 1944

Dear Mother and Daddy:

This is a wonderful field. Everyone is so swell and tries so hard to help us. They are very friendly. This officers' club is beautiful. It is finished just the way Daddy is finishing his office—knotty something-or-other below and that funny stuff in strips going around above and on the ceiling. The furniture is nice and very comfortable. I am writing in a smaller, cozy room listening to a lovely phonograph playing classical records. The fellows play them a great deal. Twice today when I came in I have

In the officers' club at the Las Vegas Army Air Base. L-R: 1st Lt. Jack Hill, a B-17 pilot, Madelon Burcham, WASP, an officer whose name I have forgotten, and me. February 1944.

found them playing. We have full officers' privileges and the commanding officer has ruled that we carry them out fully. We rate a salute and salute all other officers just as any officer does.

We have been very busy taking physicals, filling out papers, getting instructions, being fitted with our own parachutes with our names stamped on them, being fitted with oxygen masks, and just waiting wherever we go. The 5 WAAC officers with whom we live are very, very swell. The civilian personnel officer, Lieutenant Grant Dixon (a man), is our acting group commander and he is wonderful. He reminds us of one of our very favorite officers at Avenger, Lt. LaRue. We would have been ready to fly finally tomorrow, but he doesn't think we should until we have been provided with insurance. We are not eligible for government insurance so he is working his head off to find suitable insur-

ance for us. Tomorrow morning we have to take an altitude-pressure test in a test chamber in which we shall remain for an hour. In a night-blindness test yesterday I made the highest score.

Yesterday we had a very rare pleasure. Our commanding officer, Colonel Henry, asked to see us. He was wonderful. He welcomed us very warmly and wished that we would be very happy here. We certainly are. We are going to fly AT-6s for a short while, then go to AT-11s (twin engine), then to a bigger twin-engine, B-26, and probably finally to B-17s. Isn't that wonderful? We are the first WASPs on the field, and we have created a lot of interest and attention. Everyone has expected us so long, it seems.

There was a lovely dance at the club Saturday night and we were all invited. I danced with a wonderful dancer so it was lots of fun. The dances are formal so I shall have use for another dress. Please!

Another thing I need is the record of my shots which I think I sent home. Did you find my social security card or at least the number? If you can't, you probably could find out by calling that office in the Federal building.

I hope you are having a lovely trip. Your card came today from the Grand Canyon. Wish I were with you. We would have a grand time, wouldn't we? What did you find in Oklahoma City?

Bye now. Think I shall go listen to the music and then go home to bed. Sleep tight and sweet dreams.

Love,
Marie

Letter 46

O F F I C E R S   M E S S
LAS VEGAS ARMY AIR FIELD
LAS VEGAS, NEVADA

March 9, 1944
9:00 pm

Dear Mommy and Poppy:

Your letter was so sweet today. I just read it again and I was so thrilled. If everyone had parents like mine they would always do their very best.

So you finally got home! Did it seem like a long time to be gone? It was a grand trip, wasn't it? Be sure to send the car at the first opportunity, won't you? We are practically stuck here. There are buses going in

The same group outside the Officers' Club. February 1944.

in the evenings, but they go at inconvenient times and besides, I usually want to go in the daytime to do necessary shopping, etc. I have been attempting all week to get my laundry in.

Yesterday we did a short solo cross-country into California and Arizona. Remember Silver City, California, on the way here? From there we went to Kingman, Arizona. It was non-stop and required 2 hours. This is certainly rugged country. We couldn't see it well the day we drove through that country, could we? There are high peaks all around. It is amazing how great the distances are in the country. It looks as though it is a few miles between ranges, but it takes us perhaps thirty minutes to go from one range to another! It is wonderful. Did I tell you that we flew in a B-26 through Death Valley a few days ago? We saw Mt. Whitney in the Sierra Nevada that day too. We can go for rides in the B-26s and B-17s any time they are going if it does not con-flict with our schedule and there are many going up everyday. Some of the kids have been up the Grand Canyon. They let us fly the ships part of the time when we go along. They are wonderful. The ships, I mean!—and the people too.

We have finished transition on AT-6s except for instruments. It seems to be a field rule that all new pilots take transition on 6s no matter what they fly. Today we started instrument refresher. My instructor said I was good on instruments! We are taking link (trainer) everyday, too. They have finally told us definitely what our first job is to be. We are to be instrument instructors for the rest of the pilots on the field who don't have instrument ratings and most of them do not. No doubt we can do transition on the other ships at the same time. Do you know that, for the first time in our lives, we can get an AT-6 anytime we want and fly it the whole day if we wish. Golly!

I must send you a copy of a poem which was composed for me by the little fellow I have been going with mostly. His name is Lt. Dale Kreps. The poem is just beauti-ful—a masterpiece I think. Hope I don't forget to copy it when I get back to the B.O.Q. [Bachelor Officer's Quarters]. I don't want him to see me copying it now. He is writing a letter, too. We are listening to Schubert's Unfinished [Symphony] on the phonograph at the Club.

I shall enclose the check for the last half of February which I hope will cover car

expenses and what I borrowed on the trip. Please tell me what all that amounts to. The information for the income tax report is in a drawer in my desk in the book (black) of expense accounts, on pieces of paper. Each month is marked with the year. I believe the line on each month's report is the 4th line—one marked "total received" or something. The third line is total amount given (in lessons) but of course that wasn't always received. It must be the 4th line. In the desk somewhere (in the bottom drawer) are the old reports too. I made two quarter-ly installments last year—March and June.

It is getting toward bedtime. Goodnight! Sweet dreams!

Love,
Marie

You can endorse the check, can't you? I am sure the bank will allow you.

Comment

I already missed my car. The air base was located far from the city of Las Vegas and the military bus transportation provided by the Air Force to and from the city was not convenient. For social occasions the bus was impractical. Even getting around the base by bus was difficult. My car was a necessity.

The "Link" was the Link Trainer, the flight simulator for learning instrument fly-ing procedures. I had some experience with this at Sweetwater.

Letter 47

OFFICERS MESS
LAS VEGAS ARMY AIR FIELD
LAS VEGAS, NEVADA

March 14, 1944
8:30 pm

Dear Mother and Daddy,

I am writing in the record room at the club and someone is playing the march from "William Tell Overture" on the phonograph. Remember it?

Last night and yesterday we had a very good sample of a Nevada sandstorm. The wind was blowing 50-60 miles per hour and my pillow by the window was brown with dust. We flew instruments first period in the morning and quit. We gained altitude in a glide, and then we would strike a down draft and lose altitude in a climb. Lt. Skelton said he had never seen that condition so bad before. We were getting a cold front, you see—a terrific one.

This morning it was very cold, but by afternoon the terrific wind had calmed. Oh! yes, it snowed quite hard for a little while this morning.

This morning I went to the band building and listened to a brass sectional rehearsal, the woodwind sectional, then rehearsal of the complete band. I get to play with them and I can practice there. Major Philips had spoken to the director about me and the ground was laid.

I am getting into an AT-6 in my WASP uniform and parachute. Normally, I would wear a flight suit when flying, but this photo is a PR shot. February 1944.

I got a "very good" in Link this afternoon. I did an instrument letdown on our radio range into our field—supposedly.

We had a big dance at the Club Saturday night. I went with Dale and wore my new white dress. I think he was quite overwhelmed after seeing nothing but uniforms. After the dance orchestra had quit playing for the night and most people had gone, Dale sat down at the piano and played and played anything anyone wanted to hear until the colored boys finally practically pushed us out the door. We had fun. I finally didn't get that poem copied, but I shall this time.

Some of the fellows were laying bets this morning as to how soon the first girl among us would be married. They give the first one two months. But Madelon and I said, "Not until the war is over." There are lots of swell fellows here. Don't worry. I am very busy flying and crazy about it.

The dress came today. Thank you so much, but you forgot the belt. It is of the same material and is in the top drawer of the chest. Please! I need it for a week from Saturday night. May I have your locket, Mother, and my gold bracelet that Grandma gave me too, please?

I shall enclose an article which appeared in a newspaper here in Las Vegas about us. Sleepytime. Goodnight!

Love,
Marie

Isn't the poem beautiful? It is just a masterpiece, I think. It is a bit private though, you know.

Ode to a Lady Pilot

Not every miss can count the skies her playground,
And roam where shortly mortals never trod,
While some of us must yet remain quite earthbound
And muse on our resemblance to a clod.
It strikes the mind that in such carefree wanderings
Amongst the far flung reaches of the clouds
Perhaps the wanderer must indeed be tainted
With wisdom hidden far beyond the shroud.
For when I look into those eyes of azure
So knowing, yet as wistful as a child's,
I realize, My Sweet, that my description of you
Though I were fluent, would indeed be mild!

Dale

Comment

I was pleased to find a sympathetic reception from the base band and was invited to play with them when my schedule allowed.

It was only natural for speculation to develop regarding marriage between WASPs and base officers. We had constant contact with one another on flight operations and shared an interest in aviation. Madelon doubtless intended to maintain her "blessed singleness" until the war was over but she and Lt. Jack Hill were married in the summer of 1944. A few WASPs did marry officers they met on the base. Of course, I did too—but not until John returned from overseas in 1945.

I was pleased and, I think, charmed by Dale's poem. These encounters in wartime are inherently brief and often bring out feelings that in less stressful times would have been more muted, at least for those of my generation. Dale wrote at least two other poems for me but they have been lost.

Seven of the ten WASPs from our Sweetwater Class 44-1, who were assigned to the Las Vegas AAB are, L-R: Betty Wall, Madelon Burcham, Gwen Crosby, me, Jeanette Jenkins, Ida Cater, and Ruth Craig Jones. Not shown are Marge Harper, Madelyn Taylor, and Rosina Lewis. February 1944.

Letter 48

OFFICERS MESS
LAS VEGAS ARMY AIR FIELD
LAS VEGAS, NEVADA

March 20, 1944

Dear Mother and Daddy,

Today I instructed my first student in instrument flying. It was lots of fun. He has even taught instruments here himself, but he has no instrument card. I overheard him telling another fellow that "she knows more about instruments than I do!" I had him 2 hours this morning and two hours this afternoon. We had a terribly rough day for it—as bad as last Monday. We have a reputation on the field for being very good on instruments. I love to teach them. That was my favorite part of the course at Sweetwater.

Yesterday morning I went for a wild ride with Bob Shawn. Have I mentioned him to you? He is very, very nice, red headed, and married. He took me for rides on missions with him twice last week in a "6" [AT-6]. They are camera missions on which gunnery students ride in a formation of 3 B-17s and supposedly shoot machine guns equipped with film instead of shells and shoot pictures of the "6s" diving at them from all sides. We were one of the "6s" (AT-6s—what you saw me fly). It is quite a wild ride for a hundred miles up the valley and back. It is wonderful. The B-17s fly along so dignified and unperturbed and the little "6s" look like excited little birds, dashing here and there.

Thursday night I was invited to Shawn's for dinner. They are expecting a baby any day. I felt a little funny about going because I didn't know Bob well, just as I would see him on the flight line occasionally, and I had never met Bernie, his wife. But just as soon as I walked through the door with Bob, everything was O.K. because Bernie was so friendly and called

I am standing on the wing of an AT-6 wearing my parachute and approving the instructional form of one of my instrument flying students, Lt. John C. Peterson. March 1944.

me "Marie" before we were even introduced. We had a swell time.

Last night (Sunday) Dale and I went to dinner with them at the El Cortez. Dale has been in Indian Springs for a week—that is another field operated in connection with this one—about 40 miles up the valley in the God-forsaken desert—and arrived back yesterday. I took him for a very short ride yesterday afternoon. He loved it. He wanted to fly himself, but was reclassified in pre-flight as a bombardier. He leaves in one more week. He threatened to flunk his comprehensive exam tonight so he could stay another month. Isn't it silly?

Some records—good ones—are being played on the phonograph and one of the fellows is entertaining everyone with his experiences of the day flying a B-17. Everyone is in stitches.

This is a wonderful place.

Oh, yes, last Friday word came from the West Coast Command asking if we would be qualified to teach BTs [Basic Trainers] in Texas, so they sent word back that we were qualified but were emphatically unfavorable to the idea. We were scared little kids. Madelon said she was afraid being in Las Vegas was too good to be true. We hope to hear no more about it.

Love,
Marie

We were paid today, but we were overpaid last time—for Feb. 15 to Mar.1, instead of Feb. 25 to Mar. 1, so today we just received $27 and I shall need that for eating.

Letter 49

<pre>
OFFICERS MESS
LAS VEGAS ARMY AIR FIELD
LAS VEGAS, NEVADA
</pre>

March 28, 1944

Dear Mother and Daddy,

I just read through all of your recent letters and it was so much fun. They are always so very newsy and morale-building. Makes me feel wonderful.

Everything is going O.K., I guess. I still have the same student. He is a beautiful flier, especially in acrobatics. He taught me to do barrel-rolls today. They are illegal, but we go over into the opposite corner of the valley where no one can see us.

The package, which I suppose had the jewelry in it, is in the PO—has been since Saturday, but I keep forgetting it. I wanted it for the dance Saturday night.

It was a nice dance. I wore my blue formal and I felt very nicely dressed. Dale liked it too. He gave me a corsage of two camellias—and they don't give corsages around here! But it was our last party. He was shipped out last night. Betty and I saw him and Jack off at the train. It was a bit on the weepy side too.

It was too bad about Bob Compton. Accidents like that seem so unnecessary. Flying is safe as long as one flies safely and it is so unnecessary to fly any other way. "Hot pilots never grow old," they say. This is some letter, isn't it? I owe so many. I am going to concentrate on them this week. Keep writing please—and often. Tell Aunt Maple, I believe she owes me a letter.

Love,
Marie

The pictures from Lt. Timmons came today. I could very nicely use the little lamp now, but there was a short in it and all the globes blew out quickly.

Comment

Bob Compton, a USAF aviation cadet in pilot training and the son of the president of the West Des Moines Bank, was killed in 1943. My parents had mentioned his death in a recent letter.

Letter 50

<pre>
OFFICERS MESS
LAS VEGAS ARMY AIR FIELD
LAS VEGAS, NEVADA
</pre>

March 30, 1944

Dear Mother and Daddy:

My, but I have put in a hard day today. I flew 2 ½ hours. Some life, isn't it? I usually put in some extra flying, but today I didn't, and that was all I had to do.

We learned today that 5 of us have to do a ferry job and those who are about finished with their respective students were selected. I have to go. We are to be flown in a nice

Lt. Peterson, my instrument flying student, and I are prepared for an instrument flying lesson in an AT-6. March 1944.

twin-motored AT-11 to Ponca City, Oklahoma, where we will pick up PT-17s (Stearmans) to be flown to Phoenix, Arizona. There the AT-11 will pick us up and bring us back here. I don't want to leave here, but it will be fun when we get started.

I shall finish up my student tomorrow probably. He is so cute—so full of life and nervous energy. He certainly hates instruments and gripes constantly good-naturedly, but in the air he works hard and is pretty good.

There are 10,000 people on this field. I don't know whether that includes those on the field at Indian Springs—an auxiliary field—or not. That field is just as permanent as this one but smaller. Most of the "23" (AT-23, a target tow plane version of the B-26) pilots are up there where they tow targets and little gunners in B-17s shoot at the targets.

No, I didn't hear the symphony. That was the night of our last big party. It must have been beautiful.

I hope Daddy's cold is better. Please take care of yourselves. I shall mark the letter "air mail" and see how long it takes. Your letter marked 8 pm, Mar. 26, came yesterday, Mar. 29. Not bad! I shall send that clipping from the paper you mentioned. I shall enclose those snapshots too.

Mother, you and Mrs. Burcham really get together. I imagine she enjoys it. I don't write as often as I would like, either. Madelon and I see each other less frequently now than before as we are each very busy.

I need some new medicine from Miss Weiss. I think her tel. no. is 4–7211. The prescription no. is 58466. I need it by next Friday. Please! I had almost forgotten.

Please send my car whenever there is a chance. Golly, I need it! While it is there, use it all you like.

Rosie Lewis was called home by the illness of her father last Sunday morning. She caught a plane at 9:30 am, but he died before she got home to Salt Lake City. Ida Carter was in the hospital ill several days ago and while she was there, they discovered she has a goiter so she is going home to Oklahoma City with us Saturday to have it removed.

Every time we hear news of the other girls we feel lucky we are here. The girls who went to Childress to fly AT-11s have been sent to Randolph to become BT instructors and the 4 girls who went to B-26 school have been transferred elsewhere except Marge Logan who remained as co-

pilot. We are busy. Goodnight!

> *Love,*
> *Marie*

Will you please get another copy of me alone under the palm tree and I shall send it to Lorrain W. Mother, will you please call Younkers and have them send me a couple of large Coty lipsticks in "medium" shade? Don't let them send that shaped stick—it breaks—just the plain stick.

Letter 51

First Presbyterian Church
CLIFFORD W. WILLIAMS, PASTOR
Sweetwater, Texas

April 5, 1944

Dear friends,

Guess what? I went to the door a few minutes ago to find <u>Marie</u> knocking. It was such a thrill and surprise that I stood there sort of spellbound.

She was ferrying planes from Ponca City, I believe. We didn't know that she was located in Las Vegas. It was so good to see her.

Though she stayed only a few minutes, her visit was like a breath of fresh air. You are surely fortunate to have such a lovely and thoughtful daughter.

The Williams' hospital is improving. The pastor is recovering from an appendicitus operation, and Bob is recovering from Bronchitis. Mrs. Williams and Bob join me in sending best regards.

Hope this letter finds you all well and happy, and that the Lord may continue to bless and keep you all.

Sincerely your friend,

Clifford W. Williams

Letter 52

O F F I C E R S   M E S S
LAS VEGAS ARMY AIR FIELD
LAS VEGAS, NEVADA

April 8, 1944

Dear Mother and Daddy:

We arrived home this morning and I found a week's accumulation of mail including two wonderful letters from Mother and one from Aunt Maple!

I had dreaded the trip, but it was wonderful. First of all it was fun riding in AT-11s— we girls got to fly them most of the time— and then I hadn't realized before how much one misses green, green fields. They were the most beautiful sight and gave me the strangest feeling. I just couldn't get over the greenness of the ground. Even Texas was green! We got permission to land at Avenger and it was swell seeing the field again. I saw Mrs. Dalton, Mr. and Mrs. Harper, Monseruds, Mr. Morrison, Lt. Timmons, called Mrs. Urban, saw the people on the flight line, and lots of the kids. June [Braun, from Des Moines] graduates next week, her mother probably told you. Isn't that swell? And all the other Des Moines girls are still there in W-5 except the Castello who resigned before we graduated. There were 7 in W-5, you know.

Oh, yes, in Oklahoma City I found a pair of beautiful black flat-heeled shoes for flying and if you will send me a shoe stamp, I shall send for another pair just like them.

For mailing you may detach the stamp. It is airplane no. one stamp now. I still haven't dress shoes.

On west [ferrying PT-17s] we flew over the very places through which we drove. Remember that high mountain and pass between Carlsbad and El Paso? We flew through a low spot in the ridge next to that—just south. I remember how thrilled I was when we saw it because they were my first western mountains. In El Paso we stayed at the Cortez—all 5 in a room. We landed on that field just to the right of the highway on the way into town. Remember?

Next day we landed first at Deming on that field. Then at Tucson on the field south of town where there are many, many B-24s. We were scolded there for taxiing on down the runway after landing instead of turning off (we had no radio) [Primary Trainers had no radios]. A 1st lieutenant found some people without rank whom he could bully! I flew low that day where it was nice and warm and had lots of fun amusing myself, flying around the mountains and seeing them at close range (however, the altitude was always safe, Mother!). My ship was faster than some others so I flitted all about while the others flew straight— always within sight of the others however. I could see those dips in the paving which impeded our automobile progress. Remember? It was so much fun to see all those things from the air that we saw together on the ground.

Phoenix and the valley were beautiful as ever and Thunderbird Field was heaven.

I am in the cockpit of an AT-6 and Madelon Burcham is on the wing. We are reviewing the status of the aircraft prior to flight. April 1944.

Just like a big beautiful country club or should I say flying club? There was constantly in the air the odor of wet grass, fruit blossoms, and odors of the brilliantly colored flowers. We could pick all the flowers we wished, so I had a boutonnière of sweet peas. They were sweet. Thunderbird is owned by several Hollywood movie stars and producers and is a government-contract school just like ours at Sweetwater. Both American and Chinese boys are trained there. Many Chinese cannot understand English, but are very adept to hand signals from American instructors. The American boys have to look out for the Chinese boys who are playful in the air but are not good judges of distance and speed! Otherwise they are excellent fliers.

We arrived at Thunderbird Thursday night, but planes (the AT-11s from Las Vegas) did not arrive to pick us up until Friday night so we stayed in Phoenix again and came home this morning. Thursday night we girls stayed at the Westward Ho. Remember the scent of orange blossom on the patio? Last night the lieutenant called the San Carlos for reservations which was rather nice too, but more expensive than our rooms the night before.

We have always respected our reserved and dignified and young Lieutenant Pauls, transition school head and our immediate boss, but we have often wondered how much was back of it. We found out this trip in Oklahoma City. One of the girls made such a play for him, and most men would go in for a little fun—married or not—Lt. Pauls is married. But not Lt. Pauls. He was a bit amused and paid more attention to Betty and me in spite of the attentions of the other girl. It is nice to know that there are still such people as that in a topsy-turvy world and profession.

Are your colds better? Do take good care of yourselves for each other and for me. It would be wonderful if a trip would take us near Des Moines or St. Louis. If we came near, I know they would let me go the rest of the way. Sweetwater was out of the way on this trip. Aren't they swell? We don't expect much ferrying though. We were amused to hear that 15 of our B-17 and B-26 pilots had to go yesterday to ferry Stearmans (the kind we ferried—PT-17s). Ha! Ha! One of them ground looped too. Ha! And some of our girls had never been checked out in them!

Yes, I use my phonograph a great deal and I would love more records—La Mer (an album) and "The Swan of Tuonela" (a single record) if you ever have time (they are there at home). Thank you for the pictures and medicine. Miss Weiss said, "Hello, Marie, good luck," on the label.

Oh, Harpers and Williams wanted to be remembered to you. Mr. Williams is recovering from a rather serious appendectomy. Yes, that was Dorothea Norris whom you met?

Sleepy!

Love,
Marie

Comment

Shoes were rationed at this time of the war. To purchase a pair I needed ration stamps. In this case, a no. 1 stamp.

The bullying we got from the junior officer was certainly not typical of the treatment WASPs generally received. The excessive use of authority by senior officers was infrequent. We taxied our PT-17s back along the runway since, without radios, we could not receive instructions from the control tower.

Letter 53

OFFICERS MESS
LAS VEGAS ARMY AIR FIELD
LAS VEGAS, NEVADA

April 10, 1944

Dear Mother:

A very happy birthday to you! Have you had time to celebrate today? Do you feel 56 years old? You will always look and seem like 35 to me. You never change. I hadn't forgotten the important day, but last week that x-c [cross-country] came so unexpectedly and we collect per diem after the cross-country and not before and I had to borrow to complete that. Regular payday has happened now though, so I can send a gift. I am afraid again that you will have to buy what you wish because Las Vegas is no better than Sweetwater for shopping. Will you please spend it for something you would like very much?

The letter postmarked 1:30 pm, March 7 [I think I must have meant April 7], came today. Not bad, eh? I shall try to answer your questions without delay. Yes, I like very much to read letters from others which you enclose. Any that you would like back please mention. Sweetwater was quite a ways south of the trip—the distance from Oklahoma City south. It would have been quite a direct route straight west from Okla. C. through Amarillo, Albuquerque to Phoenix.

Yes, you may send the belt to Mrs. Urban. When I called her she said she had not received it. When I wouldn't let her pay for it, she wanted my address so she could send cookies. Isn't that sweet? I still don't know the street address, so just send it to Mrs. Robert K. Urban, Sweetwater, Texas.

Did you have a very nice Easter? I went to church for the first time since I have been here—in the post chapel. It was packed—it is quite large and there are several services every Sunday. That takes several chaplains. The music is beautiful—a nice organ and a small, very lovely, well-trained choir. Then I spent the whole after-noon on the flight line flying. I took Donnie [WAC Lt. Donovan] *for a ride. She loved it. In the evening we saw a very funny show,* The Heavenly Body.

This morning Rosie and I played tennis early. Neither of us is scheduled to fly until 10:30. I would like my striped denim shorts—nice ones that I made, you know, that button down the side and also my bathing suit. The officers' swimming pool is open now, but I believe it is the only one open on the post as yet.

Happy birthday again to the sweetest lit-tle mother in all the world! Give Daddy a great big kiss please.

Love,
Marie

Letter 54

OFFICERS MESS
LAS VEGAS ARMY AIR FIELD
LAS VEGAS, NEVADA

April 13, 1944

Dear Mother and Daddy:

A new experience happened to me today—one of those things you think will never happen to you. Can you guess? I ground-looped! There was no reason for ground-looping today either as far as the wind was concerned. Yesterday afternoon I shot 16 landings in wind which was very strong and gusty and constantly shifting and every landing was beautiful, but today—in a perfectly calm wind condition and smooth air! Major Mixon, the air inspector, had ridden with me Tuesday and on our landing the tail wheel kicked into full swivel and he ordered maintenance to jack it up and fix it immediately (tail wheels are supposed to be steerable). Today after my ground-loop which was apparently again a result of a faulty tail wheel, he called maintenance and ordered every tail wheel jacked up and inspected.

There was nothing unpleasant about it, but one hates to ruin a plane. I got one

125

wing-tip and an aileron. Thank goodness, the landing gear wasn't damaged—it nearly always is.

After such an experience, people are always checked on landing, but they didn't check me. Lt. Pauls said I could take the whole afternoon off, if I wished or go fly, whichever I wished. So I practiced 10 landings solo. I didn't ground-loop anymore.

Everyone was swell. They said there are only two kinds of AT-6 pilots, those who have ground-looped and those who will. Nearly every pilot on the field has ground-looped at some time.

We had wonderful news. We are all going to the Army's instrument instructors' school at Bryan, Texas, eventually. Orders came from the Western Command in Santa Ana for Ruthie Jones and Jeanette Jenkins to report for the 6 weeks of training April 21. Isn't it wonderful? We all have to take 4 weeks of Officers' Training in Orlando, Florida, too. Betty Wall, Madelyn Taylor, and I report June 21. We shall go in alphabetical order, so Madelon B. goes May 17, I believe that is the date.

I have tried to call you several times. On Monday night in Oklahoma City, last night, and again tonight. But apparently you can't hear the telephone from upstairs. Tonight the lines were very busy and, by the time the 2 or 3-hour delay would elapse, you would be in bed again, so I cancelled it after the first hour.

If we can possibly get gas, there is a way to get the car here. Lieutenant Lloyd Smith is going home to Des Moines on leave

Saturday night and would like to drive the car back. He is a pilot here. Tomorrow I shall see the adjutant about a letter from the commanding officer for gas. If that fails would you try for some? It would be better to have the letter before the ration board is approached—if I can get it. Oh, I do hope we can get it (the car) out here. Would you have the fenders fixed and the seat covers fixed first please? Have everything checked thoroughly. Bye now.

Love,
Marie

Comment

To ground-loop an airplane is to lose control of its track along the runway after landing. There are a lot of reasons this might happen to a pilot, although most of one's colleagues would call them excuses! A ground-loop usually happens when landing in a gusty crosswind and the wind lifts one wing before the pilot can use the rudder to straighten the path of the airplane. When this occurs the opposite wing scrapes the runway causing some, usually minor, damage to the wing-tip. The aircraft then goes into a rotational mode, called a "ground-loop." Of course, everyone on the flight line sees it, much to the embarrassment of the pilot. In my case, however, there was a cause beyond my control. This was an improperly maintained tail wheel, which pivoted freely instead of responding to control by me using the rudder pedals. My only alternative in this case would be to use the wheel brakes for control, but as the "loop" happens so fast it is virtually impossible to use the brakes for this correction.

My need for my car is still great. Fortunately, arrangements for Lt. Smith to pick it up at home and drive it to Las Vegas worked out fine. Gas coupons were approved by my commanding officer. I am embarrassed as I read this letter sixty years later of how much extra work I asked my parents to do. They were always loving and faithful parents!

Letter 55

OFFICERS MESS
LAS VEGAS ARMY AIR FIELD
LAS VEGAS, NEVADA

April 16, 1944

Dear Mother and Daddy:
Today we had a real sandstorm and the wind is still blowing quite furiously. I am going to bed to get warm. This was the first day for summer uniforms too!

We walked to and from church in the sandstorm and filled our eyes and ears and hair and mouths with grit. Our blue uniforms were white with sand. But the church service was lovely and we had some beautiful organ music and a tenor solo. The sermon was wonderful—something about confidence in ourselves to do our job well. The chaplain, Chaplain Gray, has such a convincing way of stating things. You could have heard a pin drop. It was the type of sermon that should send the boys' morale way up high. It did mine.

After church WAC Lt. Margaret and I went to the club and listened to Tchaikovsky, Stravinsky, and Brahms.

We are moving to a one-story building in the hospital unit. It is just across the street north from our present B.O.Q. It will be nicer because the whole building will belong to the 6 WAC officers and us WASPs. Also we have a reception room which we have had to do without before.

Smitty left last night for Des Moines with the letter for the gas. There was no argument with the adjutant for the gas whatsoever. I merely stated what I wanted and he had the secretary write out the letter. Isn't it wonderful? Smitty will be at his mother-in-law's at 1530 Lay Street. He spoke as though he would like you to go to the ration board office with him, Daddy. He will call you and you can meet him there. He probably will not have a way to get out to our house for the car either. Will you meet him please? He is a nice fellow. You will like him. You could send those records I asked for in the car. I am trying to think of other things I want. Goodnight.

Love,
Marie

The B-17F, "Flying Fortress," which I flew as copilot at Las Vegas. 1944.

Letter 56

OFFICERS MESS
LAS VEGAS ARMY AIR FIELD
LAS VEGAS, NEVADA

April 19, 1944

Dear Mother and Daddy:

This is just a short little note in answer to your question about the car. I can't stay awake much longer. (Please excuse the writing. I am writing on my lap.)

It would be better for the car to come now, because Madelon reports to Orlando May 17 and wouldn't be here to see her mother—and I report June 21 and would have the car only a few days before leaving. Now I shall have it a whole month longer. It would be nice to have you come out, but I shall be routed through Des Moines and stop off one day on the way without having to take leave for that one day. Don't tell anyone about the one day, please!

Smitty left last Saturday night. No doubt you have heard from him by this time. He is to arrive back here April 29. Don't let the ration board talk you out of that car. Transportation is a serious problem here.

I am trying to think of things for you to send in the car if Smitty has room for them. You might send the rest of my records—La Mer (a volume), "The Swan of Tuonela" (single), "Night Soliloquy" (single), and isn't there another volume or is there? I can't remember what I had—oh, yes, "Afternoon of a Faun" (single). Don't send any of Eloise's records. Please send some Kleenex. Kleenex is very scarce here. There is some in the attic. I could use a few hangers (clothes).

We shall be in Orlando for only 4 weeks. I shall answer more of your questions next time. You must have had fun at your formal birthday dinner.

Goodnight.

> *Love,*
> *Marie*

Letter 57

OFFICERS MESS
LAS VEGAS ARMY AIR FIELD
LAS VEGAS, NEVADA

April 20, 1944

Dear Mother and Daddy:

Today has been a day of funny weather for Las Vegas. The sky has been partly clear and partly covered with heavy cumulus clouds with heavy rain streaks hanging from the clouds to the earth. We watched them come over from the other side of Mount Charleston while we flew. Then the rain finally reached us so that flying was called off last period this morning. The sky is still heavy this evening and once in a while it sprinkles! It reminds me of spring thundershowers at home (without the thunder) and it looks so good.

We are all moved into our new quarters. We have a large reception room and doors on our wardrobes to keep out dust. Some of the girls are painting their walls and finishing floors, etc. I haven't decided whether to bother or not. My nice bright cretonne draperies are up and it looks so cheery.

There are 10 WASPs on this field when we are all here. Two have gone to Bryan to instrument instructors' school for six weeks and one is at home on medical leave. That leaves 7 right now. We figured out that it will be at least August before we are all together again. I doubt if we will be then though, if we all go to Bryan—two at a time—and we all expect to go.

No, Betty Wall is the one whom you met in your hotel room with Madelon—the little blonde. You met another but larger blonde on the street, Rosie Lewis. Betty and Madelon are here with me at the club writing.

Love,
Marie

If you have difficulty with our ration board about the gas, go to the state board office, and they will fix it up. A letter from the commanding officer of LVAAF is a command, but you never know about our board.

I shall enclose the paycheck I got today and hope that our travel check comes soon because I am broke.

Letter 58

OFFICERS MESS
LAS VEGAS ARMY AIR FIELD
LAS VEGAS, NEVADA

April 30, 1944

Dear Mother and Daddy:

I see there are 3 of your letters to be answered, but if I don't write fairly often I forget all the many things I wanted to tell you. And you ask so many questions (that is O.K.—please do) that I might forget a few.

Smitty came out in his own car yesterday

afternoon and took me back to his house in town to pick up my car. Was I glad to see it! He apparently drove very little extra. The speedometer was just a few miles over 29,300 and he had 40 gallons in coupons left. He had a little tire trouble. A blister formed on one tire, but he said if it cannot be vulcanized, he will go 50-50 on a new one. I don't suppose it is his fault because two of the tires have been previously vulcanized. It is so nice and clean inside and the seat covers look so nice. Thank you so much for the box. Those supplies should last for quite some time. And the cookies! They are swell. I hope you don't miss the car too much. It is running beautifully.

I must write to Aunt Maple and Uncle Elmer and congratulate them on being grandparents again. Aunt Maple must be very busy with Mary Lea.

Madelon has been walking on crutches for two or 3 days. Her knee might be a little serious because the cartilage is broken too. It is possible that an operation will be necessary after her leg comes out of the cast—10 weeks—then 4 weeks in a splint. She will probably move back to our quarters next week. She can go anywhere and do anything now. The cast is over the foot and all the way up to her hip. She doesn't want to go home.

She was supposed to go to Orlando May 17. We haven't had another directive on who will take her place. The best route to Florida is through Chicago. That is why we can stop at home. We are to take Union Pacific through Ames. I don't know about

connections with the Rocket in Denver.

Yesterday the student of mine who took his check promised me a ride in a "6" (AT-6) if he passed his check ride. He passed, so today we had a beautiful ride over Lake Mead and through the lower Grand Canyon. It was lovely. I thought of high stone castles on each side of us and the colors were beautiful (this is off the record).

This same student took me on a beautiful ride Friday, too. The sky was full of rain clouds and we dodged about them, then went over to see the cliff over which we fly everyday, but seen from below in the valley, it was a new world. Do you remember when we drove into Las Vegas, we saw the high jutting rocks on the left? That is the cliff of which I'm speaking and they have vivid colorings. That same flight my student asked me if I wanted to go under the hood, so I flew instruments and he sat in front and shouted at me constantly over the interphones the way I shouted at him, only worse. Then he gave me unusual positions and I couldn't for the life of me come out of them. I would swear we were upside down, but he says we were not. It was fun. That was George Stewart.

Everything happened that day. The next period when Randy Longinaker started flying the radio beam, he started losing altitude and he lost altitude constantly clear down to traffic altitude. He was not doing his let-down, he was just losing altitude! Once I called him up and asked if he were doing lazy 8s. He would make a large correction in heading one direction and lose several hundred feet, and make a large correction the other direction and gain several hundred. It was so funny. These students of mine! But they fly beautifully when I get through with them. Brag! Brag! The third student, Bill Catlin, president of the Ground Loop club (because he has yet to be surpassed in sensational ground-loops), has been out 4 days with a cold.

Tomorrow in addition to flying 4+ hours each day as usual, we start B-17 ground school—4 hours each day. This is in preparation for co-piloting B-17s. It will be fun.
Must sleep. Goodnight!

Love,
Marie

P.S. Yes, Daddy, this Orlando training is in preparation for our commissioning as officers. It is military indoctrination or something. I am enclosing a $25 bond. Tell Aunt Maple I shall send you copies of all those pictures and she may have the ones she spoke about. I shall get you another copy too if you want it and if it is obtainable.
Bye,

Me

Comment

Conducting maneuvers down to traffic altitude meant that an aircraft was carrying out training exercises at the same altitude other aircraft were flying as they entered the flight pattern preparing to land at the air base. This created an unsafe condition and was in violation of LVAAB regulations.

Letter 59

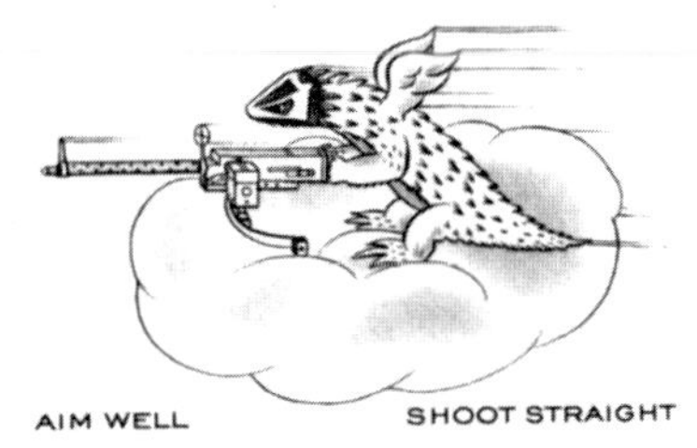

May 12, 1944

Dear Mother and Daddy:
Your daughter has been very neglectful, hasn't she? I really don't remember how long it has been.

We finished B-17 ground school today. It has been very wonderful. It is by far the best ground school and best equipped I have ever seen. Captain Shirley says it is the best in the country and I know very well it must be. The instructors were sergeants who have worked on 17s a long time and know the ship inside and out. Each sergeant specializes in one system and each has "mock-ups" of that one system set up in his room. In other words the actual system of a ship arranged in the best possible way, the way the system is arranged in the ship. And each one can be turned on so that we see the actual operation. Systems studied were electrical, hydraulic, engine, supercharger, oil, fuel, radio (there are several radios of various kinds in the 17), instruments (automatic pilot, fluxgate compass), electronics, heating and ventilation, emergency equipment, wing de-icers, propeller anti-icers;

that must be everything. Isn't that enough? It is wonderful. It is certainly a complicated airplane. We have spent 4 hours a day for two weeks in ground school as well as doing our usual flying.

All my students so far have passed their check rides—4 so far. Another will be ready in a few days. I started a new one today. The fellows are all swell and I enjoy it. They don't seem to resent us now the way we felt they did at first.

The music is playing so loudly I can't think of any of the many things I wanted to say.

I would like to bother you for my swimming cap and my two pairs of navy slacks that I sent home with my civilian clothes. I am cooking in my wools. And I would like that pair of white wedgie slippers too. Isn't this the silliest letter you have ever received from me?

Guess I had better close. Bye now.

Love,
Marie

Comment

I believe we misjudged the feelings of the male pilots regarding any resentment they may have felt about our flying with them and teaching them as well. Such attitudes did exist at other USAF bases but rarely at LVAAB.

Letter 60

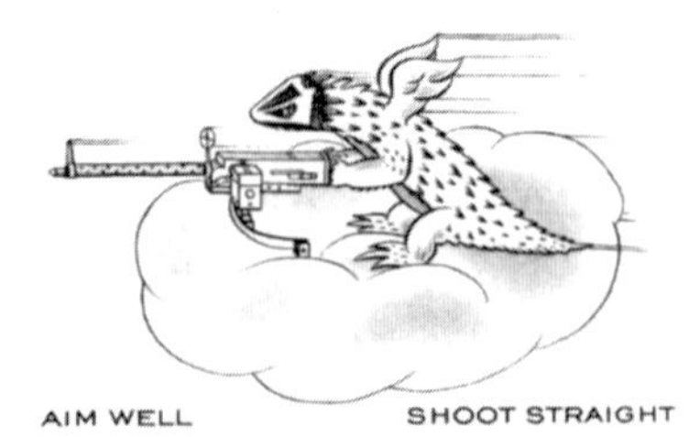

May 16, 1944

Dear Mother and Daddy:

Madelon is sitting on the davenport at the club waiting for Jack so I am sitting with her.

We had a surprise tonight. It is raining! Very lightly but steadily. Rain is quite an event in this desert. It is cold too.

We are having another surprise now—a very pleasant one. A fellow is at the piano playing and playing nice classical music. Madelon said he had played for an hour a while ago. Today I went into the music store to buy records, but they didn't have what I wanted. I would love to have Brahms's First Symphony, if you would have time to call Younkers and while you are calling, ask the cosmetics department to send Max Factor's pancake makeup in tan rose shade. Madelon wants one too. I found some lipstick, so don't bother with that.

Mother, I have an apology to make to you. I thought of Mother's Day Saturday night, and that, it seemed, was too late. I am so sorry. I thought about you hard all day Sunday though.

Sunday I had the nicest time I have had since coming here. Marj Harper and I went with a couple of fellows to Charleston Park up on the side of Mount Charleston (11,910 feet high). You wouldn't believe there was such a place in Nevada. The place was covered with huge white pines and quaking aspen. We parked the car as far as we could go (my date had the car—a former student of mine, George Stewart) and walked up very steep paths—over snow part of the way—to the top of cathedral rock. Then we came down a steeper path—I should say we slipped down. It took the whole afternoon. Then we had a wonderful steak dinner at the lodge, which is run by the Last Frontier Hotel in Vegas. Our field runs a camp up there too. You know how I love that sort of thing. Oh, we saw two waterfalls too and drank from one of them. When there wasn't a waterfall we wet our throats with snow. George is such a nice fellow without the "wolfish" tendencies of most fellows. He flies AT-6s and P-39s.

Saturday night I went to a nice quiet steak house for dinner (instead of to the usual nice hot spots, of which I am extremely weary) with Madelon and Jack and a little friend of mine, John Clark. He is only 21, but is about the nicest fellow I think I ever met. He has been here in co-pilots' school and all last week he followed me around "like a puppy pattering along behind" as his fellow classmates described him. He is an engineer in civilian life. He has eager eyes, a determined chin, a charming nonchalance as well as a charm-

Lt. George Stewart in front of his car at Mount Charleston. May 14, 1944.

Me in front of Lt. George Stewart's Ford at Mount Charleston. May 14, 1944.

ing "line." He is cute. This week he is at Indian Springs but will tear the Army down to get here Saturday night next. Did I tell you what he and I did a week ago? We went through the Basic Magnesium Plant [located in Henderson, NV, not far from Las Vegas]. I think I told you. One night we took sandwiches and limeades from the club and had a moonlight picnic by the pool.

This morning I shot my first landings from the backseat of a "6." One student was not there so the other one, Ken Sarchet, rode safety for me in the front seat while I flew the beam under the hood. Then he made me shoot a couple of landings. It was fun.

Oh, I should have told you. About a week ago John was confined to post for something he was perfectly innocent of (not appearing on flight line when not scheduled to fly) but he didn't do anything about it—just took it. Saturday he wanted to take me off the post for once so we got Jack (Madelon's Jack, the other officer in charge of the co-pilots) to get John excused.

I am debating whether to stop for that one day on the way to Florida or put it with several other days and take a leave after Florida. Madelon's mother may come out June 1. Why don't you come with her, Mother? You too Daddy?

Thank you so much for all the colored pictures. May I have one of Dolores and me to give to Dolores? Guess I had better sign off. Bye.

Love,
Marie

P.S. Enclosed you will find a $50 bond and a money order for Mother's Day. Mother, I would like an inexpensive light blue chenille bedspread—72 inches wide. Did you find a swimming cap among my things?

Me

Comment

Two very important events occurred about the same time in my life, one happy and the other sad.

The happy event was meeting that "little friend of mine, John Clark," whom I described to my parents as "cute." John's attention to me was evident to all and I found it flattering. The description of his following me around like a puppy was petty and misleading. John obviously saw the potential depth of our relationship much sooner than I. He never uttered a word of resentment to the puppy analogy probably because, if he even heard it, his own determination to enlarge our relationship simply rode over it. I have learned over the years that this is one of his strong personal characteristics. Once he decides on a course of action, very little will deter him. He usually succeeds where others have failed.

The sad event was the death of my former student, Lt. George Stewart, in the crash of a B-26 in Arkansas about ten days after this letter was written. He was with a group of five or six other LVAAB pilots flying to Georgia to pick up P-39s to ferry back when they encountered severe thunderstorms over the Ozarks. The aircraft apparently broke up in flight as no one parachuted out and all were killed. George was from Chattanooga, TN. I was told that his father came to Las Vegas to pick up his car.

The first date I had with John was a visit to the Basic Magnesium Plant in

Henderson, Nevada. Here they made magnesium by using electricity from Boulder Dam. We both were curious about the plant since we could see it from the air. We arrived at the plant after dark and were told at first that the plant was closed to visitors. I was quite surprised, impressed, and pleased at how John managed the situation. He explained to the guard that we were both pilots at the air base and could not get away during normal visiting hours. This was the only time we had to visit and we were very interested in the operations. The guard was friendly and after checking with his supervisor, admitted us to the plant. Inside we were turned over to the shift supervisor who gave us a personally guided tour. One thing I recall is that the electrical conductors transmitting the electricity to make the magnesium carried 50,000 amperes of current. They were made of pure silver borrowed from the US Mint! Their safety was assured!

Letter 61

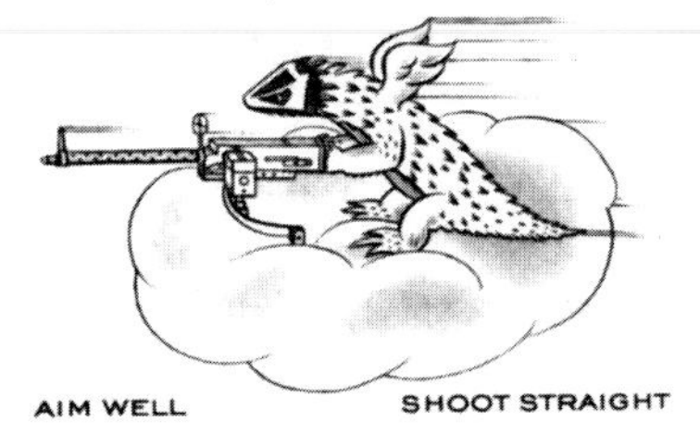

May 18, 1944

Dear Mother and Daddy:

I look very beautiful now. I am sitting under the drier at the Sal Sagen Beauty Shop in Las Vegas. It is the first time for some time that I have had to come in for they are open only during the day. They do beautiful work here.

Las Vegas is having its yearly spree of several days' duration—the Helldorado. All the men have beards (the townsmen only, thank goodness!) and wear western clothes. They have a barbecue, parade, and several rodeos—two rodeos each day for 3 days. I am afraid it doesn't attract me.

Last night was my first experience with bowling. Gee, it was fun. And such high scores I made—17! the first game, but the second was 54. Al Cummings was highest with 189. Both he and George [Stewart] are pretty good, I think. They were certainly patient trying to teach poor dumb me. It was a little hard on my left hip and the two middle fingers on the right hand. But they are pretty good today.

I gave Sarchet his last ride this morning

This is the only photo I have of John in Las Vegas. It was taken at the Dunes, a quiet Las Vegas restaurant. L-R: Madelon Burcham, WASP, 1st Lt. Jack Hill, me, and 2nd Lt. John Clark. May 13, 1944.

Fifty-eight years later at a WASP reunion in Tucson, Arizona, we posed for the same photo taken in Las Vegas in 1944. October 2002.

before his check. He flew beautifully and I was really proud. Forbes did well on basic this morning so I shall start him on radio tomorrow.

Yesterday I received the pictures that were taken of the 4 of us at the Dunes last Saturday night. There was an extra copy—a very poor print—but the pictures are very good—so I shall send it and show it to Madelon's mother please. We each have a copy so you may keep yours.

I haven't had a letter from you for days but I know you are very busy. You have certainly had a lot on. Please don't wear your-

selves out. I am so glad, Mother, that you can be out easier, because I know you love it. The Klechners must be very swell. I would love to see them when I come home. And Uncle Elmer and Aunt Maple. Those are the only ones.

How about Mother's coming out? Don't you think it a wonderful idea, Daddy? She won't be traveling alone either.

My hair must be about dry. Madelon and I are going out in the sun when I get home.

Love,
Marie

Comment

I have always loved this photo as it shows John as he actually is: happy, eager, and bright. John had been confined to the base this weekend for some minor infraction of the rules. I don't think he even knew what the rule was. However, Jack Hill, who had a lot of authority over the copilot training program which John was in, intervened and freed him to join us for this memorable dinner. Jack and Madelon were married in the summer of 1944 and John and I were married a year later. Each couple will celebrate their sixty-first and sixtieth wedding anniversaries, respectively, in 2005.

We had an opportunity to repeat this 1944 Las Vegas pose at a WASP reunion in Tucson, Arizona, fifty-eight years later, in 2002. We are seated in the same order as in 1944 and the passing years are evident!

Letter 62

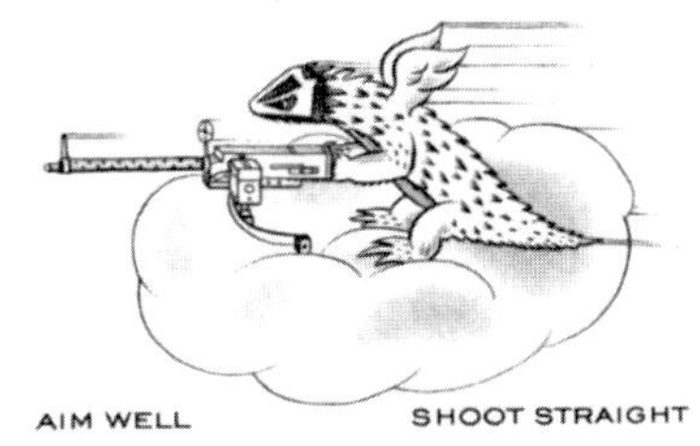

May 23, 1944

Dear Daddy:

Happy birthday! It seems as though I always write on the important day and not *before so that you can get it on time. Anyway you know that I am thinking about you, don't you? I shall enclose a very original gift, a money order, and hope that you buy something for a very special daddy. Please don't forget about it. Just sending money seems so queer, but I hope there is something you want very much, but perhaps wouldn't buy otherwise.*

You sound very, very busy, Daddy, from Mother's letters. I suppose it is all piled up from the delay caused by the rain. Please don't wear yourself out completely.

Your picnics at the field would be fun. May I come? We used to have fun doing that, didn't we? Does Mother still take lemonade to you at 3:30? Wish I could. Mother's description of the flowers, garden, birds, etc. sounds wonderful to us. In fact, we can hardly imagine such a thing out here. Green growing things must be the most beautiful color there is.

John and I drove up to Charleston again last Sunday. It was beautiful as ever and so cold we wore jackets. We climbed the mountains and then had a lovely steak dinner at the lodge and made wishes by heating pennies in the candle flame and sticking them in the heavy, multi-colored, tallowed candle stick—what I mean is, the sticks are bottles—wine bottles, etc., I suppose, over which they have dripped lots of tallow of different colors. In the bottle is a white candle. The hot pennies can be stuck in the tallow on the bottles. It is fun anyway, even if it is silly. John is the finest boy I have ever known. I wish he were only

On the road to Mount Charleston. May 1944.

A view from Mount Charleston down the valley toward Las Vegas. May 21, 1944.

about ten years older! On the way down we stopped the car to examine the millions of flowers along the road. Then we saw many other kinds back away from the road—so tiny that you couldn't see them until right upon them. There were all kinds, all colors, and so many of them very, very tiny. You would love them in a rock garden. Mother would go nuts to see them.

Is Mother working on that invitation June 1? I hope she comes. Madelon hasn't heard from her mother for 3 weeks. What is she so busy doing?

The white lady who was our maid last week while awaiting another job on the field came back today to do shirts for us. Starting last Friday, we have a colored man, "Striker" as the Army calls him. He cleans and makes beds and does many things for us. He is wonderful. He does a beautiful job. He regrets not having a brush so he could clean behind radiators! He probably has one by now. He washed my car Saturday. Clarence is an enlisted

man—I don't know his rank. Every B.O.Q. on all Army posts has one, but they hadn't gotten around to us girls before. We certainly got a jewel.

The car was simonized today by a colored fellow—$8.50. He did a beautiful job. He did Jack's car [Madelon's Jack] *and Jack got him to do mine.*

Another student passed a check ride Saturday. He was my best. There is just one more to go and that will be next Saturday. I have been very lucky not to have a student flunk a check ride. Our instrument job is about finished. The next job is still in the rumor stage. I shall tell you more about it later, when we know more ourselves. Please excuse the writing. I am sitting on Madelon's bed.

Goodnight, Daddy.

Love,
Marie

Comment

I always felt badly about sending my parents money to buy themselves gifts, but shopping away from home was difficult during the war since goods were scarce, I was not familiar with the shops, and I had very little time to get away from the base.

John and I began spending more and more time together and I realized that we shared a great many hopes and aspirations. Driving to Mount Charleston was one of the things we both enjoyed. Here we could explore the beautiful landscapes and scenery of the mountains. It was much too early in our friendship for me to have any thoughts of a more permanent relationship, but the seeds of one must have been in my mind when I wrote my parents that "I wish he were only about ten years older." He certainly seemed to me to be a fine person who stood out among the others I knew. His time at Las Vegas was rapidly coming to an end so we made a point to be together as much as we could. We both sensed that our friendship was something we wanted to mature.

On the way down from the mountain we stopped by the roadside to look at the wildflowers. Further off the road, on the desert floor, we found a multitude of blossoms so small that we had to crouch down to even see them. On my final flight at LVAAB, months later, as I soared high above the desert, I remembered these miniature flowers, bringing back the memory of our happy Sunday afternoon together. By that time John was flying combat missions over Germany and faced an uncertain future.

Letter 63

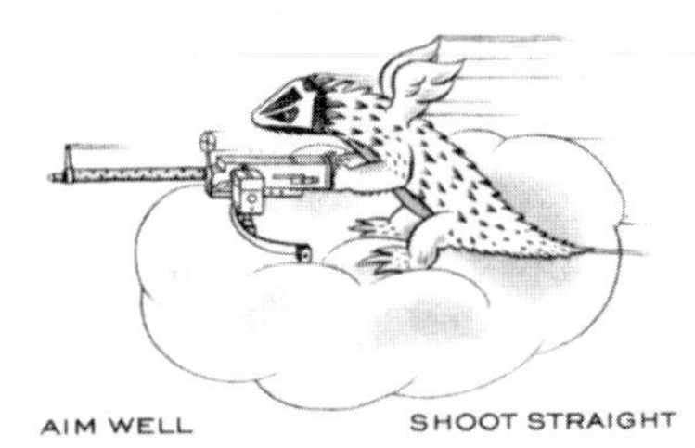

May 25, 1944

Dear Mother and Daddy:

This has been a very nice day. This morning one of Betty Wall's students was given to me so I flew the two students a total of 3:25 [hours]. Then right after lunch I got the sudden notion that maybe I could start AT-11s today, so I called Lt. Skelton in our transition office, and he called to see if a ship would be available and I drove to the flight line and we went right up. I co-piloted for awhile, then we landed and I took the pilot's seat. I taxied to takeoff point, called the tower and took off and flew out in the practice area awhile and came back and landed with Skelton as co-pilot. It was my first experience of being the real pilot of a twin-engine ship. I have a total time of 1:10 at present. The AT-11 is a beautiful ship in which to start one's twin-engine experience. It is a cabin ship with twin tails too. 900 HP altogether.

Madelyn Taylor and I went swimming later. The water was cold and very invigorating so tonight I am sleepy. That sentence is a bit contradictory, isn't it?

Betty Wall is going home on 3 weeks' sick leave tomorrow. They say she has "pilot's fatigue." She loves to fly like I do so I suppose she must just be tired. It is too bad. I shall miss her. She and I will go to Florida together though at the end of that time. It is a bit of a tragedy because her friend, Hal, thinks he will be shipped out in July before Betty arrives back and they had planned on being married, though John and I are the only ones who know. Hal is stationed at the Springs [the auxiliary field 43 miles up the valley] *and John has been there last week and this—and next, too—so the two fly down to see Betty and me as often as they can. John will be gone after next week.*

Are you coming June 1, Mother? I suppose you will not want to leave Daddy while he is so busy, but I would love to see you and have you see the field and everything. Of course, I shall soon be home—in July. Don't tell anyone now. I haven't asked for leave, but I am quite sure of it. I have some coming—at the rate of 26 days per year (civil service). After Florida would be a perfect time because it would be a "delay en route" and travel time would not come out of leave time.

Did you find the $60 money order? I couldn't quite spare the whole check. There was something else—Oh, yes, I don't believe I told you how much I appreciated the cookies and your sending the box of stuff. Thank you so very much. Of course, you know that those are my favorite cookies.

Sweet dreams!
Marie

Letter 64

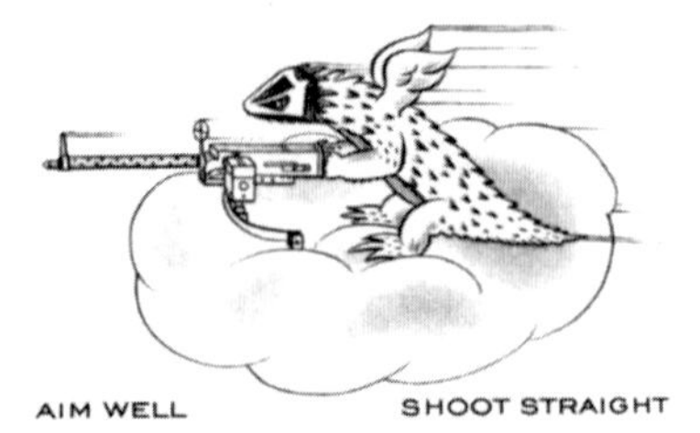

May 29, 1944

Dear Mother and Daddy:
Such a beautiful day! The valley has been full of heavy clouds and heavy rain showers. I flew with a new student from 7:30 to 10:00 this morning and we were in rain nearly all the time. Some showers were so heavy that we had to avoid them completely because visibility was absolutely zero. There was real lightning too, though rather scattered, and on the ground we heard thunder. When we landed there was the most delicious odor of wet pine in the air. I couldn't see any pines, but the odor was beautiful. It brought back memories of Minnesota in the rain.

This afternoon Gwen Crosby and I started out shooting landings in the "11" with Pulling. She flew first to be sure to get her flight in because she leaves Thursday. I stood between her and Pulling just in back of the pilots' compartment. She did 4 or 5 and the tower called us to fly to Kingman, Arizona, to take someone down, so my "11" flying today consisted of flying to Kingman. Gwen flew back.

This was a lovely weekend. John was down from the springs and being with him is so satisfying whether we do anything or not. We did errands in town—mostly laundry and cleaning—for everyone—Jack and Madelon and Oscar and my stuff—then had a picnic with stuff from the grocery store and sandwiches and tea from the mess hall. We saw fresh strawberries in the kitchen in preparation for breakfast so we went to bed early and got up for breakfast and sat beside the pool awhile and went to church at 10:00. We had dinner and called on Bob Shawn's wife (Bob is away with a group to fly back P-39s) to see their red-headed baby. Then I slept awhile and dressed and we went to the Dunes in town for steak and sat there most of the evening. It was fun. I still wish 21-year-old John were about 10 years older. Mentally he is old, but he looks like such a boy. You would think him O.K.

We had a blow here last Friday. One of the B-26s, which was carrying the pilots to Georgia to fly back P-39s, crashed in Arkansas and George Stewart, of whom I have written, was aboard. It was quite a low blow to me because he was such a swell person. He had about the highest ideals of anyone I know besides John. It was the first B-26 ever to be lost at this station. If you go down flying your own ship it isn't so bad. But George was a passenger this time. It is just hard to believe—George of all people—because he was so conservative in every way—particularly in flying, because he loved to fly and he didn't want ever to do anything that might mean being grounded. Things like that are all in the course of events, of course.

You must have had a wonderful time in Lincoln, etc. I am so glad you could go. Perhaps you weren't so tired as usual in summer so that you did have more fun. You always sound as though you are having fun no matter what it is. That makes me happy. I am sorry about the fieldwork though. We have been reading about the floods and rains in Madelon's Registers [a newspaper, the Des Moines Register]. She still hasn't heard from her family. Her cast came off today but she is still on crutches.

I am glad you sent Eloise's letter. That is the only way I hear. Of course, I owe her a letter. Poor little Suzie had really been ill.

Yes, I would like The Hearthstone. John is always giving me clippings which his aunt and mother send him. We haven't heard more about Bryan [instrument training at Bryan AFB, Bryan, Texas]. What we hear about the WASP controversy is mostly from you. I am glad to hear.

Love,
Marie

Comment

I still was thinking about John and considering how we might maintain our relationship. My observations about him to my parents, pro and con, indicated that I was becoming more serious about him, in weighing the prospects. I was preparing them for more news about him by suggesting that they "would think him O.K."

The crash of the B-26 in Arkansas, killing all the LVAAB pilots aboard including Lt. George Stewart, was a severe blow to us all. His death was a great loss and something that was very difficult to explain. I believe there may have been two B-26s on that ferry mission, as I mention that Lt. Bob Shawn "is away with a group to fly back P-39s."

The status of the WASP was becoming national news. We were so busy that we really knew little of it and depended on news from home. It became a major controversy in the Army Air Force, resulting in our deactivation in December 1944.

Letter 65

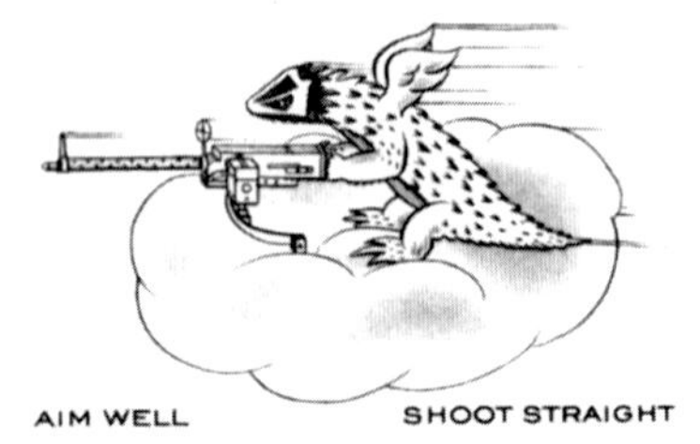

May 30, 1944

Dear Mother and Daddy:

I went to rail transportation today to make arrangements for the journey to Florida. I shall leave here at 4:10 am June 13 and arrive in Des Moines at 2:46 am on the Rocket on June 15. I shall leave on the Rocket at 7:15 am June 17 and arrive in Orlando June 19 at 12:30 pm. Will it be all right with you? Please don't tell a soul because I don't want to see anyone but you and Aunt Maple and Uncle Elmer, and you wanted me to meet Kleckners, but please, I only want to meet them. I would like to do some shopping, but the rest of the time let's just be at home or at Uncle Elmer's. That is a horrible time to have to meet a train, isn't it? But the next best was to meet me in Ames at 1:00 something am. I shall ask for a leave of several days on the way back too. I think I shall try to go through St. Louis on the way back. That is, if it will be convenient with Eloise and Johnny and Suzie. I could stay there a day or two and then be at home for 4 or 5 days. It sounds exciting. Golly!

Madelon has a long distance [telephone call] from home waiting and I have looked all over for her.

Love,
Marie

Letter 66

June 7, 1944
Dear Mother and Daddy:
Your last letter isn't anywhere where I can see it, Mother. John was with me at the time, so I read just yours and saved Eloise's and Aunt Clara's until later to read. Gee, I hope I find them.

Last weekend was John's and my last together. He came down from the springs [Indian Springs] Saturday morning and apparently arrived about the time I left in a "6" for the springs but I was there only 30 minutes. We had lunch together and did a few errands in town then spent the rest of the afternoon in our reception room. We chattered and read and I sewed shoulder patches on my uniforms. We ate dinner and dressed and went to the El Rancho Vegas Hotel and ate shrimp salads and saw the floor show and went home. Sunday, we had the most glorious time. We drove out to Lake Mead and got stuck in the sand and couldn't get a boat and drove along the lake to Boulder Dam. We drove across the dam and back and once a guard drove up beside us because we were not keeping directly behind the preceding car. It was the little car's second trip across, wasn't it? Do you remember Boulder City? I had never been there before nor John either. It was paradise in the desert. Did you ever see greener grass? Such a beautiful little town! It is a government reclamation project. We had so much fun there. We ate in a lovely little restaurant and played our theme song over and over on the jukebox, then walked to the park and swung, and teeter-tottered then sat down on the grass and took our shoes and stockings off and put our bare feet on the cool, green grass and even ran around on it barefooted. It was evening then and it became cool so we walked around the streets lined with green grass and trees and shrubs and got a soda at a drugstore and drove home in the moonlight. It was very special, but everything we did together was so special. John left Monday evening for the replacement center at Lincoln, Nebr. I do hope you meet him someday. I still wish he were ten years older and from 3 to 6 inches taller. If he ever goes through Des Moines he will call you and you may invite him out if you wish and treat him like a member of the family. His name, in case I haven't told you, is Lt. John Alden Clark. He is 5'9," 21 years old, has a very clean face, is highly energetic, is a perfect gentleman, and very charming, has a brilliant mind, and a deep, deep voice, and I think he is swell. But he is gone now.

Hal came to see me last night and we cried on each other's shoulders. It was his birthday and Betty was not here to help him celebrate. I was ready for bed so I didn't go. Hal and John saw a lot of each other at the springs as well as on double dates here. Hal and Betty are to be married in the fall but John and I are the only ones who know.

Lt. Siveright hasn't been able to get reservations for me so he asked how early I could go. Anytime from Saturday night on. I shall let you know. Goodnight.

Love,

Marie

Comment

John flew down from Indian Springs with Hal in a B-26, picking up some copilot time in that bomber. He and Hal had become pals and double dated with Betty Wall and me.

For us, as with most young people in all eras, popular music often stimulated sentimental and sweet memories. For John and me, our theme song was "I'll Get By" ("as long as I have you") from the 1944 movie *A Guy Named Joe*, starring Spencer Tracy, Irene Dunne, and Van Johnson. The story is about a bomber pilot who is killed flying out of England and goes to "pilots' heaven" where he sends emissaries to earth to aid pilots encountering trouble in flight. He is in love with an English woman pilot. The correspondence of their story with our own was probably one reason we liked the movie. We saw it at the Las Vegas AAB theater and to this day we recall our wartime memories whenever we hear this song.

I continued to express my wish that John was a little older and taller. I am happy to report that he has more than exceeded my earlier specifications! I included his full name and rank in my letter as I wanted to be certain my parents knew this, as well as his personal qualities. They then would be comfortable should there be an opportunity for him to visit which, I suppose, I hoped would happen some day. As things turned out, he did visit and, to date, has stayed sixty years!

Letter 67

PALMER HOUSE
CHICAGO

June 17, 1944
Father's Day, Chicago, Illinois, 20:00

Dear Mommy and Poppy:

I have a reservation (Pullman) for the first night out of here! I am surprised because the first time I tried today there were none available. At 5:30 I obtained this one.

As you probably have guessed I have a room at the Palmer House and your daughter is scrubbed and fed and in very good spirits. Downstairs there is a sign saying, "No accommodations without confirmed reservation." So I walked up to the window anyway. All I wanted was a room until 9:30 and they said they always try to take care of service people. Isn't that nice?

None of the girls have appeared. Hope they are on the train. Wouldn't wonder if a person has a better chance at reservations on everything, if alone.

I saw a show—Passage to Marseilles or something like that with Marseilles in the title with Humphrey Bogart. It was one of those super-specials. Very good.

No, you are not second choice. John has been neglected for you. I won't have time to write him.

Please take very good care of each other. Goodbye.

Love,
Marie

P.S. Mother, please exchange Suzie's dress so I shall have something to give her. Thank you so very much. I had a very special time at home as you already know.

Me

Comment

I spent a very short two days at home on my way to Orlando. Most of the time I just rested in the warm surroundings of my home with my parents. This was the first time that I'd come home in almost a year and it was refreshing to be in green and verdant Iowa. We paid brief visits to my Uncle Elmer and my Aunt Maple in Des Moines and made short stops to see local friends.

Letter 68

AIR CORPS, UNITED STATES ARMY

Orlando, Florida

June 22, 1944

Dear Mother and Daddy:
Your lovely letter came today, mailed Tuesday. You were very kind about my selfishness, Mother. I did have such a perfect time at home. Please keep yourselves as well as you looked last week.

This post is a dream with buildings as nice as Army posts go, lovely lakes and beautiful pines with long needles—pine trees as thick as any place in Minnesota. Our B.O.Q. is right on the shore of the large lake and has a nice dock handy for us. Every evening the lake breezes blow right through my window. Our B.O.Q.s are large rooms with twenty girls in each one, but each room is lined on both sides—all sides, I mean, with windows and it is so bright and cheery.

Ground school is extremely interesting, though long—8 hours per day. The courses are given by experts.

The mess hall is a cafeteria and the food compares with a cafeteria like Bishop's (in Des Moines) except that the food is even better prepared. It is really wonderful.

Dolores, Kay Murphy, Rosemary Hall, and so many others we know are here.

You probably heard about our bill's being defeated by 20 votes in the house [U.S. House of Representatives] yesterday, but the opinion of the experts here is that it will eventually go through because General Arnold and the War Department get what they go after. General Arnold is out of the country right now.

I am so sleepy. Sleep tight and sweet dreams, Mother and Daddy!

Love,
Marie

Comment

Unfortunately, the US House Bill did not ultimately work out in favor of the WASP. The failure of the WASP to be granted military status led to its deactivation just before Christmas 1944. It was a deep blow to the women pilots, of course, who had demonstrated their ability to fly successfully all aircraft in the USAF inventory. The unsavory political actions aside, it must be recognized that there were, in fact, many more male pilots returning from overseas combat than had initially been assumed when the WASP was created. The details of the political maneuvering on this matter are included in several of the books I cite under "Selected Reading."

Letter 69

AIR CORPS, UNITED STATES ARMY

Orlando, Florida

June 25, 1944
5 pm

Dear Mother and Daddy:
Such lovely hot weather and such very high humidity! We are wringing wet all the time. Nights, however, are comfortable and often at night a lovely lake breeze blows through my window.

This afternoon we had a surprise. A very mild thunderstorm blew up and rained a little and the air is actually a comfortable temperature.

This place is a dream. I have told you about it before, but everyday I drink it in all over again. Beautiful tall white pines very thick, the lakes, one at our backdoor with a dock for good swimming, buildings green [colored] to fit in with the landscape. Our lake is quite large—a mile across at least and the water is warm and fresh. There are two boats and a canoe at our dock.

The roughest part is sitting in ground school 8 hours each day, even on Saturday. But every instructor is such an expert and, in spite of the possibility of boredom in all these subjects, the classes are extremely interesting, partly too because every instructor is such a fine personality. Just listen to this array of subjects: Army orientation, Air Force administration, military courtesy and discipline, base and staff functions, group, post, and squadron duties, AAF communications, military law, AAF weather, recognition of aircraft, organization of War Departments and AAF, Air Force supply, safeguarding military information, chemical warfare, aero-medicine.

It is really raining hard now.

Scotty, a 43-W-6 girl, and I went over to the airbase today to arrange to fly an AT-11 next Sunday. I shall try to get a ride on a plane out of here. I shall finish at 3:00 pm Thursday, July 13. Getting a ride is quite certain but it is hard to tell when within two days. I can't get a train reservation until Saturday afternoon. Then I wouldn't get to Dyersburg [Tennessee] until Sunday night. It will work out.

It is raining very hard now and blowing. The lights went out. The rain looks wonderful.

Please tell Aunt Maple and Uncle Elmer "hello" for me.

Bye.

Love,
Marie

Comment

I traveled by train from Orlando to Des Moines, stopping to visit John at the Dyersburg AAB at Dyersburg, Tennessee, where he was in combat flight crew training in preparation to go overseas to join the Eighth Air Force in England.

Letter 70

AIR CORPS, UNITED STATES ARMY

Orlando, Florida

July 2, 1944
7 pm

Dear Mother and Daddy:
Such a time to do my laundry today! Part of it was ready to put on the line but it looked like rain and it did pour very hard.

Then I put it all out and it has been raining lightly ever since. We have lovely thunderstorms every afternoon or evening.

As usual we have sat in classes from 9:00 to 5:00 every day and right now we are in the midst of exams. Dolores and her class finished and left Friday and a new class will be in in a day or so.

I plan to leave here July 15 and arrive in Dyersburg on Sunday night—stay Monday and Tuesday (John will be off from Monday noon until Tuesday noon) and take a train at 8:30 Wednesday morning for St. Louis, arrive Wednesday night and stay until Friday and arrive home Saturday morning. There should be 2 or 3 days then to spend at home. I asked for 7 days' "delay en route."

This has been a very special week. Do you know that Orlando has a symphonette whose members were all symphony men before going into the Army and they are all stationed here as musicians? A fellow who knew that I liked music and who knows these fellows took me to hear a quartet, violin, viola, cello, and piano, and introduced me to all of them. Do you remember the violin and viola who played a concerto grosso with our orchestra about 3 years ago? The principal second violin and principal viola from the Minneapolis Symphony? That viola was the one I heard Tuesday night. I asked if I could ever hear them practice but they work when I am busy too. So he (the violinist) said he would arrange a group some evening. So that was last night. It was a string quartet and it was at the cellist's home and I took Rosemary, and Ed, the fellow who took me Tuesday, took us in. It was a perfectly wonderful evening in which they played constantly Haydn, Mozart, and Schubert quartets. I sat on the floor beside the viola so I could get as close as possible to the music. Thursday night the symphonette of 25 pieces played a radio concert from the auditorium (one of the several auditoriums) and then played a short concert afterward for the audience. They were wonderful—as would be expected from all such marvelous professionals. I met the flutist, Opava, who was first flute in the Minneapolis before entering the Army. The viola player's name is David Dawson, and after leaving Minneapolis 3 years ago, he played in the Coolidge Quartet, and among other things has made recordings for Victor. He is 31 years old and looks the way Billy would have. He is 31. I have a date with him tomorrow night which should be very special. Rosemary and I are going to a symphonette concert tonight at 8:15. Isn't it wonderful that they have all this music here? And to think it is the only time in my life to be without my flute!

This morning another girl and I flew a C-78 [Cessna UC-78, a twin-engine advanced trainer and utility aircraft] *and saw Florida as beneath us and the Atlantic Ocean stretching out as far as we could see. It really is against regulations to fly to the coast but it was too beautiful to resist. The airdrome officer, who was on duty for the day, rode along in back and it seemed to be*

O.K. with him—in fact, he suggested it.

John is very busy, but he seems to find time to write every day faithfully. He is so swell and I am becoming very eager to see him again. Rosemary received a diamond through the mail a few days ago and she is going to see her Johnny on the way from here. We have so much fun talking together about our going. We think it would be so much fun if they were in the same places— but they aren't. You remember Rosemary, don't you? We are together most of the time.

I can hardly wait to see Eloise and Johnny and Suzie. I just can't imagine what Suzie must be like. She is such a special little niece.

Mother, would you call Younkers and ask them to wrap as a gift a copy of On Being a Real Person *and send it to John right away please? His birthday is July 9. His address is at the bottom. Please write oftener. But who am I to ask that?*

Love,

Marie

I would love to have the Kodak. May I please so I can take a few pictures of John, etc. And if you can find some film too, it would be swell. Thank you so much.

Lt. John A. Clark 0-774946
C/o Commandant of Crews
Box #1933
Dyersburg, Tennessee

Squabble Over WASPs

★ ★ ★

BY DREW PEARSON.

Washington Merry-Go-Round.

WASHINGTON, D. C.—Air Forces Commander General "Hap" Arnold may not know it, but he is facing trouble from Capitol Hill as soon as congress gets back to a full-time job.

The congressmen are aroused over Arnold's efforts to side-track the law by continuing to use the WASPs while more than 5,000 trained men pilots, each with an average of 1,250 flying hours, remain idle. All this has happened after congress refused to let the WASPs be incorporated into the regular Army.

PEARSON.

The government has spent more than 21 million dollars training women flyers, primarily at the behest of Aviatrix Jaquelin Cochran, wife of Floyd Odlum.

Though not generally known, 25 WASPs have already been killed while ferrying planes in the United States. Further, after almost two years of training and the expenditure of millions of dollars, only 11 WASPs are able to fly twin-engine pursuit planes and only three are qualified to pilot four-engine bombers. Bulk of the WASP work has been on training planes, production of which has been practically eliminated.

Air Corps pilots and transport flyers see red. Hundreds retiring from active combat are anxious to stay in the Army as transport ferry pilots. More than a thousand discharged pilots are unable to get jobs with the air transport command.

Last May, the Ramspeck civil service committee began a determined inquiry into the WASPs, was ready to recommend that they be dropped immediately.

★ ★ ★

They Buried Colonels.

The infantry replacement training center at Fort McClellan, Ala., is blessed with a colonel, Carl F. Duffner, whose gospel is that good soldiers in wartime are those who salute snappily, keep their shoes shined and their neckties straight. He has courtesy squads roving the nearby streets of Anniston looking for soldiers—and officers—who miss a salute or have a cuff unbuttoned in the murky Alabama heat.

In camp, both Colonel Duffner and the commanding general insist that enlisted men salute every civilian car with a white tag (enlisted men's tags are blue, officers' tags are white), even if there is a woman at the wheel.

A lot of war casualties are at Mc-Clellan—men from Italy, North Africa, Guadalcanal—recovering from wounds or malaria. One of these, a little private from Italy, was upbraided by Colonel Duffner for returning a sloppy salute.

The colonel made the private salute properly, then barked: "Have you anything to say for yourself?"

"Yes," returned the little private. "Sir, at Cassino, we buried colonels."

*Article from the
Des Moines Register.
June 1944.*

Comment

Musicians enjoy a special fellowship. Even when in new and unfamiliar surroundings they seem to find one another. I believe I probably went to a concert given on the base and recognized David Dawson, a violist, from hearing him play at Drake University in Des Moines before the war. Naturally, I introduced myself and David saw that I was musically entertained all the time I was in Orlando. He was among a group of professional musicians recruited by the Air Force to provide music at the base. Most of these musicians were former members of the major symphony orchestras in the country.

Comment

Drew Pearson was a nationally syndicated columnist who tried to give the inside story on events in the nation's capitol. His reporting was usually of the sensational variety and in this article he got several of his facts wrong. Pearson was no friend of the WASP. In the end, unfortunately, his prediction turned out to be correct.

Letter 71

Orlando, Florida

July 11, 1944
Tuesday, noon

Dear Mother and Daddy:

I have been a very bad daughter, I know. Between studying, exams, tests, etc., and trying to take in all the advantages of this post, we keep ourselves very busy. Even John has been neglected, so please don't feel too badly.

This last week has been extremely interesting. The last week and a half of the course is by far the best because the dry stuff is finished and we have lectures and demonstrations on all kinds of Army equipment. It is amazing.

I have had lots of music too. Concerts, as well as evenings at the Sopkins with David [Dawson] listening to records. I have met so many of the musicians and their families and been to their homes with David. We haven't gone everywhere we have been invited because David would rather swim or play tennis. He is a beautiful tennis player and has played with many professionals. I am so very lucky for music. It has made so many nice contacts for me.

I received word today that only 5 days' leave would be granted. Don't you think I had better still spend the two days with Eloise and one day at home? Two days will be necessary with John, because of train times. I am so glad that I had that 6 days at home on the way down.

I shall leave here Saturday, July 15, at 2:18 pm to arrive in Dyersburg Sunday evening, at 10 or 10:30. John is free from Monday noon until Tuesday noon, and Wednesday morning at 8:30, I shall start for St. Louis to remain from Wednesday night to Friday night. Saturday morning I shall arrive home and Sunday morning I leave Omaha at 8:30. I don't know how or when it will be necessary to go to Omaha.

Thank you for the Kodak. I hope we can find some film.

I am anxious to get home again. At the same time I shall be very sorry to leave here—this beautiful place and all its music. Time to go to class.

Love,
Marie

John says my address in Dyersburg will probably be at the Forked Deer Hotel, but he isn't sure. They wouldn't take reservations this far in advance.

Comment

As it turned out I actually stayed at the Cordell Hull Hotel in Dyersburg. Rooms were very difficult to get during wartime at hotels near military bases. I believe John had to make advance payment and register the room in my name as his "sister."

Southern customs discouraged single women from staying at the hotel.

Letter 72

AIR CORPS, UNITED STATES ARMY

Orlando, Florida

On way to Jacksonville
July 15, 1944

Dear Mother and Daddy:
We left Orlando at 2:18 this afternoon and I must say I was reluctant to leave. It is a beautiful post and the life there has been wonderful. I shall arrive in Dyersburg tomorrow night and shall leave Tuesday morning and arrive in St. Louis at 3:45 Tues. pm. The route had to be directly from St. Louis to Omaha where I shall arrive Friday morning, July 21, at 8:30 am. Here is what I wondered. The soonest I could get home would be at 6:00 pm by bus. Could you come for me in Omaha please? I shall be on the Wabash.

This is so difficult—later—in the restaurant in the depot at Jacksonville.

If you haven't enough gas or it isn't convenient I shall come the best way I can. Connections going back to Omaha won't be quite so atrocious. I can take a bus at midnight from D.M. and arrive in Omaha in time for the 8:30 am train.

Guess I had better eat. Betty Wall, Lynn Nichols, and Kay Stark are with me.
Bye now.

Love,
Marie

Comment

Asking my parents to drive to Omaha to pick me up was doubtless an imposition on them as they had many things to look after on the farm, and gasoline was rationed. I do not recall if they did pick me up there or if I got home by other means. My even asking them to do this indicates what generous parents they were.

John and I had a wonderful time during my Dyersburg visit. Because of his flight schedule we had only a day and a half to spend together. It was good to see how much he had matured by the six weeks of combat flight training. We talked of many things but what I remember most was our discussions of the "permanent things." Our relationship had developed to the point where we felt comfortable discussing marriage. We both agreed that marriage should be postponed until after the war or, at least, until John returned from combat. We also agreed not to impose the restrictions of an engagement on each other but to maintain our commitment. Because he was about to go overseas I was aware my visit could actually be my last chance to say "goodbye." We both were happy to have the opportunity to bring this important topic up and resolve it as best we could.

My stay at home was extended by a tragedy at Las Vegas. Beverly Jean Moses, a WASP in class 44-5 from Des Moines and recently assigned to the base, was killed July 18 in an air crash in the mountains near Indian Springs. She was flying as copilot in an AT-11 piloted by an officer I thought to be reckless. There were four others on board—all from the Link Trainer detachment on the base. All died in the crash. It was the custom for a WASP to attend the funeral and interment of a colleague so the WASP coordinator at Las Vegas asked me to do this, which I did. Before the funeral I visited her father, who was living alone in a single room in Des Moines, to convey the official condolences of the WASP. I believe Beverly's mother was dead. Beverly was buried in the Oakwood Cemetery in Youngstown, Iowa.

Letter 73

Cheyenne en route to Las Vegas
July 31, 1944
15:10

Dear Mother and Daddy:

Please forgive the stationary. It is the best Cheyenne drugstores could afford. And the pen is acting up because of the high altitude. For a long time at Sweetwater I wondered why my pen leaked. Finally someone informed me that it was the change in altitude—for I always had it in my pocket while flying. Trains aren't particularly conducive to legibility either. Can you make out my scribble?

Last night the Rocket made up 10 minutes—for me to catch my train I was told—so I did make the Union Pacific. I didn't get the reservation because the drafts [travel authorizations] were already down at the train but my space wasn't taken anyway.

We have just stopped at Laramie and I wish this were ready to mail to you. The trip has been very uneventful after making the U.P. in Omaha. The girl across from me is an Army nurse from Esterville on her way to Muroc, California. And the two girls across the aisle are from Fort Dodge and some other place in Iowa. Can't remember where.

I had such a wonderful stay at home. Isn't it nice that it was so long? Hope you aren't completely worn out from your guest. I am sorry I was so crabby before leaving. Seems as though I always am. Mother, you looked so sweet and so smart. Daddy, you could finally have come with us after all. We are moving again now.

Love,
Marie

Mother, I looked all over Cheyenne for Busille thread, but there was none to be found.

Letter 74

Las Vegas AAB
August 5, 1944
Saturday, noon

Dear Mother and Daddy:

Please forgive me for not writing sooner. I have been quite weary of evenings and last night I went to bed before 8:00 to get up at 5:00 this morning.

I am flying to and from work everyday. Wednesday Pauls told me I would be assigned to fighter squadron which was exactly what I wanted, but Gwen Crosby and Marj Harper were fussing so much about being left on range estimation so long that they sent me up to relieve them. So every morning I fly up to the springs—50 miles away—take another ship and fly a mission, wait in the officers' club until time to fly the next mission then fly home again after the second mission. Two of us, Madelyn Taylor and I, alternate on the 4 missions a day—7:00, 9:00, 1:00, and 3:00. One day she flies at 7:00 and at 1:00 and the next day I fly those hours while the other flies the other two. We are not allowed to fly two in succession because they are too grueling they say. We each fly a ship up here so that neither has to come until just in time for her mission and can

leave again right after her last mission.

Range estimation is a series of dives—shallow dives at 180 miles/hour—no lower than 75 feet—toward a shed on the ground which shelters gunnery students tracking our ship as it snakes a pass toward them. It is supposed to be very dangerous, but it really isn't because, if you haven't altitude, at least you have speed, which is a lifesaver because if your engine quits, with speed you can gain lots of altitude before making the forced landing or giving yourself more time to get the engine started again. Can see how it would be dangerous for anyone who lacked judgment and coordination, but I have coordination and a normal amount of judgment, I think. Everyone hates it because it is monotonous and hot and the air is so rough so near the ground, but so far I like it because it is improving my flying. I try to perfect the pattern over the ground, judging the dive to make it just the right angle for the gunner and just the right height when I pass over the shed—I haven't taken any shingles off yet!—and perfecting coordination. It is fun.

We had a thorough checking-out on the job. The first mission I just rode along in the backseat with Lt. Bushire. Then I flew two missions with him in the backseat. He seemed pleased with my job. Today I am by myself. We are left on this job only two or 3 weeks at a time and alternate with fighter missions for a much longer period of several weeks. Please don't worry about my fatigue because it is just that flying is an exertion after such an inactive life. I am soft.

Marj Harper was just told that she is on the list of two to be transferred to Deming, New Mexico. She is just sick about it. The other is one of the two Taylors—don't know which one.

It is absolutely wonderful to be back. The girls are such a swell group and get along so well and everyone on the flight line seemed just a bit glad to see me. I love this place. I am so much happier here now than ever before—if that is possible.

The records and bedspread came. The bedspread is beautiful and there are draperies to match. Mother, would you see if Younkers carries the draperies? Mrs. Murray on sixth floor sold me the spread called "Painted Desert" and could tell you, no doubt, if Younkers have the draperies. She might remember the sale since it was sent to Las Vegas. I need one pair, blue background. I forgot to order Gwen's name tags too—O. Gwen Crosby in red.

Please! I don't know how many—perhaps 3 dozen. Charge them to me and I shall collect from her. Address would be the same as mine—just leave out the box no., for I don't know her number.

I had such a swell time with you. That is why I am so happy here, I suppose. Oh, we have a piano in our reception room now—very poor, but it is a piano. I would like to have all that piano music on the piano when it is convenient. There are two other things which are not on the piano—probably in the piano bench—The White Peacock by Griffes and a yellow album of

Brahms. I would appreciate it so much. It must be about time for the next mission so goodbye.

Lots of love,
Marie

P.S. I saw Beverly's [WASP Beverly Moses] *wrecked plane yesterday. It was in a very inaccessible spot for rescue. Difficult job.*

Mother, the telegram said, "Marie writes of your untiring efforts." That was why Ernie [Lt. Ernie Maulsby, a Las Vegas pilot from Des Moines] *said, "What have you been writing about me?"*

Letter 75

Las Vegas AAB
August 7, 1994
Monday morn, 0900

Dear Mother and Daddy:
I am in the club at the springs and have just finished a mission and shall wait until 1:00 to fly another. It was smooth as glass this morning and lots of fun. Flying the early mission means getting up at 5:00 to be at the springs just before 7:00.

Saturday afternoon was just as rough as could be. The only time I have ever flown in such rough air before was through a cold front at night while still in training. Rough air adds a little interest in the flight just to see what the ship will do. It bounces all over like a poor helpless butterfly and I fasten the safety belt tight to avoid hitting the top of the canopy.

Saturday night John sent me a dozen red roses. I don't know what prompted the gesture but they were beautiful. I put them in a vase and set it on the chest in front of the large round mirror and put John's snapshots on either side. It made a very pretty picture and the kids teased me about my shrine.

Last evening Rosie and I decided to drive to Charleston's lodge for a steak but our plans were thwarted. When we were beyond town—west—about 8 miles or so, we had a flat. A sergeant, who is in LVAAF convalescent camp at Charleston came by on his motorcycle and changed it for us. The spare was the one with the blister so I was afraid to drive on it far. We went back to town to have the tire repaired (there was a nail and 3 holes in the tube) and by that time we were too hungry to drive to Charleston so we had a steak at El Cortez. We had a nice time anyway. I would like to have two new tires but the inspector said that he would rather have any of my old tires—with the exception of the spare— than any new synthetic. What would you advise, Daddy?

Mother, I believe I would like black gloves with the blue and gray—except perhaps with the gray when there is no color in any other accessories, then you might wear fuchsia gloves. That, to me, would be the only time.

Madelon sees a lot of Jack Hill and they seem nicely suited to each other. He brought his mother here when he was on leave and they have rented a house in town. I have seen her (Madelon) twice for only a minute. We are all very busy. She is co-piloting AT-11s and "6s" on cross-countries and is waiting to be checked out as 1st pilot on the "11." Her job is quite different from mine partly, I think, because her leg still bothers her.

Love,
Marie

I just figured up the nos. of pictures—size 8x10—1 of each picture—5x7—12 in full uniform and 4 without the hat. That includes 2 or 3 extra in full uniform. Remind Mrs. Bushnell that I want the pictures in folders the same size as the picture itself so there will be no mat. We talked about that before. Bye—Be sure to use the proofs I marked with "x" on the back.

Me

Letter 76

Las Vegas AAB
August 9, 1944
Wednesday, 11:30 am

Dear Mother and Daddy:

The air was smooth this morning and lovely for flying. It was the longest mission I have flown yet, 07:10 to 09:00. I clocked a few passes this morning and it took 5 minutes to fly 4 passes—making 88 passes (I think) in 1:50. I get lots of practice on them, don't I?

Madelon and Marj fought their transfers so hard that they were cancelled for the present, at least. Madelon told them that she and Gil were planning to be married, and Captain Watson, with whom Marj goes, told them she was "too good flying material for the field to lose." A nice compliment! Madelon flies range estimation up here with me. One reason we should be militarized is so that our responsibilities can be clearly spelled out and obeyed according to military discipline. I think the WASPs here are a well-organized group but I hear that is not the situation on other bases.

Rosie left this morning as co-pilot in an AT-11 to take General Stenseth, who is on our field, to Orlando. Golly, would I have liked to go!

Rosie said last night, thinking that I had known about it, something about my transfer of a month and a half ago. It seems that orders came out of West Coast Headquarters then for me to go to Colorado somewhere to B-25 school in a general shakeup in the Western Training Command but it was all cancelled, it seems. That was the first I had heard. It seems that we are getting so much flying time here that Cochran [Jacqueline Cochran, Director of Women Pilots] wants some other girls to have the opportunity also. So it seems, according to the latest rumor, that some of us are to go out each month and others are to come in. The field is disgusted about our transfers because they have us all trained for our jobs and that will mean training new ones. We don't want to leave, needless to say. Right now they say they won't check us out on P-39s because WASPs are too valuable. That makes us mad. About the time we get them worn down to the idea, we shall be gone and the new girls can take advantage. Gripe! Gripe!

I just wrote to Bill answering his letter of July 30 saying that he probably could come out in a couple weeks. Hope he can.

John wrote yesterday about his first flight in a Cub! Some difference from a B-17. He had so much fun. I feel sorry for him. I am afraid he is getting an inferiority complex about being a co-pilot. He wanted to fly the Cub partly because he wanted to feel that he was really flying himself. Of course, he flies half the time as co-pilot, but the pilot is responsible.

Madelon B. told me that she and Jack may be married next month. It will be swell and she looks quite happy. Take good care of yourselves.

Love,
Marie

Letter 77

Las Vegas AAB
August 11, 1944
10:00

Dear Mother and Daddy:

This is a beautiful morning to fly. I just came down about 9:00—from the 07:00 mission. Someday I shall take a thermometer up in the cockpit to see just how high the temperature is behind the engine. There is a thermometer on the instrument panel indicating outside free air temperature but it is much hotter inside. The hot air burns my legs. But it is still fun and wonderful practice in coordination.

Yesterday I was so disgusted and sick of all the wrangling about the WASP [militarization] that I would have resigned if I hadn't been so crazy to fly. On our field they seem to be so afraid that we would risk our necks that they wouldn't check us

out on other ships, but last night 4 girls had orders to attend B-26 school on our field so perhaps things aren't quite so conservative as they have sounded. Madelyn Taylor, Marj Harper, Jeanette Jenkins, and Rosie Lewis are the 4, and they can take it right here in our own transition school, so they are happy. So now the rest of us are more hopeful for the P-39 and P-63.

After Cochran's statement a few days ago that either the WASP will go into the Army or disband, we wonder just what will happen. We wouldn't be a bit surprised if we were on our way home soon. Don't know.

Wish I had known about Edith. I would have gone to the train. She would have been through here Sunday night at 7:30, I suppose.

John wrote that he flew just about over our house last Saturday night. It must have been about midnight. Did you hear a B-17 fly over then? They fly all over the country on navigational and bombing training hops.

Madelon's Jack Hill is slated probably to go to B-29 school in about a month. His whole class—all those on our field—42-A—are to go. Don't know whether Madelon knows or not. Haven't seen her since last Sunday morning.

Six of us celebrated our one year in the Army, August 9, Wednesday, by eating dinner in town in civilian clothes. Pat Carmody, who washed two weeks before graduation, the one who wrecked two planes—remember?—was going through with her husband and ate with us too.

Helen Goodman, the WAC officer who works in civilian personnel and who is so jealous of us and does us dirt at every turn, although she is sweet to our faces (breath!), reported us to the air inspector for being in civilian clothes, even though Ruthie Jones, that same night, picked her up with all her clothes from the cleaners and took her home!

Anyway, Lt. Pauls was sent a letter of endorsement and we all meet with him this pm at 5:00. We would like to shoot Helen. She has no authority over us but seems to think she is God. Enough dirt!

How soon will the pictures be ready? I shall send you a list of people. Be sure you get the right two pictures.

I shall enclose two fifty dollar bonds. Another one is due now.

Bye now. Be careful.

Love,

Marie

Comment

Ruth Peacock is an old friend from the Fine Arts Department at Drake University. We met when we both were instrumental music students, me on the flute and Ruth on the oboe. For a time she lived with us in West Des Moines. She spent most of her career playing oboe with the Indianapolis Symphony Orchestra and was one of the first women in the US to play in a major symphony orchestra. We still see each other regularly.

Letter 78

Las Vegas AAB
August 15, 1944
09:30

Dear Mother and Daddy:

How are you this morning? Keeping busy as usual, I suppose. You sound terribly busy in your letter. It was a beautiful morning to fly—I had the 07:00 mission and will again fly at 1:00 pm. My two weeks at this job will be up Thursday. Crosby, who will take my place, is on x-country and may not be back by Thursday though. I shall fly fighter missions next, the job which I had expected to do upon arrival back from home.

Miss Cochran is to arrive tonight. Every time I get disgusted with this business, I try to remind myself that everything worthwhile or big has gone through the same growing pains and criticism, and the big things have lived through it because they were big and there had to be loyal people to carry it through each time. We would just as soon not have Cochran come. All she did on her last trip (I was in Orlando) was to stir things up. She decided we needed more girls here because we were all getting so much flying time, but we have enough here and the field doesn't want more. We wonder what she will do this time. The girls say she has no sense of humor whatsoever. It seems that she was a foundling and practically grew up by herself and has always had to work hard. All her wealth she has achieved by herself. Life to her has been too serious for any sense of humor. We had all always thought that her wealth was her husband's but it seems that she had all this before her marriage.

I forgot to measure to see if the spread would be wide enough for draperies, Mother. I shall do so tonight. They would be plenty long enough, I am sure. My windows are high. But they need to be wide enough to use as shades.

Helen Grote is the WAC captain on our field. She is commanding officer of the WAC company here and lives over in the WAC area. She has nothing to do with the WACs with whom we live. It is a funny marriage. She is five years older than her husband. She outranks him because he is only 2nd lieutenant, and she is much taller than he!

No, the plane is still up in the mountains alone with all the other wreckages scattered here and there. It was supposed to be blown up but the last I heard it was not yet.

I finally heard from David concerning the pictures he wants. He wants both views in 8x10. His address is—

Sgt. David P. Dawson
902nd A.A.F.B.U.
Squadron E
O.A.B.
Orlando, Florida

John wants the one without the hat in size 5x7. His address is—
Lt. John Alden Clark 0-774946
C/O Commandant of Crews
Box 1933
A.A.F.
Dyersburg, Tennessee

You may give yourselves one of each in 8x10. Give Aunt Maple a 5x7 with the hat (if that is the one she wants—and I think it is). Send Bill H. [Bill Hinkhouse, my Iowa cousin] *the same—also Eloise—also Doris Van Fossen (1302 Evelyn, St. Perry)—also Helene Siedenfeld (1528 Carpenter, D.M.)—and Mr. Leach (805 ½ Locust)— and Ruth Peacock (she has asked for one several times)—and Dolores Meurer (Moore Field—Mission—Texas). Save one of each in 5x7 for me. Be sure all the folders are just the same size as the picture, won't you? I would like John's and David's to go in leather folders—David's a double folder. Mrs. Bushnell had some but you might find better looking ones downtown. It isn't so important for David's to go in leather but John will be on the move so much that the leather will be better preservation. Put both in leather though if you think they look O.K. that way.*

You will find enclosed my "per diem" check. Please put the picture bill on my account with you. The $7 sitting charge is paid. I didn't need the other check, Daddy. Thank you.

Did you ever figure up how much I still owe you? Please, I would like to know. Goodbye.

Love,
Marie

Hurry and send John's picture. He will leave Dyersburg very soon. An x-ray of Madelon's knee showed that it was not all completely healed, so all she can do for awhile is co-pilot on the "11" on x-c [cross-country].

I told you about training WASPs here on B-26 (AT-23), didn't I? It turned out to be as co-pilot, so I am very glad my name was not included.

Letter 79

Las Vegas AAB
August 17, 1944
Thursday morning, 10:00

Dear Mother and Daddy:

Miss Cochran arrived the day before yesterday and last night we all (just WASPs) had dinner with her and a nice discussion afterward at the Last Frontier. She is such a charming person and yet she has such a driving personality and is beautiful besides. She is wonderful. She scolded us and built up our morale and explained things, too. First of all she scolded us for letting our personal affairs interfere with business—some of our girls threatened to quit if they were transferred away from their fiancés here, etc.—also Rosie had threatened to flunk out of this B-26 deal if they didn't take her out in the first place (these are just examples of personal feelings in the matter). She reminded us that when we first went in we were tickled with the prospect of flying PTs and now the girls were kicking about flying BTs. On the subject of going into the Army she reminded us that when we were first interviewed we were told about prospects of going into the Army and we were favorable then (many girls object to our going in). This was just what we needed—the talk about personal affairs. The girls took it beautifully. I should say Miss Cochran did it so beautifully that we all loved her for it. She reminded us that this is war and that we had gone in to help.

Then she gave us facts and figures which we needed for morale. We knew that facts have been so misrepresented in publicity and that many statements are so false and yet we didn't know how much they were wrong and they were wearing down our morale because we had no official facts to take their place. The first girl to be perma-

nently maimed or injured put her arm in a prop just the other day. I don't know where. More than half the girls who have been killed were with men pilots. We have a remarkable safety record. Concerning these 4,672 civilian flyers about whom the CAA was worried when we wanted to go into the Army, they were doing the civilian instruction to avoid the draft in the first place and now 90% refused commissions anyway. She gave so many astounding facts and figures that I can't remember them all and other things we can't tell.

The Bill [legislation in Congress] was not completely thrown out. It was sent back to the committee. She says we will either have to go in or disband for many reasons. She also told of a number of openings that will be opened to us as soon as we go in. It sounds wonderful. We just wish that she could talk to all WASPs as she did to us. It would make an entirely different organiza-tion out of us. Miss Cochran holds all but one of women's flying records.

This B-26 deal sounds good since she explained it further. We train as co-pilots only until thoroughly familiar with the ship and then check out as first pilots and will be sent to the Second Air Force which is the one just east of here and goes over toward the Mississippi somewhere with headquarters in Colorado Springs.

They want a lot of the girls and the open-ings were all read to us last night. I would-n't mind being on the list now. We are all to be eventually. Rosie was scratched from the list yesterday and is to be one of two

Photo courtesy of USAF Museum via Bob Parmerter

The AT-11 I flew at Las Vegas. 1944.

girls to check out on P-39s for engineering hops. We don't know who the other girl is. Rosie wanted it badly but not particularly for engineering hops. She wants to fly fighter missions as she does now in AT-6s.

I don't feel like asking for a choice. I have the feeling that whatever I am assigned to will be the best. But I am very partial to pur-suit ships. Miss Cochran says that eventual-ly all B-26s in the 2nd Air Force are to be exchanged for pursuits. So that deal sounds better than ever. I am just sitting tight and waiting to see what happens.

Daddy, the cold air is turned on in the cockpit and the canopy is partly open, but the engine heat hits the pilot before it goes elsewhere and besides the desert air is pretty warm (understatement!).

Lt. Pauls was wonderful. He naturally realized the gross injustice and we have found that even the WACs can't live with Helen. They have been most sympathetic as has everyone else.

The P-39 Bell Aircraft Corporation single engine fighter.

The P-39 Bell Aircraft Corporation single engine fighter. Photo taken at the Kalamazoo Air Zoo, Michigan. 1992.

When my bills are paid to you (if ever!) please start putting my money where yours is, Mother. The account books are in the desk (mine).

Love,
Marie

Letter 80

Las Vegas AAB
August 17, 1944
Thursday night, 10:30

Dear Mother and Daddy:

I am sleepy but you must hear the news. Tonight when I came home from the Springs I went into Paul's office to say "hello." He detained me and Major Gribble came in and they started asking questions such as "Do you want to fly professionally after the war or are you flying for fun?" Do you guess what they were leading up to? I can have my choice of either P-39 or B-26! If I wanted to fly professionally they suggested B-26, if for fun, P-39. You know my choice, P-39, although I will not tell them until morning. So Rosie and I are to be the two to check out on P-39s. I am so thrilled. I shall fly just one last mission at Indian Springs tomorrow, then Gwen will take over, and I shall start studying tech orders on P-39 and studying the cockpit. Believe me, I am going to know it thoroughly before taking it off the ground. Of course, it is just a one place fighter plane. It has tricycle landing gear.

Ernie Maulsby wanted me to apologize for him for his not calling you before he left. He was married while at home. That is a good reason, don't you think? His wife is in nurses' training until February and then will come out.

Goodnight and sweet dreams.

Love,
Marie

Letter 81

Las Vegas AAB
August 21, 1944
Monday, 3:00 pm

Dear Mother and Daddy:

You now have a P-39 pilot in your family! I checked out this morning—flew 35 minutes—and it was wonderful. It is smooth and fast and so very light on the controls. I flew out in the area until they called me in because it was about time for missions to come in. I am the only one so far. They wanted me to check out first and then Rosie second, but because missions were about to come in she couldn't then, so she will tonight or in the morning. She was quite disappointed.

It was really very funny to watch, because—in that tiny, tiny cockpit—Lt. Marshall, who is in charge of P-39 transition, had his head in one door and Major Gribble, director of flying, had his head in the other door getting me all fixed with shoulder straps, parachute, safety belt,

working the new kind of radio, making a cockpit check, starting engine, etc. They were just like two fond, concerned fathers—both younger than I, no doubt.

We have a huge cooler now in our quarters and the place is actually cold sometimes.

We are being allowed to fly at night— tonight for the first time. Isn't this field getting wonderful?

The flowers sound wonderful to me. Do you have just lots and lots? A blade of grass is such a treat out here.

Thank you so much for bothering with my pictures. I hope John gets his before he leaves. I still don't know how much longer he will be there. It just can't be more than a few days.

Bye now.

Love,
Marie

P.S. Did I tell you we get personal cross-countries now just like the rest of the pilots—on weekends?

Enclosed will be a check and a $50 bond.

Letter 82

Las Vegas AAB
August 29, 1944
Tuesday evening, 9:30

Dear Mother and Daddy:

You have been very sweet to keep writing even though your neglectful daughter hasn't. It seems as though the time has been very full. I have to date eleven hours on the P-39. It is a sweet ship to fly. Now they will put me on fighter missions. I was to do ten hours transition first. Today I flew fighter missions in a "6" as a sort of check out on fighter missions since I had never flown them before.

Rosie has had a bit of bad luck. She finally checked out last Wednesday, but on her second ride the next day, she broke off the nose wheel on an unfortunate landing. She was so afraid that that would put an end to P-39s for us. But it was decided that all the girls would check out on them! Then yesterday a call came from Santa Ana to discontinue our P-39 flying. But after a big conference yesterday morning during which the tower gave me a call by radio (I was in a P- 39) to see how much time I had, it was decided that only Rosie and I would fly them. Today Rosie went out to check out again—(her first flight since her mishap)—

and she had difficulty taxiing—the nose wheel goes crosswind if you are not careful and you can only go in a tight circle. Trying to get out of that, the engine heated so much she had to shut off the engine to let it cool—and then it wouldn't start again. Then Gribble was so disgusted he wouldn't let her fly again. Poor kid! Everything happens to her. But we are relieved because we do not want anything to happen to her. She is much disappointed, of course.

John called me Saturday night, which was the 4th evening he had spent in the attempt. We talked for 20 or 25 minutes and we could hear each other quite well. He had received my picture that day and seemed very pleased. Tonight some perfectly beautiful gladiolas were sent by telegraph—from John, of course. They are in a gallon fruit can with the green wax paper flower wrapping around the can. His picture came last week—did I tell you? Thank you so much for taking care of my pictures.

David has been very busy playing nearly every night as well as every day. It is fun to hear about what they play and his comments on the programs. He often suggests recordings for me to buy. His leave will be October 18 instead of in November. He doesn't know his plans in detail yet however. Did you send him the two large pictures?

I had such a satisfactory weekend. Saturday night after John's call—by the way I tried to call you, too, and at 8 or 8:15 (10 or 10:15 your time) the information came that you didn't answer the phone but your letter today told me you were not at home—I went to Bob Shawn's and stayed all night and Sunday (with Bob and his wife, Bernie). Saturday night we lay out on a blanket on the lawn in the moonlight and talked, then Bernie fixed waffles, then we went to bed. Sunday we drove to Charleston in Phil Rust's car (Bob has it while Phil is on leave) and had a steak fry. We slept and read on blankets all afternoon and went back to their house and I lay on the davenport and read and then we sat on the floor and ate lunch spread on the coffee table and talked. It was lovely and comfortable.

The whole weekend was so relaxing and we had such fun together. Their baby is a doll and looks exactly like Bob with red hair and everything. Bob is a good pal. I see him on the flight line every day and he helps me out often with flying problems, etc. He flies P-39s and the new P-63s. One of the 63s spun in yesterday and the pilot apparently did not jump in time and was killed. His body was found just a few feet from the wreckage. Too bad he stuck with it so long.

No, don't send pictures to me. Gwen's name tags haven't come yet, but they probably will soon.

Your letter, Mother—that is, the last two—I have received the next day. Good service! How soon do you receive mine?

I shall take your word about the amount I owe you. It will be nice to finish it.

Uncle Elmer has obtained $1,000 of life insurance for me—has he told you? At $25 per thousand more it will cover flying. Will you see if perhaps I could have $2,000 or $3,000 worth? I shall feel quite relieved to have even $1,000. It is nice of him to do this.

You are always having the most fun together. Do your dresses look nice, Mother? Do you like them, Daddy? Have you worn your new hat, Mother? Wasn't Ladies Courageous [a movie about women pilots in England] *terrible?*

Must go to bed. Very weary from flying 5:40 hours today.

Love,
Marie

Letter 83

August 29, 1944
Tuesday evening

Officers Club
ARMY AIR FIELD
Dyersburg, Tenn.

TUESDAY EVENING
AUGUST 29, 1944

DEAR MRS. MOUNTAIN,

ARE YOU SURPRISED TO GET A LETTER FROM ME? I IMAGINE YOU ARE AND I HOPE IT IS ALL RIGHT FOR ME TO WRITE. EVEN THOUGH YOU DON'T KNOW ME I FEEL AS THOUGH I KNOW YOU BECAUSE MARIE HAS SO OFTEN TOLD ME ABOUT YOU. SHE IS SO VERY PROUD OF HER FAMILY.

I'VE WANTED FOR A LONG TIME TO WRITE YOU AND THANK YOU FOR BEING SO KIND IN MAILING THE BOOK AND MARIE'S PICTURE TO ME. I SURELY DO APPRECIATE IT VERY MUCH. MARIE'S PICTURE IS CERTAINLY A TREASURE TO ME. IT'S A VERY GOOD LIKENESS, DON'T YOU THINK? THAT IS JUST THE WAY SHE LOOKED WHEN I SAW HER FOR THE FIRST TIME LAST MAY IN LAS VEGAS AND THAT IS A SPECIAL MEMORY OF MINE. BY GOING TO LAS VEGAS FOR TRAINING, I BECAME ONLY A B-17 CO-PILOT BUT BY MEETING YOUR DAUGHTER I BECAME MUCH RICHER THAN IF I HAD GONE THROUGH

THE FINEST FIRST PILOT SCHOOL IN THE COUNTRY. NEEDLESS-TO-SAY I AM VERY FOND OF MARIE, TO PUT IT QUITE MILDLY, AND I ALWAYS SHALL BE REGARDLESS OF WHAT COURSE OUR FUTURE RELATIONS MAY TAKE. HOWEVER, THE PURPOSE OF THIS LETTER IS NOT TO TELL YOU THIS, ONLY.

SATURDAY NIGHT I CALLED MARIE IN LAS VEGAS. IT WAS SURE GOOD TO HEAR HER VOICE. SHE IS VERY WELL.

VERY SHORTLY WE WILL SHIP FROM THIS BASE. FROM HERE WE WILL GO TO SOME BASE IN NEBRASKA FOR A FEW DAYS AND THEN FLY OVER. OF COURSE, NO ONE KNOWS WHERE WE WILL BE SENT BUT MOST OF US ARE HOPING IT WILL BE THE EUROPEAN THEATER OF OPERATIONS. EUROPE HAS SUCH A WEALTH OF ARTISTIC BEAUTY THAT CERTAINLY ALL CAN'T HAVE BEEN DESTROYED. I SHOULD LIKE MUCH TO SEE THE FAMOUS CAPITOLS OF THE OLD WORLD.... AND NOT THRU A BOMBSIGHT!

I AM GOING TO WRITE TO MARIE TONIGHT AND IT'S GETTING LATE SO I WILL CLOSE. AGAIN, THANKS FOR ALL YOUR KINDNESS. VERY RESPECTFULLY,

John

Letter 84

Las Vegas AAB
Sept. 10, 1944
Sunday evening, 7:30

Dear Mother and Daddy:

This is Sunday but most of LVAAF works just the same. This morning I test-hopped two P-39s and then slept a couple of hours this afternoon until I was called to the line to fly another one. But when I arrived most of the mechanics had gone home so I shall fly that one tomorrow morning first thing.

Last Wednesday I was pretty sick of all the bickering over whether we should fly "39" missions or not so I went to see the chief engineering officer, Major Mixon, whom I like very much. And Thursday I was in engineering test-hopping and slow-timing 39s. It is very interesting and I should learn a lot about the ships.

Madelon Burcham went home Friday, as well as Madelyn Taylor, who has resigned and will be married when she comes back. Marj Harper was married Thursday night and is gone a few days for a honeymoon.

There are two new girls on the field who are B-17 pilots. They are very good, they say. They are in engineering too. The 3 of us are the only ones [WASPs] in engineering so far.

John's letter was very nice—all his letters are. I received a telegram today which he sent from New England on their way across. He has a first pilot's rating now and will probably have his own ship and crew very soon. He is a very wonderful person. I am afraid I am a bit partial to him. The last week I have been going with a very swell person. You would like him very much.

I am very weary and feel very uneager about letter-writing tonight. Last night the gang we were with stayed out so late and then they wanted to go to Lake Mead which is a one-hour drive each way, but Doug [Lt. Doug Holt] put an end to that. He told them I had to work this morning.

Mother, would you please call Mrs. Shriner or Miss Lorenzen and ask them to send some night cream, please?

Goodbye for now.

Love,
Marie

Letter 85

OFFICERS MESS
LAS VEGAS ARMY AIR FIELD
LAS VEGAS, NEVADA

September 14, 1944
Thursday evening

Dear Mother and Daddy:

It sounds so strange to hear you speak of rain and cold weather at home—and Eloise speaks of it too. It is still clear weather and 105° every day. But it is September and I guess it is time for rain and cool weather in well-regulated countries. But you know how I like hot weather so I love it here.

Today I had some interesting flights. The first one was to test an engine that was reported to cut out at high altitude so I climbed up to 23,500 feet and flew awhile and couldn't make it cut out (that was right over the field in case it did cut out) so I went back down. Then I took up a ship that was supposed to cut out on left tank and reserve tank but at 9,000 feet it wouldn't cut out for me. The third ship didn't check well on the magneto check just before take-off so I didn't fly it. No ships were ready after lunch so I told them to hold any that did come in until morning because I was going to knock off for the afternoon. Independent me! That first flight would

have been very interesting but the hook on my helmet for the oxygen mask came off and one hand was busy constantly holding the helmet and oxygen mask together where the hook should have been.

Rosie and I were asking for a personal cross-country to Sacramento this weekend but Major Mixon doesn't want me to go for a very good reason—I am the only P-39 pilot in engineering at present—Chonoski is in the hospital and Berry is on leave. So I shall take one when one of them is back.

Tuesday night we had the most wonderful steak fry on the beach at Lake Mead. The beach is taken care of by rangers and has tables with built on roofs overhead, bathhouses, water, stoves, etc. and is very nice. It was a gang of 8 and 3 of the fellows are the 3 nicest here, I think. The one with whom I have been going recently, Douglas Holt, is a fine Virginia gentleman. You would like him.

Last night Rosie and I had a long talk. Her life seems to me to need more direction right now. She seems restless and needs to focus her interests more concisely, I think. So I talked to her as a friend, almost as a sister, which in many ways we are. She seemed to enjoy it and was very cooperative. I don't think anyone ever really talked to her understandingly before. Her mother always just says, "I just don't understand you, Rosina."

I am so thankful for my understanding parents who worked with

Two of the B-17 girls, Charlotte Mitchell, 43-5, left, and Pat Bowser, 43-6. Las Vegas. October 1944.

me positively instead of negatively to mold my philosophies. They are wonderful people. Now don't be too puffed up. I guess maybe you have a few bad points, but I can't think of any right now.

Tell Aunt Maple and Uncle Elmer to take a vacation in Las Vegas this fall when they want some sunshine. They are working much too hard. You may come too, if you wish.

Love,
Marie

P.S. Mother, will you please call Miss Wiess and ask her to send more pills immediately. I shall need them Monday but I guess they will still be too late. But please. Thank you.

Me

Comment

On this flight I needed to use oxygen since it was at an altitude above 10,000 feet. Oxygen was breathed through a mask, which was held on my face by attachments to my flight helmet. Sometimes these attachments do not fit properly and the mask has to be held on the face by one hand. This adds a complication to flying, as can be imagined!

Photo courtesy of Al Hansen via Paul Minert

The B-26, Martin "Marauder" which I flew at copilot at Las Vegas. 1944.

Letter 86

Las Vegas AAB
September 21, 1944

Dear Mother and Daddy:

This is a very quiet evening at home. Doug is writing letters too here in our living room. I was afraid to go to the club for that purpose because I might stay too long and I am too sleepy. We (the girls) are going to B-26 ground school now all afternoon (we fly in the morning our regular duties—me on the P-39s) and I get so sleepy. Can't get my usual after lunch nap. This ground school will last only a few days.

Madelon and Jack arrived back last night. Jack couldn't find his car anywhere on the post so he borrowed mine to drive

170

into town for the night and he picked me up this morning before driving to the line. I am glad you liked him. He is a very swell person. Did the Burchams like him?

Madelyn Taylor's nerves were getting tied up in knots. She had been grounded for several days before leaving. I think she had been very much worried because she and Gil had planned to be married and she was put in B-26 school to be shipped out at the completion of it. She didn't know what to do. I am glad she did resign because she and Gil are just right for each other and she is the type to be homemaking instead of flying anyway. She will be a good little homebody.

Yes, the church bulletin came and I was glad to receive it. Did I tell you that Mr. Kleckner sent a letter a couple of weeks or so ago? I appreciated it very much. Next time I shall read a note from my father, won't I? Do you think the amount on the pledge card is O.K.?

This morning I went to the dentist. My jaw (hinge) has been bothering me for a couple of weeks and yesterday high altitude bothered one of the teeth. The difference in pressure can play havoc with fillings. I am very glad to have such good ones. X-rays showed nothing wrong. We have very good dentists. One is a high altitude specialist and took care of me today.

I am becoming very sleepy and this letter is pretty dopey, I guess. Goodnight.

Love,
Marie

Letter 87

Fairmont Hotel
NOB HILL
San Francisco

September 24, 1944
Sunday pm

Dear Mother and Daddy:
Surprised? We have had a very nice personal cross-country to San Francisco this weekend. We left Las Vegas at 10:35 yesterday morning, had lunch at Bakersfield, and arrived in San Fr. at 3:05 pm. We flew an AT-6; I was pilot and Doug Holt was my passenger. It was a lovely flight. We didn't have reservations here, but Doug was able to find space in an officers' dorm in this hotel and I shared a room here with 4 other girls. It was a very nice arrangement.

We must go now to the field which is built out into the bay. We shall stop in Reno and hope to arrive in L.V. at 6:00. Will tell you more about it tonight in a letter.

Love,
Marie

Letter 88

United States Army
Air Forces

Las Vegas, Nevada

September 30, 1944

Dear Mother and Daddy:

I believe I haven't written since the note in San Francisco. That was a wonderful x-c. There are so many things to do in San Francisco and we had 24 hours exactly from landing time to takeoff time. Before leaving L.V. Doug had asked one of his friends where all we should go in S.F. so on the way between Bakersfield and S.F., he called me on interphones and asked me to have dinner with him in the Mural Room at the St. Francis Hotel. So after we had obtained rooms we dressed and went out into the cold fog—gee, it felt good—to the St. Francis for dinner to Ted Weems's music. Then we walked down more terrifically steep hills to the theatre district to see Wilson, *the story of Woodrow Wilson, which is termed as political propaganda and is not to be shown in Army camps until after the election. It was very fine. There was a good stage show in connection with it. We wanted to go to the "Top of the Mark" after that where you can see all over the bay area, but it had just closed at midnight, but we were sleepy anyway so we didn't care.*

Next morning we ate breakfast in the Fairmont Coffee Shop and went to church at the First Baptist in a taxi. We rode back to the hotel up the steep hills in a cable car—my first ride in one. We stood on the back platform and hoped the car wouldn't slide backward or that the back end wouldn't fall off.

Then it was time to begin the long trek to the field again—after packing, of course. We took off at 3:00 and landed in Reno at 4:25. The flight between Sacramento and Reno was over some of the most beautiful scenery I have ever seen. It was quite rugged and covered completely with green pines. Lake Tahoe is nestled there among the highest of the peaks. It would be a beautiful place for a vacation for you. That whole area is dotted with lakes. The desert began just before Reno and continued all the way from Reno to Las Vegas. We were on the Reno field exactly 20 minutes, leaving there at 4:45 and arriving in L.V. at 6:50—twenty minutes after sundown. I hadn't flown a "6" for several weeks and it felt good to be in one again. All our "6s" are being shipped out and are being replaced by BTs which I dislike very much. That was the last weekend for "6" x-cs. We were lucky, especially when 4 other applications had been made from our field for S.F. Only one ship from our field can go to each field in the coastal restricted area at one time. Besides that we were given the choice of ships too. So we chose the best instrument ship on the field.

Doug is not checked out on "6s" so it was rather nice for him to be able to go along with me. But he will be checked out on BTs right away. He has been night flying every night this week so I hardly saw him all week long.

We have a swell bunch in engineering. I like all the B-17 girls who are down there and it is a good bunch of fellows, too. We have gay old times. Ernie Maulsby is down there, as you may know.

It is wonderful that you spent some time at Aunt Clara's. You both always have such fun with them. It sounded like a very busy time.

We are beginning to have winds and the resultant sand and dust. A good time to have a forest fire, too—which we do have on the west side of the valley at the base of one of the peaks. It started yesterday afternoon. Did you ever smell a forest fire? It is a beautiful odor. Ernie and I were one of the first to spot it when we were flying a "6." Not so long ago there were bad forest fires in California and the air here was very hazy with smoke.

Tonight Doug and Pete, Doug's pal, were supposed to fly because the air was too smoky last night, but Pete's gal friend is going back to L.A. tomorrow and they had counted on tonight; so this morning they got excused, and the 4 of us are going to El Rancho.

I am spending a lazy Saturday. This was the first morning I haven't been on the line by at least 8 o'clock for weeks. We (all pilots on the field) are limited to 50 hours

a month now and I have in 54:30 and there were no ships to be test-hopped anyway.

They are serving lunch now—so 'bye.

Love,
Marie

Letter 89

Las Vegas, Nevada

October 10, 1944
Tuesday evening

Dear Mother and Daddy:

I can't remember the last time I wrote you, but it must have been long ago. So many things have happened since then—so many things happen every day that I would like to tell you, but when I wait so long to write, you hear only a few surface things.

We had quite a gay weekend. The whole engineering department from Major Mixon on down had a weekend party at Charleston. I believe I have told you that the Last Frontier Hotel runs a nice lodge on Mount Charleston with rooms as well as lots of little cottages. We 5 girls in engineering had a cottage (just like a hotel suite with living room, two bedrooms, and bath), all the single fellows had a cottage, and all the married couples had rooms and cottages. We arrived in time for a delicious steak dinner Saturday night at the lodge and then went to one of the cottages for the evening. It was a highly successful party. My date, Don Douglas, (another Doug! confusing isn't it?) stayed sober with me and we had an awfully good time just watching the others who were quite hilarious. Late in the evening Don and I went walking in the cold mountain air. The moon was just coming up and was shining only on the upper part of the rugged peaks all around little us down in the canyon. The clouds were blowing fast from behind the ridge and looked stormy in the moonlight but they quickly disintegrated in the dry air this side. It was a beautiful sight and we were both thrilled to death.

Sunday morning Don and I followed a path a ways up the canyon. I wish you could see those beautiful white pines and the quaking aspen trees with golden yellow leaves.

After starting home Sunday afternoon we branched off on a road that followed around on the other side of the ridge very high up. We could see for miles and miles. We saw many deer, a coyote, and an elk! He was beautiful and stately with a buff-colored body, and very dark head and legs. The first I ever saw. Then, of course, on the drive down into the desert, we were thrilled to death again with the expanse and beauty of the desert and the mountains at sundown. Don is about as much taken with this country as I am.

Doug Holt asked me to go x-c with him to El Paso this coming weekend, but the oper-

Lt. Donald C. Douglas standing by my 1941 Chevrolet Deluxe Coupe. October 1944.

ations officers tell me that field is closed to us for x-c but Doug doesn't believe it. He will find out tomorrow. His brother is there and will soon go overseas. It will be too bad if he can't go. Don [Douglas] put me on his x-c application to Denver for the weekend, too. I have never been there and would love to go. I had planned that for my next x-c in another week. So perhaps I shall go x-c someplace this weekend unless they both fall through.

Today Major Mixon told me to co-pilot on B-26s and B-17s if I wished, so I co-piloted with Don for two hours in a B-17 this morning. We slow-timed a new no. 2 engine on it. I flew a P-39 for an hour this afternoon and then I let Don take it for the second hour. He has just checked out on it and likes to fly

Lt. Donald Douglas and me in front of the lodge at Mount Charleston. October 16, 1944.

them occasionally. Major Mixon told me today to check out on a P-63 so I hope to do that tomorrow. It is the Bell King Cobra (Bell also makes the 39s). It is one of our fastest fighter planes and is much easier to fly than a P-39, they say.

Gee, I am sleepy. Goodnight.

Love,
Marie

P.S. We have heard for several weeks that we would disband about the first of the year or whenever Germany is taken care of because then there would be a big surplus of pilots. The date of December 20 for disbandment is official. I shall be home for Christmas. Isn't that swell?

Mother, my medicine hasn't come yet.

Bye now,
Marie

The pines on the snow-covered, forested slopes of Mount Charleston. October 16, 1944.

P.S. again, There should be enclosed a check and a bond. I haven't thought of anything for Christmas yet. What would you like? Please tell me.

Me

Letter 90

October 21, 1944
Saturday morning

Dear Mother and Daddy:

It was nice talking to Mother Thursday night, but I wanted you to be there too, Daddy. I tried to call you last Saturday noon, but for some reason the call didn't go through.

Please excuse the pencil because my nice little pen disappeared about two weeks ago. Even though my name is on it I prob-

ably will never see it again. Optimistic, aren't I?

I am just ill about this deal of having to come to Sweetwater. I had planned to make the most of our last two months and fly those little P-39s hard. It was a wonderful set-up at Las Vegas and I had everything my own way. Just after I went to engineering, the officer in charge of the P-39 hangar asked Major Mixon for me to be assigned to his hangar exclusively and ever since then they wouldn't let anyone else test-hop their planes without my permission. The mechanics and all thought I was a little tin god or something. When I left they all told me they surely hated to see me go. Weren't they sweet? The other engineering pilots told me they thought hangar 4 would just fold-up when I left. But I guess they are still going.

Did I tell you that two of the mechanics on P-39s worked on my car and tuned it all up—for nothing, too. One worked in a Chevy garage in civilian life and the other worked in some other kind of garage. They got the 39 electrician to fix the radio too. Don Douglas is driving the car while I am gone. Did I tell you I have co-piloted some for him in a B-17 in the last several days? Sunday he and I took up two 39s and flew formation and had a dogfight together. We had so much fun.

Sunday night we went to Charleston and came back Monday morning and started the tongues wagging although they had absolutely no reason to do so. But then,

their evil minds seem to have to work on something. I wanted to go up just once more before leaving. It was cold up there with ice cycles and everything. We had a big breakfast in the lodge with the warm sun streaming through the windows. It is beautiful up there. You must see it sometime. High rocky cliffs surround the lodge and the white pines are so thick and so big. Las Vegas is so hot still and dry but I love the desert and the mountains in the distance. I shall become very homesick for that place after Dec. 20. How about your coming out and driving back home with me?

After yesterday I don't feel quite so badly about being here [Sweetwater]. I love to fly instruments and I concentrated hard yesterday morning. In the afternoon we had a wonderful ground school—two hours of lectures on the psychology and physiology of instrument flying and on the analysis of maneuvers. They were by Captain Wallender, an expert in instrument flying from Bryan, the Army's instrument school. He is one of many Bryan men who are here in charge of our instrument school. This morning were lectures by Lt. Romney from Bryan on suction systems and on the theory of gyroscopes. They were the finest lectures I have ever heard on those subjects.

You see, our 3 most important instruments, the flight indicator, the directional gyro, and the turn and bank indicator are really gyroscopes inside and the gyroscopes are turned by suction rather than by positive air pressure to prevent collection of dirt and oil and for smoother flowing of air through the instruments. The first two instruments require a differential suction pressure of 4 inches of mercury while the turn and bank indicator requires a suction of only 2 inches of mercury.

The psychology in instrument flying is interesting and is the biggest problem. We have the same sensations flying under the hood as one has when flying contact, but while flying contact you are unconscious of those sensations because you are flying with reference to the ground. Under the hood or under actual instrument conditions those sensations come to the fore and you think the ship is in an altitude entirely different from the altitude it is actually in. The problem is to ignore your own sensations completely and to believe in the instruments all together. It is fun.

What would you like for Christmas? Please tell me. And what should I get Aunt Clara? What would Eloise and Johnny and Suzie like? Of course, here I am in Sweetwater again just before Christmas— a very poor place to shop.

Bye now. Enclosed will be a bond.

Love,
Marie

P.S. Mr. Harper, my primary instructor, is teaching instruments in my flight. He tried to talk my present instructor into trading with him, but he wouldn't do it! Ahem!

Me

Comment

I had arrived at Avenger Field, Sweetwater, Texas, on October 20, 1944, for a four-week advanced course in instrument flying. This course was identical to one given at the Bryan, Texas instrument flight school, the principal center for instrument flying training in the USAF. Instructors from Bryan were flown to Sweetwater for the course.

Letter 91

October 31, 1944
Halloween

Dear Mother and Daddy:
You must hear the wonderful news. Today we had check rides which finished the basic [first half] phase of our course. My check was with Captain Ware who is at the head of our instrument school and he said it was a "very satisfactory" ride. I wish he could ride with me on just an ordinary day because today was the worst I have ever flown in several ways. And yet at other times during the ride it was very good. It was alternately very, very good or very, very bad. Never in between. It is wonderful to have it over. And to think that we are already halfway finished! It is supposed to be a 5-week course, but the weather has

been beautiful, warm, and clear every day—just like Las Vegas except that Las Vegas is hot yet.

This is a wonderful course. It is being given to us by men from Bryan, the Army's famous instrument school. As we were told, there wasn't room for us at Bryan so Bryan came here. I have wanted to go there so this is my chance.

This is Halloween and one of the boys in our barracks is having a party. All the girls are dressed in very clever costumes of just things they happened to have plus plenty of very clever makeup. It is a good party. I was there for awhile.

The girls in my bay are swell. We also have, besides six girls, 3 pups. Two are cocker and the other is Heinz. They weren't completely housebroken at first, but now they are much more pleasant to have around. They are very cute.

Please tell me what you want for Christmas. The girls want to go to bed so goodnight and sweet dreams.

Love,
Marie

"Peek-a-Boo." Not all was work at Sweetwater. Classmates Elizabeth Watson, middle, and me, behind her with another WASP (unknown). November 1944.

Letter 92

Avenger Field

November 5, 1944
Sunday evening

Dear Mother and Daddy:
I just looked up your letters, Mother and find that there are questions in 3 of them which I have not answered, so here are the

answers before I forget to answer them. First of all, I voted a straight Republican ticket because I hadn't studied the candidates except the candidates for president and knew absolutely nothing about any of the others. The medicine has come just since coming to Sweetwater. I shall let you know if two come since they seemed to be rather certain that they had sent two.

You mentioned reading Dragon Seed. I have never read it but I saw the movie and it was very fine, much finer I have the feeling than the book. I have been reading several books since coming to Sweetwater. I am afraid I do that instead of studying, but so much of the stuff is repetition—not all of it—that I listen in class and sort out the information and what has not already been put back in pigeon holes and find a place for the other. So it isn't hard. I read Brave New World by Aldous Huxley which is a bit startling but in a way is very good. It is the story of a civilization of several centuries to come whose ultimate goal has been happiness and the tragic end for having that aim in mind. Then I read Time Must Have a Stop by the same author which I enjoyed more. The philosophy in the last chapter is worth the reading of the whole book. The story is about a boy who is sensitive, temperamental, and a poetic genius. The theme seems to be our wishing to make the world a better place to live in for the next generation—the usual theme isn't it? The last book is Time for Each Other by Runbeck which is another book about Miss Boo but this time she is 8 years of age instead of 4. It is a sweet book for anyone who loves children. It makes you feel very good after reading it.

Saturday nights around here are pretty awful. I really get into the dumps but last night was a pretty good one. I went into town just long enough to buy some V-Mail stationary and came right out again. Then about 9:30 Ava Hamm and I started out for a walk—she is one of my bay mates. We crawled across the fence on the west side of the field and walked through the cactus and sagebrush and rattlesnakes in the dark down into a pretty little gulley. Then we crawled through the fence again farther up and walked all around the field which in spots is a pretty rough trip because the field is lined inside the fence line with gullies, etc., just as all west Texas is full of them. After awhile the moon came up. We took a blanket along and for a little while found a sheltered spot from the cold night wind and watched the stars and the clouds racing across them. For a long time neither of us said a word—each lost in her own thoughts. We finally arrived at the bay at midnight with our legs about ready to give way to fatigue. We did have a very nice time and we slept like logs—the rest of the night I mean.

This morning it was beautiful. I didn't like to waste it inside but I went to church anyway—to the Presbyterian. Then I heard some wonderful music this afternoon, the [New York] Philharmonic on the radio and wrote some letters and then a bunch of us had a picnic. We went over to the gulley that Ava and I found last night and had a swell steak fry. She and I came back early and I believe we hear them coming now. The rest of them I mean.

Our good weather finally broke Friday. We had a very low ceiling and on Saturday morning was a very thick fog which didn't clear quite in time to fly in the afternoon and for some reason they decided to let us have today off. That didn't make me particularly happy. I am crazy to get back to Las Vegas.

Captain Monserud's lost a baby yesterday morning. Isn't that too bad? Two of our bay mates just arrived home from a weekend in Big Spring and it seems that they had a wonderful time. Their eyes are just beaming.

Thursday night a cablegram came from John. He hadn't heard from me in a month and seemed to be quite worried. He asked for an answer right back. I hadn't heard from him in about that long either, but in the last 3 days six letters have come from him, but the last date on them is October 15, which was quite some time ago. He has been writing airmail as have I, and I remember hearing that airmail is no longer to be carried across by plane so I suppose that is why, so I shall send them V-Mail now. For about 3 weeks now he has been on bombing missions. But evidently everything is going quite well and there isn't much opposition. That is good.

Getting sleepy now and must still write a birthday letter to Don [Douglas] whose birthday is Wednesday. You still haven't told me what you all want for Christmas.

Ask Eloise and Johnny what they want and what shall I get for Aunt Clara?

Goodnight and love and kisses,
Marie

Letter 93

November 15, 1944
Wednesday evening

Dear Mother and Daddy:
Your daughter has been very neglectful but we have been so busy.

Yesterday was my final check ride with Captain Wallender—and I passed! He is another of the fellows from Bryan. Then today was a 4-hour instrument cross-country to Waco and this afternoon I did my last hour of Link. We shall finish ground school Saturday noon and I still have 4 or 5 hours of flying to do.

We were all extremely unhappy last night when a notice came out that no WASP could leave until Monday, November 20, by order of the C.O. I was especially unhappy because Don [Douglas] is hoping to get a x-c to come get me Saturday and he has to be back Sunday night. But tonight they said they are hoping to get those who have finished released before. So I am keeping my fingers crossed.

We are to be given a full dress uniform and beret, whichever we choose—summer or winter—and a slack and battle jacket outfit, and our topcoats, and we may buy anything we wish for half price. Oh, yes— we are to have given to us all our insignia. Isn't that nice? How much do you think I should keep? I mean buy? I thought about another 2 slacks and a battle jacket and perhaps a dress uniform of each material— one to be given and one to buy. That would mean a dress uniform of each material, one winter slack and battle jacket and 2 summer slacks and one summer battle jacket. They are all beautiful material. Please tell me what you think.

Sunday our instructor invited his three students to his house for dinner. It was a lovely chicken dinner. He has two little girls who were cute—7 and 5. His wife is nice too and is a very good cook. We took her a box of candy. Our instructor is very swell.

My next mail should go to Las Vegas, I think. Would you do a very special favor and send a few things? I would love to have the Kodak and some film if you can find any, and my pretty blue nightgown with the tulips on it, and that periwinkle blue sweater—that big fluffy one—all washed and fresh—and is that big yellow one still fit to wear? Oh, yes—do you have any gas coupons extra? Some perhaps that do not have a license number on them? I would love to have a few. Send them to Las Vegas and tell them to hold the package until my return from Sweetwater. Please?

John is flying bombing missions over Germany. He had quite a close call on his 4th mission which was now about a month ago, but that is the last letter I have had. They had engine trouble over Germany. One engine went out completely and another was in very bad condition on the same side. If it had gone out they would have been completely out of luck. They nat-

My instrument class at Sweetwater, L-R: Elizabeth A. Watson, WASP, Class 44-5; Mr. Kenneth G. Fincher, instrument instructor; unknown; and me, Class 44-1. We had been invited to dinner. I had forgotten to put my WASP wings on my uniform. November 1944.

urally couldn't keep up with the formation so they were escorted home by several fighter planes. He sent a cable on November 2, so I know he was O.K. then.

David [Dawson] is making arrangements for his divorce while he is on furlough now. He wanted to spend as much time as possible with his son on Long Island and his mother in Florida, and he didn't have the money either, so he couldn't come, but I didn't want to come home now anyway. He is mentally very low now, poor fellow!

It is raining outdoors tonight—the first I have heard since Florida. So all the kids want to go to bed to listen to it, so I shall leave you now. Goodnight and sweet dreams!

Love,
Marie

P.S. Mother, about the spread. I shall leave it up to you now. Do you think we could use a pair of them? Several weeks ago one of the WAC officers said she would like to have it if I decided not to take it, but I shall not know if she has purchased another in the meantime until I get back. Shall let you know.

Me

Letter 94

Las Vegas Army Air Base

December 6, 1944
Wednesday evening

Dear Mother and Daddy:

I would just die if you wrote to me no oftener than I seem to write to you. I love to receive your letters. And I was so glad for the snapshots. Of course, you want them back, but I wish I could have prints of Suzie's and Eloise's pictures.

Before I forget, I shall not need that bedspread unless you want to use the two of them at home.

Yesterday Don [Douglas] and I flew a B-26 to San Bernadino (remember that place this side of L.A.) for a new-type radio installation and we were supposed to pick up another to bring back, but it wasn't ready and we had to wait until this morning for it. So of course we had to R.O.N. [remain over night] there. We had a very swell time. We ate Chow Mien and shrimp at a Chinese restaurant and then went to see Topper at the California Theatre. We couldn't get two single rooms so we had to get two double beds and sign in a roommate for each of us also (OPA regulations).

This morning our ship was finally ready about 11:00. While we waited we looked at the new Bell jet-propulsion ship. It is one *which uses no propeller. Last night we watched one take off and its sound was just a soft "whirr." Nearly every day 26s go down* [to the San Bernadino depot] *and others come back, so I have gone as co-pilot two or 3 times before. Remember the San Bernadino mountains? They are so green after flying over our desert mountains. We fly over them and then let down into the beautiful green valley onto the field. Lake Arrowhead and Big Bear Lake are in the mountains, you know, and we can always see them. It takes an hour to fly the 200 miles. We came back today by way of Blythe and then up the Colorado River to Las Vegas. That trip took almost two hours.*

I have been co-piloting on B-17s, too, a little for Don when there isn't a 39 to fly. I love to do it because there are so many gadgets for the co-pilot to work and I can fly part of the time too. Don is a wonderful pilot.

So much has happened since I last wrote. Did I tell you that Don tried to get to Sweetwater for me the weekend of November 18, but the weather was very bad east of El Paso. But we had been weathered in for 3 days and I still hadn't flown the last 4 hours of required time, so I couldn't meet him there. As you know from my phone call, I left Sweetwater on Tuesday night, and as the train stopped in San Bernadino Thursday morning a telegram from Don was delivered saying that he would come get me there in a B-26. So I got to fly part way anyway.

We have spent the last two weekends at Charleston. It is beautiful and all covered with snow which is quite a novelty to us desert rats. The sun is warm up there so I can enjoy the snow without getting cold. I wish you could fly over Charleston in a 39 with me. The peak and the ridges are bald and glisten with the purest, whitest snow you ever saw. The desert always looks wonderful though after the snow and pine scenery.

Monday I checked out in the P-63 which is another Bell ship similar to a 39 but more powerful and faster and much safer. It has 1550 HP in its one engine. It flies more the way an airplane should fly. Major Mixon is keeping one 63 in the engineering department until we leave so that I can fly it all I want. I am the only girl on the field flying either P-39s or P-63s.

Madelon received her gift from you. But she is having such a time getting all her thank you notes written. She flies part of every day.

Daddy, I shall send back the B [gas] *coupons. I didn't realize you were cut so low. Don was able to get some C* [gas] *coupons while I was gone, but we loaned the last one of those to one of the fellows last Saturday because his wife had their coupons in her purse, but he hasn't paid us back yet. Tonight we parked the car in front of the quarters registering "empty," so it will have to sit there until someone comes across. Tomorrow I shall apply for extra. The car looked beautiful when I came back from Sweetwater. Don hired our favorite P-39 mechanic to simonize it and Don washed it again just before I came.*

Daddy, you asked about Thanksgiving. That was the day I arrived back in Las Vegas. I didn't know it was Thanksgiving Day until that morning. I had lunch by myself—a turkey sandwich and orangeade—in the Red Cross Canteen (for pilots) in the operations office on the field at San Bernadino while waiting for Don. I felt just a little queer about being alone on that day. But he finally came about 3:30. We arrived back on our field in time for the most beautiful turkey dinner you ever saw in the mess hall all beautifully decorated—with Major Mixon and his wife. In the evening we called on Lt. and Mrs. Collier in town where Don and Ernie had been invited for dinner—Ernie was there though to eat. Then we went to the club for a while where a Thanksgiving party was in progress and saw everyone there. So it turned out to be a very thankful Thanksgiving Day—thankful to get back to L.V.

Some of the WASPs are to be married before leaving. Milly Taylor will be married December 15. It will be a beautiful white wedding in our chapel. Betty White just told us Monday that she will be married December 19—both girls to fellows on the field. I wouldn't be surprised if Betty Wall were married soon. She and one of the fel-

Lt. Donald Douglas on the wing of a Bell Aircraft Corp P-63 "King Cobra." I checked out in it on December 4, 1944. Las Vegas, Nevada. December 1944.

Another view of the P-63 "King Cobra" with Don in the cockpit. Las Vegas, Nevada. December 1944.

lows who shipped out several weeks ago planned to marry after the war, but today he surprised her by being shipped back here again permanently. I hope they decide to do it up right away. 3 of the girls have already married fellows on the field you know, Madelon B., Marj Harper, and Madelyn Taylor. Don't worry about me. I shall not be. I want to go to school at Drake next semester—more music.

Mother, that periwinkle blue sweater should be in the civilian clothes you took home from Sweetwater.

I shall enclose two checks, a money order, a bond, Herbie's letter, and the two gas tickets. Thank you anyway, Daddy.

Love,

Marie

P.S. Daddy, you said Mother might accept my invitation and come out, but after our trip back from Sweetwater, I certainly don't want her to have to suffer train travel. I shall soon be home anyway. I shall probably leave here Dec. 21 and spend about 4 days on the road. No doubt one or two girls would like to ride with me so I shall have company.

Me

Comment

Recently a remarkable coincidence occurred that stirred up memories of a friendship from long, long ago.

In the summer of 2004, John's brother Bob and his wife Mary were walking along a deserted beach on Orcas Island in the San Juan island group of Washington state, where they have a vacation home. Here they encountered an elderly gentleman who was walking very slowly in the same direction. As they came up to him they stopped to talk. He said he used to have a place on Blakely Island not far from Orcas Island. As most of the residents of Blakely Island have their houses on an airstrip at the northern end of the island, Mary asked if he was a flyer. Yes, he answered, adding that during World War II he had been a test pilot at the Las Vegas Army Air Base at Las Vegas, Nevada. Of course, they then asked him if he had known a WASP who also flew there named Marie Mountain. Yes—yes, indeed he had known Marie, he said, adding, "All the male test pilots there were especially fond of her, myself perhaps more than most!" He said his name was Donald C. Douglas. He was overwhelmed when Bob told him that I had married his brother John.

I was deeply touched by this chance meeting and John and I have since exchanged letters with Don expressing our pleasure of knowing that he had met John's brother and his wife Mary. Certainly, old acquaintances are not forgotten!

Letter 95

U. S. ARMY AIR FORCES

Las Vegas Army Air Base

Dec. 10, 1944
Sunday evening

Dear Mother and Daddy:

This has been a wonderful day, warm and perfectly calm with a clear blue sky. I slept ten hours last night and flew 5 wonderful hours in P-39s today. And all the landings were just "snitzy." The first period up, Don was up in a B-26 so I made lots of passes on him and shot him down over and over. He was a dead duck. Another period we each had a P-39 and we flew formation, showed off with acrobatics, and had a good rat race.

Tonight I am having a concert on the phonograph of the music of Sibelius. There are several of his things in my collection. And I am writing to you and John and then I shall go to bed early.

John sent a few snapshots, the first of several he will send. One is of him and he looks so different in it. I can hardly wait to see what he looks like when he gets home. He said perhaps he will be here by Easter. I hope so. He is still the finest person I have met in the Army.

Thank you so much for sending the package. I have fun being a lady in my room in the evenings dressed in the nightgown.

I did a very foolish thing. I thought I had some money in my bag, but it seems that I sent it all home. May I please bother you to send back $50? I am having to borrow and I hate that.

This town is no better than Sweetwater for shopping for Christmas. I guess we shall have to do as last year. Heck! I hate to do that.

Isn't it just terrible about Henry? It affected me as it did you, Mother. It sent shudders from my head to my toes. I guess this is really a war? Every time I hear news like that, I thank my lucky stars.

I am becoming very sleepy. Goodnight!

Love,
Marie

John sent me this photo after his fourth mission. He looks so much older! They had lost their no. three engine before the target (Cologne) and were deep in western Germany, alone. P-51 Mustang fighters escorted them to safety. October 1944.

This is a photo John sent me of his B-17G on his Christmas Eve mission, flying in support of the Battle of the Bulge. John is the copilot in the plane. December 24, 1944.

Comment

This is the last letter I sent home to my parents from Las Vegas. I had ten more days before the WASP was deactivated and I had to leave Las Vegas, the WASP, and my military flying. I spent almost every one of those days doing the thing I loved most and for which I had been trained: flying. On many of these final days I flew three or four different missions. My flights were mostly in the P-39 and P-63 fighters but I also flew the BT-13 and, as copilot, in the B-17, "Flying Fortress." In the last ten days I flew twenty-six hours or an average of 2.6 hours per day. My last flight, described in Part III, "Denouement," was on the day the WASP was deactivated, December 20, 1944, and was very memorable.

Thoughts at the End

I was very saddened to have to leave the Air Force and relinquish my opportunity to fly the most modern and powerful aircraft in the world. After a year and a half of the most intensive, satisfying, and fulfilling experiences I have ever had, it was a great letdown to give it up. I spent little time trying to understand, let alone justify, the reasons the Air Force took this action. Such concerns had no relevance to me and, anyway, I could not affect the outcome. Being civil service employees, the Air Force had no responsibility other than making sure we had returned all government supplied equipment, were paid all that we were due, and that we paid any outstanding bills we had. We were then escorted to the gate. We found our own way home.

In the post-war period we had no entitlements under the G.I. Bill—no educational grants, government health care, home loans, etc., as we were not veterans. Veterans' status was ultimately granted to the WASPs, but not until 1977, thirty-three years later. By this time, about a third of the WASPs had died. Today it is inconceivable that women would be treated this way. There certainly has been significant social progress on that score in the past sixty years. The WASPs were, in fact, pioneers. Today, women fly as equals with men in all branches of the military and are recognized and honored for their service.

The Las Vegas WASP (Class 44-1) final goodbye dinner, L-R: Gwendolyn Crosby (Barthelmess), Ruth Craig Jones, Jeanette Jenkins, Marie Mountain (Clark), Ida F. Carter, Marj Harper (Watson), Madelon Burcham (Hill), Betty Wall (Strohfus), and Madelyn Taylor (Eggleston). Hotel El Rancho Vegas, December 19, 1944. WASPs Crosby, Jones, Jenkins, Carter, and Harper (Watson) have died.

I do not want to dwell on this aspect of the WASP experience, as it is only a small part of the overall story, at least to me. I felt greatly privileged to have had that wonderful opportunity to go through US Air Force flight training and then fly as an Air Force pilot while serving my country in wartime. My assignment to the Las Vegas AAB was a much-desired duty. At Las Vegas the WASP were not only welcomed and respected, but if she could qualify, a WASP could fly any aircraft on the field. I took full advantage of this enlightened policy!

In the end, I think my WASP experiences are best summed up in the expression we are so familiar with from the military: "An opportunity of a lifetime." I have always been grateful for this opportunity.

Final Goodbyes

The Las Vegas WASPs of Class 44-1 had formed a close sistership much like that of a college sorority. We all got together for a final dinner at the Hotel El Rancho Vegas in Las Vegas on our last night as WASPs. The next day, December 20, 1944, we bade farewell to our close friends and flying companions on the base and then left, taking incredible memories with us. It was over.

Part III
Denouement

The deactivation of the WASP just before Christmas 1944 did not come as a surprise. Rather, it was more like the end of a long goodbye. The basic issue concerned the militarization of the WASP and the appointment of the women pilots as officers in the USAF. This required congressional approval. A bill for this purpose was introduced in the House of Representatives in the spring of 1944 but it was defeated by a narrow margin in June. Another factor was that combat losses of male pilots were much lower than had been expected in 1942 when the women pilot program was established. While this was good news in itself it did mean that by mid-1944 the USAF had a sufficient number of trained and experienced male pilots to meet its needs. Hence, the trained WASP pilots were considered superfluous. There were other factors, too, many of which were political. One of these was pressure from civilian pilots employed in the USAF Training Command. They were fearful of being drafted into the Army if the Air Force replaced them by militarized WASPs.

In retrospect, it seems clear that the seeds for disbanding the WASP were planted in the original organizational plan in that the women were classified as Civil Service employees. This put them into a separate administrative category from those in the military. As a result, the WASPs were not entitled to the benefits normally accorded military personnel such as life insurance, medical care and hospitalization, travel authorizations, military funerals, death benefits, veteran's status, the G.I. Bill, etc. They were subject, however, to all military regulations and orders issued by commanding officers and were subject to court martial. In the end, the barrier to attaining military status was too much to overcome and deactivation was the only course left to the USAF. Hence, the Commanding General of the USAF, Henry H. Arnold, issued an order terminating the WASP, effective December 20, 1944. The nine hundred sixteen women pilots then on active duty were sent home. It was by chance that this occurred on the first day of winter—the day of the year having the longest night. To my mind, this was an apt coincidence because the long, dark night appropriately represented the saddened spirits of the disbanded women pilots.

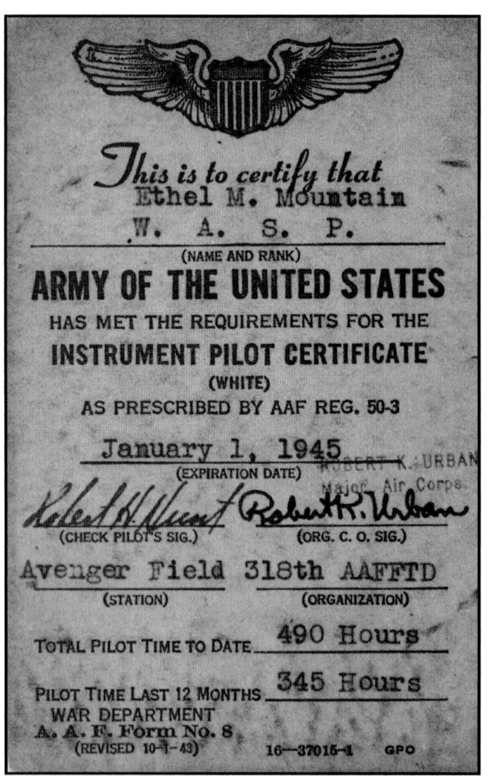

My (white) Instrument Pilot Certificate. The total pilot time was that at Avenger Field Only. January 1, 1945.

During the last six months of active WASP service most of us were relatively unaware of all the higher level negotiations regarding our future. We knew that our service time would probably be shortened, but we were too busily engaged with the important and interesting challenges we faced each day for it to bear much impact on our lives. Termination seemed to us only a remote possibility in the future. The responsibilities of daily flying consumed too much of our time, talents, and energies for us to become entangled with speculation and rumors about our future. There were conflicting factors as well that seemed to suggest that the WASP would have a longer tenure. For example, in July, I was sent to Orlando, Florida, for officer training in preparation for becoming a commissioned officer in the USAF. In October, I was detached to Avenger Field, Sweetwater, Texas, to take a month long course in advanced instrument flying and to upgrade both my instrument rating and my qualifications as an instrument instructor. Hence, with these fundamental enhancements of my qualifications, I entertained a vague notion that the WASPs were being prepared for a more permanent place in the USAF. Unfortunately, it did not work out this way.

The command at the Las Vegas Army Air Base was exceptionally cooperative in helping the WASPs there to make a smooth transition to civilian life. The operations officer arranged to check-out and provide as much flying time as possible in multi-engine aircraft for those entertaining plans for post-war commercial flying. For those whose post-war interest was in personal flying, which included me, he allowed great freedom in flying any single-engine aircraft for which we could qualify.

I checked out in the 1300 HP, Bell Aircraft P-39 "Airacobra" fighter in August and flew it consistently until the end as a member of the Engineering Flight Test Group. These test flights were usually made to determine, under actual flying conditions, the source and severity of a reported malfunction in the aircraft. In December I checked out in the 1550 HP, Bell Aircraft P-

63 "Kingcobra" fighter and flew it several times in the region around Las Vegas, southern Nevada, Arizona, and California. I also flew many times as copilot, or as "Qualified Dual," in the twin-engine Beechcraft AT-11, the Martin B-26 "Marauder," a twin-engine bomber, and the four-engine Boeing B-17 "Flying Fortress." In the meantime, I continued to fly gunnery missions and instrument instruction flights in the advanced trainer: the beautiful, much-loved North American AT-6.

My last flight as an active member of the WASP was on December 20, 1944. I took off from Las Vegas AAB in a P-39 and flew for a few minutes in the local area before venturing south along the Colorado River into Arizona. I knew that this would be my last flight, and I wanted it to be memorable.

After take off I made a wide circuit of the air base and climbed to two or three thousand feet above the hills surrounding the city of Las Vegas. Looking down on these hills, they seemed much smaller—almost insignificant—compared to their appearance from the ground. They displayed a characteristically wrinkled, reddish-brown texture laced with cracks and canyons that converged into dry streambeds and arroyos on the desert floor. The desert itself was tan, its surface mottled by green sagebrush. From my height I could not see the tiny desert flowers, but I knew they were there. To the east, outlined by a treeless Nevada wasteland, I could see the bluish-green water of Lake Mead formed by Boulder Dam. Boulder City, with its irrigated lawns and ordered street patterns, stood out as an emerald jewel in the desert. The Basic Magnesium Plant in Henderson, where John and I had had our interesting first date, on the other hand appeared in stark contrast in colors of deep brown and black. As I swung south away from the dam to follow the silver thread of the Colorado River, I could see across the arid desolation of Death Valley to the southern ranges of the California Sierra. I continued following the Colorado River a few miles beyond Needles, California, and then I turned back. Flying north to Las Vegas, the snow-capped peak of Mount Charleston and its forested slopes appeared off my left wing. This beautiful panorama brought back many pleasant memories of happy hours spent there with John and other friends. I then turned toward the air base in a slow descent, radioed the control tower for landing instructions and, with great reluctance, entered the landing pattern of the active runway.

As I landed, taxied to the ramp, and shut down the engine, the finality of it all struck me with a deep and profound feeling of sweet sadness. It was over. At that moment my opportunity to fly the world's most modern and powerful aircraft, to "slip the surly bonds of earth," to "wheel and soar high in the sunlit silence" of the sky, past billowing white clouds, was gone. Over the next several weeks these personal reactions developed into a more permanent sense of loss—similar to the feeling one has after

USAF women pilots and me in front of the Lockheed C-141 transport they flew. The WASPs were flown in this aircraft by an all-female crew during the WASP reunion in Charleston, SC, October 1988.

The all-female flight crew of a USAF Northrop B-1 supersonic bomber based at Dyess AFB, Abilene, Texas. This photo was taken during the WASP reunion in Sweetwater, Texas, October 2000.

the death of a loved one. But beautiful memories remained. I realized in my heart that I had been greatly privileged to have participated in the first USAF women's pilot program and afforded an opportunity for great personal fulfillment. I was profoundly sad but, also, sincerely grateful. To serve my country as a military pilot in wartime had truly been "an opportunity of a lifetime."

The permanent legacy of the WASP is found today in the complete acceptance of women as members of that special fellowship, US military pilots. Women now routinely fly US military aircraft on all types of missions, including combat, in each of the service branches. I am especially proud to have served sixty years ago in the pioneering effort that has made this possible today.

General Arnold acknowledged the achievements of the WASP program and their contribution to the war effort in his address to the final WASP graduation class, 44-10, at Sweetwater, Texas, on December 7, 1944. He said:

I am glad to be here today and talk with you young women who have been making aviation history. You and all WASPs have been pioneers in a new field of wartime service, and I sincerely appreciate the splendid job you have done for the AAF.

You, and more than nine hundred of your sisters, have shown that you can fly wingtip to wingtip with your brothers. If ever there was a doubt in anyone's mind that women can become skillful pilots, the WASP have dispelled that doubt.

General Arnold concluded:

Well, now in 1944, more than two years since the WASP started flying with the Air Forces, we can come to only one conclusion—the entire operation has been a success. It is on record that women can fly as well as men.

The detailed story of the 1944 disbanding of the WASP is found in many of the publications cited in the "Selected Reading" section, especially the books by Jean Hascall Cole, Bernice "Bee" Falk Haydu, and Sally VanWagenen Keil. In early 1945 Jacqueline Cochran, the Director of Women Pilots, wrote the most authoritative and definitive history of the WASP in the

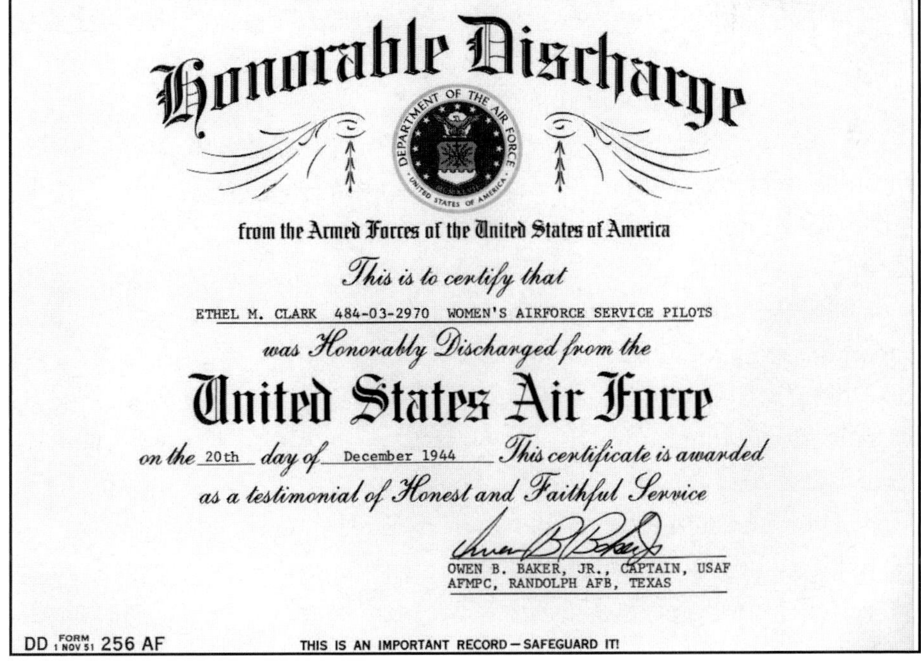

My Honorable Discharge from the US Air Force, backdated to December 20, 1944.

Betty Wall (Strohfus), my WASP 44-1 classmate in 1944 and a long-time friend. Betty is today an ardent spokeswoman on behalf of the WASP. Her book about her WWII experiences is cited in the section "Selected Reading."

"Final Report on Women Pilot Program," a USAF report published in 1945 and cited in the "Selected Reading" section.

The WASP ultimately were also awarded formal veteran status in 1977 and given honorable discharges from the US Air Force, backdated to December 20, 1944, the date of their deactivation. My Certificate of Honorable Discharge, shown here, was granted in 1982, thirty-eight years after leaving the service.

I left Las Vegas in my car on December 21 and arrived home in West Des Moines on Christmas Eve. Betty Wall, a Las Vegas WASP from my 44-1 class at Sweetwater and a dear friend of long standing, traveled with me. We also had one of the B-17 girls with us as far as Denver. We then continued on to Omaha where Betty was to have boarded a train for her home in Fairbault, Minnesota. However, it turned out that there was no train going to Fairbault from Omaha, but she could get one at Des Moines in a few hours. To make the train we drove at top speed—establishing some sort of a speed record, I am sure, but Betty made her train on time.

After dropping Betty off at the station, I drove home and was welcomed joyously by my parents. They were expecting me but were uncertain of the exact time, as I'd had no opportunity to call them since leaving Omaha.

Being home on Christmas is always a happy occasion, but this was especially true during wartime when the celebration of deeply shared joys took on a special significance, particularly after having been away many months on hazardous duty. Many of my parents' generation believed—with some reason—that flying airplanes was an invitation to eternity. I think Mother and Daddy never expected to see me again when I left for Sweetwater in August 1943. Doubtless, my parachute jump had only added to their worries. I have often thought of the immense emotional burden that my parents must have carried while I was flying with the WASP. Yet, never once did they try to transfer their

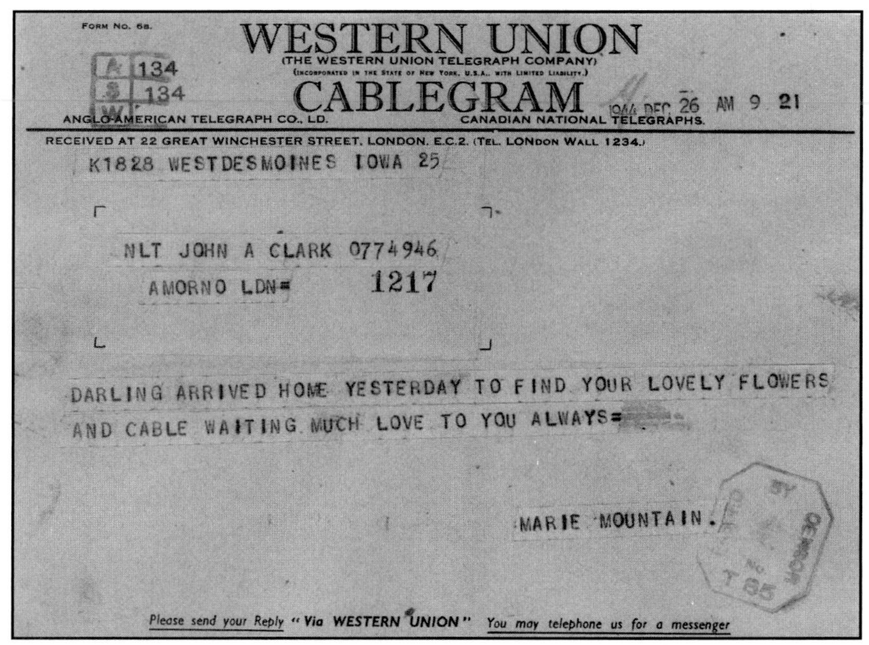

My cable to John thanking him for his Christmas roses. Christmas Day, 1944.

fears to me or discourage me from flying. I recognized this as the manifestation of the genuine faith, love, and courage of parents, something not often mentioned or acknowledged in chronicles of war. Their belief in God and trust in His divine plan always sustained them throughout their lives. The realization of their trust and sacrifices gave me a deeper understanding and respect for my parents and their generation. Their lives have served as a model for my family and me.

Some memories that I kept particularly close to my heart were those of John, that young Air Force pilot whom I did not yet know would become my husband but whom I had met and fallen in love with at Las Vegas in 1944. He was at that time serving with the Eighth Air Force flying combat missions in a B-17 "Flying Fortress" over Germany from his base in England. On Christmas Day, to my great delight, I received a cable and a dozen red roses from him. I think he had arranged for his mother in Royal Oak, Michigan, to have them sent to me. What a wonderful surprise! I answered immediately by cable and as my reply suggests, I was "pondering this thing in my heart."

I do not recall many of the events that happened during the weeks following my return home. It did take some time to readjust to civilian life after the busy and ordered life with the military. I suppose I gave some thought to what my life should become now that I was free of wartime obligations. Naturally a desire to keep flying dominated much of my thinking but just how this could be brought about was unclear. Many WASPs entertained thoughts of returning to military flying in some capacity and rumors spread about these possibilities. One hope that circulated was that former WASPs could serve in some flying capacity with the Women's Army Corps (WAC). To clarify the situation, Miss Cochran sent a memorandum to all WASPs in February 1945 that stated:

The Army Air Forces investigated every possible avenue for utilization of its women pilots before inactivating the WASP on 20 December 1944. The situation which then existed has not changed. There are sufficient trained male pilots to handle all the domestic flying assignments of the AAF. There is not now any military requirement for women pilots, nor is there any foreseeable requirement for them in a pilot's capacity.

That lack of requirement provides an answer to the question of the possible use of former WASPs as pilot officers with the Women's Army Corps. There are now no direct commissions in the WAC, officer status being given only to a very limited number of enlisted WAC who are selected from the ranks and then graduate from an officers' candidate school.

No hope can be held out to former WASPs of a return to military flying through the WAC or through any other civilian or militarized arrangement now visible.

Miss Cochran's bleak assessment put an end to all the WASPs' speculative hopes for a return to military flying. If flying was to be in our future the WASP needed to look to civil aviation for opportunities.

These were scarce to non-existent. I considered the possibility of becoming a flight instructor, as I certainly had more than sufficient qualifications. When I left the WASP I held both the Commercial Pilot Rating and the Instrument Pilot Certificate. In addition, I had almost one thousand hours of flying time in aircraft of major significance. Nevertheless, the prospect of flying a small, single engine aircraft, like the J-3 Cub, instructing a beginning student from the rear seat was simply unappealing. I felt it would be too much of a let down after flying modern, fully equipped, powerful, combat qualified military fighters in all weather conditions. Beyond that, for private flying the rental cost of such an aircraft was quite high for little benefit

I did have one more opportunity to make a few flights in a military aircraft. The Des Moines Flying Service was asked to help in the distribution of war surplus aircraft. The task was to fly them from a storage field in Ponca City, Oklahoma, to Des Moines where they would be available for inspection by buyers. The owner of the Des Moines Flying Service knew of my WASP service and asked if I would serve as a ferry pilot. I was happy to accept and during the last ten days of March 1945 I made five flights ferrying PT-19s from Ponca City to Des Moines. The total flying time for this was twenty-one hours. This was the same type of aircraft I was flying when I made my parachute jump at Sweetwater in August 1943. It felt good to be back in the air again even if it was only in a Primary

Trainer. I suppose I was paid for this service but I have no recollection of it. I probably would have done it for nothing just to fly again!

In early March, John cabled me that he had finished his combat tour with the 100th Bomb Group, Eighth Air Force, on March 8 after flying thirty-two missions. The normal combat tour at that time was thirty-five missions but his crew was released early since they had served faithfully and well and replacement flight crews were then readily available. This was especially good news. He said he would be seeing me soon, as he expected to be back in the US about the middle of April. As it turned out he crossed the Atlantic in great style aboard the *HMS Queen Elizabeth*. He has described this thrilling voyage and triumphal entry into New York harbor in his WWII memoir, *An Eighth Air Force Combat Diary*.

At the end of March, I also received a letter from the Finance Officer at Las Vegas, a Lt. Col., informing me that I owed the United States fifteen dollars. It seems that I had been reimbursed more than I should have been for a trip I had taken ten months before! I found this very amusing since even at the time of the trip I never thought of questioning the settlement and at this late date I hadn't the foggiest clue about the details. Of course, I immediately sent the LVAAB Finance Office a postal money order for fifteen dollars and have a receipt for this in my files! I include the letter here mostly for amusement since it is a good example of the slow but thorough grinding of the wheels of a bureaucracy. I suppose the USAF spent many times more than my debt to collect the fifteen dollars.

During the spring of 1945 there were two events that revived pleasant memories of my recently ended career as a military pilot. In April, Lt. Donald Douglas, a friend from Las Vegas Army Air Base, flew into Des Moines in a B-17 for a short visit. His copilot was also a Las Vegas acquaintance. This huge four-engine bomber caused quite a stir at the airport, drawing a lot of attention. I was really happy to see them both and to relive for a brief moment my exhilarating life of military flying. The sight of this aircraft, the roar of its Wright-Cyclone engines, the sounds of the equipment on board, the squealing of the brakes and the fragrance of hot engines, exhaust, oil, and gasoline brought a feeling of great nostalgia for times now gone. It seemed like a dream that only a short time before I had really flown that aircraft. Don stayed only a day and we had a short visit. The next day he flew low over the farm in an impressive aerial display that thrilled us all.

A few days later Lt. Ernie Maulsby, also a Las Vegas pilot and friend from Des Moines, flew into town with four or five others in a caravan of Curtis C-46 twin-engine transports. When they left later in the day they also provided us with much excitement by flying in trail one after the other in parade formation low over the farm as a sort of flying circus. It was a dramatic way of saying farewell, I thought.

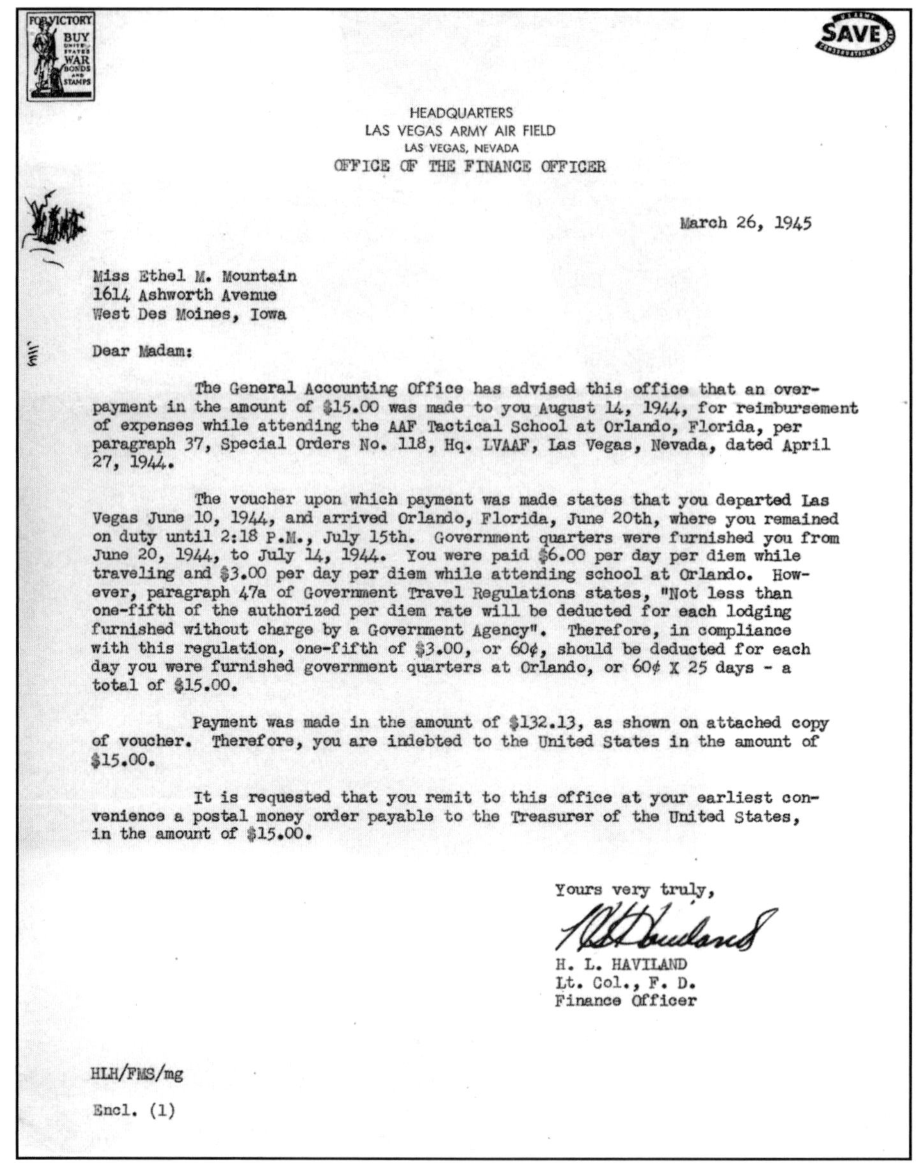

HEADQUARTERS
LAS VEGAS ARMY AIR FIELD
LAS VEGAS, NEVADA
OFFICE OF THE FINANCE OFFICER

March 26, 1945

Miss Ethel M. Mountain
1614 Ashworth Avenue
West Des Moines, Iowa

Dear Madam:

    The General Accounting Office has advised this office that an over-payment in the amount of $15.00 was made to you August 14, 1944, for reimbursement of expenses while attending the AAF Tactical School at Orlando, Florida, per paragraph 37, Special Orders No. 118, Hq. LVAAF, Las Vegas, Nevada, dated April 27, 1944.

    The voucher upon which payment was made states that you departed Las Vegas June 10, 1944, and arrived Orlando, Florida, June 20th, where you remained on duty until 2:18 P.M., July 15th. Government quarters were furnished you from June 20, 1944, to July 14, 1944. You were paid $6.00 per day per diem while traveling and $3.00 per day per diem while attending school at Orlando. However, paragraph 47a of Government Travel Regulations states, "Not less than one-fifth of the authorized per diem rate will be deducted for each lodging furnished without charge by a Government Agency". Therefore, in compliance with this regulation, one-fifth of $3.00, or 60¢, should be deducted for each day you were furnished government quarters at Orlando, or 60¢ X 25 days - a total of $15.00.

    Payment was made in the amount of $132.13, as shown on attached copy of voucher. Therefore, you are indebted to the United States in the amount of $15.00.

    It is requested that you remit to this office at your earliest convenience a postal money order payable to the Treasurer of the United States, in the amount of $15.00.

Yours very truly,

H. L. HAVILAND
Lt. Col., F. D.
Finance Officer

HLH/FMS/mg

Encl. (1)

The letter from the LVAAB Finance Officer informing me of my $15 debt to the United States. March 1945.

In the meantime, I was giving serious thought to my own life and career. I was coming to accept that flying would not be a part of it. Meanwhile, the acting-supervisor of music of the Des Moines Public Schools had called me in December when I arrived home asking if I would return to teaching flute in the schools, basically picking up where I left off in 1943. There had been no flute teacher in the system during the time I was away. This was the work I enjoyed and was most qualified to do, so I did give the proposal serious consideration. I concluded that if I were to have a career in instruction it would have to be in music, where I had excellent qualifications, reputation, and experience. I thought also of returning to private teaching or, perhaps, combining private and public school teaching, much as I had done before the war. There were other possibilities as well. For a time I considered serving in some capacity in the American Red Cross in an overseas assignment. I made a few inquiries about this but decided against it. My greatest qualifications, motivations, and experience were in music where I had an established career before going into the Air Force. Flute teaching and performance were clearly my strongest talents so, in the end, I decided that I would return to that activity.

There was, however, one other factor in my thinking that I knew held wonderful prospects but was unresolved. This was my relationship with John. He and I had talked very seriously about this the previous summer and were of a single mind about it, without any significant doubts. At the time, he was headed overseas to a combat assignment filled with great danger and an unpredictable future. We both agreed that it would be better not to become committed to each other under those circumstances. Waiting would not only settle any uncertainty issues but would also provide us the opportunity to consider our relationship after the passage of several months and from a distance. John was returning home now, and I knew that much of my own future would depend on how both of us now viewed our relationship. Because of

My sister Eloise Mountain Wright (L) and me on Easter Sunday 1945 at our family farm home in West Des Moines, Iowa. Note that I am wearing my WASP wings on my blouse.

this, I think I delayed making any fixed plans for my immediate future until John and I had the opportunity to decide if our futures were to coincide. This would be soon, as John cabled me that he expected to leave England by sea about Easter, which was the first Sunday in April in 1945. Depending on how he traveled, he could be expected to arrive in the US sometime before the last week in April. After spending time with his family in Michigan, he would come to visit me in Iowa. I thought that we would be meeting again about the first of May, and that is pretty much how it worked out.

I kept active during this period with family visits, particularly on Easter Sunday,

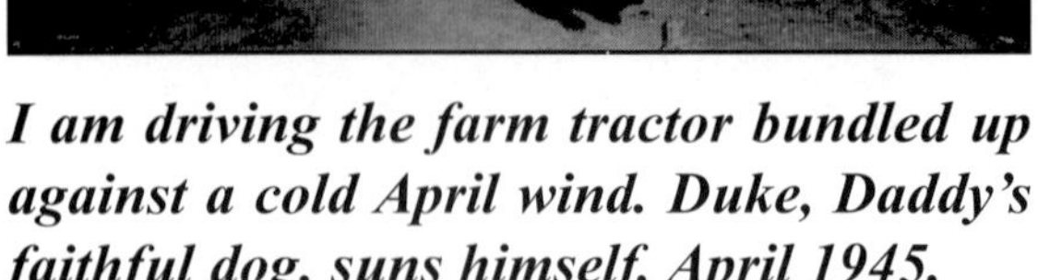

I am driving the farm tractor bundled up against a cold April wind. Duke, Daddy's faithful dog, suns himself. April 1945.

Daddy loading corn using the elevator he designed. April 1945.

and by reacquainting myself with neighbors and friends. They all wanted to hear of my flying experiences, which I tried to relate to them. On Easter, my sister Eloise, her husband John Wright, and their three-year-old daughter Suzanne came home for a few days. This was the first I had seen them since the previous summer and we had a very happy reunion.

From time to time I would help Daddy around the farm doing what I could to be useful. Occasionally, I would drive the tractor, hauling corn or silage to the feed lot for the cows.

About this time I was invited by the West Des Moines Rotary Club to be the guest speaker, wearing my WASP uniform, at their regular April meeting. I told them about my WASP experience, from training at Sweetwater, Texas, through my active service as an Air Force pilot at the Las Vegas Army Air Base. My talk included the structure of the WASP organization, the number of applicants (25,000), the number who graduated, earning their wings (1,174), the type of aircraft the women flew, and their various mission assignments. It was surprising to those attending that women actually served as Air Force pilots and that they were not formally members of the military but were Civil Service employees. I think my talk gave the Rotarians an entirely new perspective about the organization of the US Air Force in the war. They had little or no idea about women serving in the military and were impressed that women actually flew the powerful aircraft that in the pre-war mindset were strictly a male domain. When they learned that I had parachuted from an airplane over Texas they were really convinced that the war certainly had changed the way the country worked! Although I did not know this at the time, this was the first of many such talks that I would give over the next sixty years about the WASP.

Usually they would be joint presentations with my husband, who would speak about his combat flying experiences in Europe.

John arrived in New York City on April 13 aboard the *HMS Queen Elizabeth* and called me the next day from Camp Kilmer, NJ. It was a thrill to hear his voice again. He sounded older, more seasoned, and contemplative—signs of increased maturity, although he was only twenty-one years old. Eight months of combat flying during a harsh English winter had changed him noticeably—for the better, I thought. I couldn't wait to see him but had to put that off for a couple of weeks while he spent time with his family in Royal Oak, Michigan. We arranged that he would come by rail to Des Moines on May 3, where I would meet him. The date was significant, as it was exactly a year to the day that we had first met at the Officers' Club at the LVAAB. The next day was his mother's birthday, although I did not know it at the time!

The time did fly by and we probably talked by long distance telephone a couple of times. Finally, the big day arrived and I could barely hide my excitement as his train pulled into the station at Des Moines. I was almost overwhelmed when I first saw him. He seemed taller and somewhat heavier but he still looked young and vital. His step was firm and he walked with confidence and determination. His face, however, was that of a man—more sober, a little thinner, and slightly wrinkled with crowfoot crinkles around his eyes, as pilots

often have. The man I saw approaching me was a handsome, combat-decorated officer now matured far beyond his years! What a difference a year had made! We embraced on the platform for a long time, shedding a few tears and finding it hard to speak at first. I tried to welcome him home as best I could and I believe he understood my feelings. I was very anxious for him to see me in my home setting and meet my parents and for them to meet him. He was to stay at our farm home, something that never happened before for any of my visiting male friends. John's visit was a special occasion!

We had five important days together. My parents were much impressed with him and he blended easily into the family and farm activities. In turn he was very much impressed by my parents and could see that their strong, honest personalities came from a life of hard, productive work tempered by genuine Christian love. I introduced him to all my Des Moines relatives, who liked him too. One afternoon my Aunt Maple visited and asked me if I had ever played my flute for John. She suggested that I do. Perhaps Aunt Maple had some intuitive insight as to the effect my playing might have on John. He later confided to me that if he had still entertained any doubts about asking me to marry him, they were dispelled by my playing that day. He possessed a sufficient appreciation of music, particularly the flute, which he had played briefly in high school, to recognize a level of accomplishment that indicated talent, training, and achievement, which

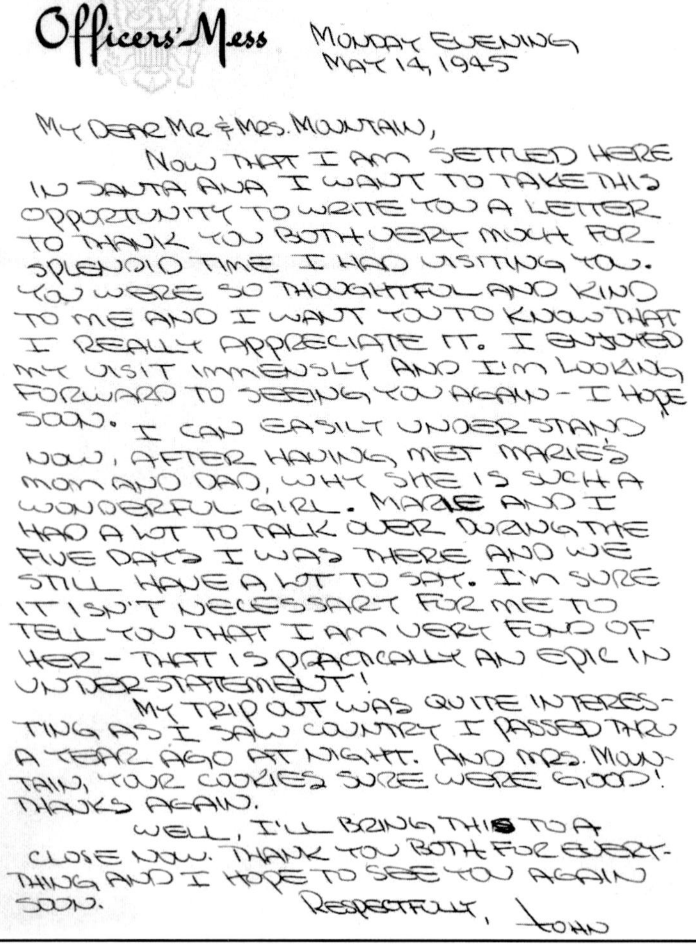

SANTA ANA ARMY AIR BASE

Officers' Mess

MONDAY EVENING
MAY 14, 1945

MY DEAR MR & MRS. MOUNTAIN,

NOW THAT I AM SETTLED HERE IN SANTA ANA I WANT TO TAKE THIS OPPORTUNITY TO WRITE YOU A LETTER TO THANK YOU BOTH VERY MUCH FOR SPLENDID TIME I HAD VISITING YOU. YOU WERE SO THOUGHTFUL AND KIND TO ME AND I WANT YOU TO KNOW THAT I REALLY APPRECIATE IT. I ENJOYED MY VISIT IMMENSELY AND I'M LOOKING FORWARD TO SEEING YOU AGAIN - I HOPE SOON. I CAN EASILY UNDERSTAND NOW, AFTER HAVING MET MARIE'S MOM AND DAD, WHY SHE IS SUCH A WONDERFUL GIRL. MARIE AND I HAD A LOT TO TALK OVER DURING THE FIVE DAYS I WAS THERE AND WE STILL HAVE A LOT TO SAY. I'M SURE IT ISN'T NECESSARY FOR ME TO TELL YOU THAT I AM VERY FOND OF HER - THAT IS PRACTICALLY AN EPIC IN UNDERSTATEMENT!

MY TRIP OUT WAS QUITE INTERESTING AS I SAW COUNTRY I PASSED THRU A YEAR AGO AT NIGHT. AND MRS. MOUNTAIN, YOUR COOKIES SURE WERE GOOD! THANKS AGAIN.

WELL, I'LL BRING THIS TO A CLOSE NOW. THANK YOU BOTH FOR EVERYTHING AND I HOPE TO SEE YOU AGAIN SOON.

RESPECTFULLY, JOHN

John's thank you letter to my parents from the Santa Ana AAB, California, after his visit to the farm. May 1945.

marked a person having a genuine, personal dedication to an art. It was, in effect, his way of measuring character. In all my years of playing it had never occurred to me that my playing would have such a profound effect on another person!

A day before John had to leave to report to his next duty station he asked me if I would marry him. Although I had prepared for this possibility, I was still deeply moved when he actually asked me and I assured him that it was my greatest desire to be his wife. However, since this was a big step and one I knew had to be for a lifetime, I told him that before I answered "yes" I wanted to discuss our marriage with my parents. This would take a little time, as there was much to talk to them about. John fully understood and suggested that I take as much time as I felt to be necessary but that he hoped my answer could be given in a few weeks. In the meantime, we could keep in close contact by phone and letter. The next day John left for the Santa Ana Army Air Base in California where he would be reassigned to new duty. To extend his visit as long as possible, we drove in my car to Omaha to meet his train. Our parting this time, though filled with a sweet sadness, was also marked with joy and hope.

After about two weeks at Santa Ana, John was sent to the Goodfellow AAB at San Angelo, Texas, not far from Sweetwater. This base was a bombardier training school using the twin-engine Beechcraft AT-11. There were many other former combat pilots there, too, doing the same thing. He more or less filled in his time flying this small aircraft as a way to maintain his flying skills. He really had no other responsibilities. After flying a combat tour in B-17s, he found the assignment undemanding. This was one way the USAF kept their pilots occupied until they could be given more permanent assignments.

About this time, however, the USAF realized that it had many more trained pilots than it needed to meet its requirements. It then began a determined effort to release its surplus pilots from active duty. This was done by a point system in which points were granted for length and type of service, awards, decorations, combat service, overseas duty, etc. Because John had completed a combat tour with the Eighth Air Force and earned many decorations, he had accumulated more points than the minimum necessary to be released from military service. He immediately applied for release, which was promptly granted.

In the meantime, after talking it over with Mother and Daddy, I realized that my future was to be with John, as his wife. I immediately wrote to him, accepting his proposal of marriage. From then on we devoted all our efforts to planning for our wedding. John informed the command at Goodfellow AAB of his plans and they were unusually cooperative in issuing orders for his release from active duty. We set the date for our wedding as Sunday, July 8, 1945, in our church, the West Des Moines Christian Church.

OFFICERS MESS
LAS VEGAS ARMY AIR FIELD
LAS VEGAS, NEVADA

Part IV
Epilogue

The preceding sections of this memoir cover the first thirty years of my life with the principal focus on the year and a half I served as an Air Force pilot as a member of the WASP, the Women's Air Force Service Pilots of World War II. This section, "Part IV, Epilogue," is an account of my life and that of my family during the sixty years following the war, beginning with my marriage to John on July 8, 1945. In order to keep this book to a reasonable length I will include in this part only the significant events of this period, giving as much detail and as many photos as are appropriate.

Our Wedding

Our wedding day, Sunday, July 8, 1945, was a beautiful Iowa summer day in complete harmony with my spirits. All our plans worked out perfectly in spite of the usual wartime uncertainties about travel. John's sister Alice served as my matron of honor and was accompanied by her husband, Dr. Earl Watch, then on active duty as a Lt-JG as a dentist at the Great Lakes Naval Training Center at Highland Park,

Illinois. John Wright, my brother-in-law, was John's best man and his charming three-year-old daughter, Suzanne, was our flower girl. Both of John's parents, his younger sister Doris, and his aunt Bessie were able to attend. All of my Iowa family was there, too.

John's sister Alice and her husband, Dr. (Lt-JG) Earl Watch. July 8, 1945.

John's arrival schedule in Des Moines was the cause for some concern because of administrative delays at Goodfellow Field, San Angelo, Texas, in getting approval for

John and me just after church. Mother is next to the house. July 8, 1945.

John's parents, left, and mine. July 8, 1945.

John and Suzanne, newfound friends. July 8, 1945.

both travel and separation from the Air Force. The approvals came through more or less at the last minute and John got to Des Moines as fast as he could, arriving on the Friday before our wedding! He and I spent Saturday picking out our rings and other things, including a few gifts for the members of the wedding party.

Daddy had suggested that I wear my WASP uniform as my wedding dress but I felt that a civilian dress would be more appropriate. I wanted to begin my new life dressed like a lady from civil society. John, of course, would wear his Air Force uniform, as he was still on active duty. I had selected a modest, chartreuse, silk crepe dress of street length, belted, with short sleeves. It was trimmed in white and had embroidered shoulders. For accessories I chose matching shoes, elbow length gloves, a choker necklace, and a small white headpiece. My bridal bouquet was a spray of lilies of the valley with a purple orchid corsage attached.

The wedding party, L-R: John Wright, Alice Watch, me, John, and Suzanne. July 8, 1945

Our flower girl, Suzanne Wright, age three. July 8, 1945.

John and me leaving the church following our wedding. July 8, 1945.

The new bride on the steps of our "Honeymoon Cottage," Clear Lake, Iowa. July 20, 1945.

John striking a "manly" pose in front of our cottage. July 21, 1945.

We were married at four P.M. in our church, the West Des Moines Christian Church (Disciples of Christ) by the Reverend Clarence S. Kleckner, our pastor. (Forty years later, our daughter Eloise married Philip McKenzie in this same church.) The church was full of friends and relatives. After the ceremony a reception was held at our farm home surrounded by the expansive green lawns, trees, beautiful shrubs, plantings, and flowers Mother and Daddy had put in. I recall the hollyhocks, especially. They were in full bloom and today whenever I see this flower I think back on that happy occasion.

John and I planned to take a honeymoon but it had to be delayed until John was separated from the Air Force. This was scheduled for July 15 at Fort Sheridan, Illinois.

We took a train to Chicago on July 14 and stayed at the Allerton Hotel where John's Aunt Alice lived. We visited with her briefly the evening we arrived and went to Fort Sheridan on July 15 to complete all the procedures for return to civilian life. The next day we boarded the Rock Island "Rocket" for Des Moines. We now were both civilians, even though the war was still raging in the Pacific.

Our honeymoon was spent in Clear Lake near Mason City, Iowa, where we rented a cottage for the week of July 16–24. It was next door to a dormitory of a girls' camp so our presence stirred quite a bit of curiosity from the teenagers. We had no fixed schedule and devoted most of our time to becoming used to being married. It was a very happy time for us and I found my new husband to be a very perceptive, understanding, loving, and patient person. We prepared our own meals, went out on the lake in a rowboat, and listened to classical music on my record player. We had taken about a dozen albums with us.

After a week at the cottage we returned to West Des Moines and began planning the next steps of our lives. John had almost two years of college before the war at the Lawrence Institute of Technology in Detroit and planned to continue his education. I had graduated from Drake University before the war with a degree in music and wanted to continue for an advanced degree. Since the time we had started school, however, the war had changed our perspectives and personalities and given us greater maturity. Now that we were married, we shared a determination to work and study hard and to find our place in society.

John initially considered enrolling in aeronautical engineering. He had even visited the California Institute of Technology when he was stationed at Santa Ana in June to explore studying there. However, after discussing engineering careers with his new brother-in-law John Wright, who was an experienced engineer, he decided to continue his study in mechanical engineering, as it would provide a broader foundation of technical knowledge. We finally decided that we would return to Michigan and apply for admission to the University of Michigan in Ann Arbor. UM also had a widely respected School of Music and we were sure that I would find study opportunities there, too. John applied for admission to the College of Engineering at Michigan in August and was immediately accepted. His academic record at Lawrence Tech was excellent—virtually all As—though he had to make up some course deficiencies, mostly in humanities and English composition. Classes started in the first week in October, as UM was still on a wartime schedule. John was admitted to the second-year undergraduate class.

The government's G.I. Bill provided funding for tuition and books for those ex-soldiers who could qualify academically for college admission. It also provided a monthly living allowance of seventy-five dollars. This assistance was a great help, probably essential, in allowing John to complete his education. I am uncertain if he could have finished his studies at Michigan and later at MIT if we did not have the support from the G.I. Bill. Unfortunately, former WASPs were not entitled to this assistance. We had to find alternate ways of financing my education.

We stayed at the farm with Mother and Daddy for all of August, John helping with the farm work as best he could. During the first week of August, the US exploded the atomic bombs over Japan, which ended the Pacific War and changed the world. We first learned of this when John returned to the barnyard after raking ("side-delivering") hay with the tractor in one of the fields. One of the farm hands asked him if he knew of the "big bomb" the Air Force dropped on Japan, probably thinking that a former Air Force pilot would know about such things! It was, of course, as much of a surprise to us as it was to the rest of the country.

John after raking hay, dressed half as a farmer. August 1945.

John and me at his parents' house in Royal Oak, Michigan. September 1945.

The First Ann Arbor Years at the University of Michigan

We packed up and left West Des Moines in early September 1945 and drove to John's home in Royal Oak, Michigan, in our 1941 Chevrolet Coupe, which had become family property. John had arranged to work as a layout draftsman and designer with the H.E. Farmer Engineering Co. in Detroit for a short period before we settled in Ann Arbor. He had worked for this firm before the war. We lived with John's parents during this time and he commuted by train to Detroit.

The housing situation in the Ann Arbor area is always tight but with the return of the veterans, many of whom were married with children, it became even more difficult to find an affordable place to live. The population was already inflated with war workers at the Willow Run bomber plant and other local industries. By late September, however, we found a small, second floor room in a house at 401 North Fourth Avenue in Ann Arbor. It was our first home. Two other families also lived there. The rent was thirty-two dollars per month. A closet had been remodeled to become our private bath and a small "kitchen," also private, was formed by a tiny enclosure near the bath. We slept on a Murphy bed which folded up against a wall in the daytime. In cold weather the room could be heated by a boiling tea kettle. We often resorted to this, as the landlord was stingy with the heat. After we moved in, we discovered that we were living in a predominantly black neighborhood. This was a surprise at first but it worked out fine. The neighbors were helpful and friendly. We were probably safer there than in the area closer to the UM campus. The farmers' market where we could get fresh produce at reasonable prices was just across the street.

John enrolled in the Department of Mechanical Engineering for a full academic load of eighteen semester credit hours and quickly made up his course deficiencies. I was admitted as a graduate student in music and took courses in music theory, music history, composition, and opera. It was an exciting and exhilarating time for me. In addition to my studies, my musical life was enriched by the concerts of the University Musical Society which presented some of the finest performances west of New York City. We heard all the great European and American symphony orchestras, many chamber music concerts, and the world's outstanding soloists. As venues for musical performances, Hill Auditorium and Rackham Auditorium at the university were among the best in the world.

Before classes began, the university gave an orientation program for new students which included a welcome to the university by the various deans and an overview of the academic programs and services available to the new students. For the returning soldiers who had not been in a classroom for many years, it was helpful to hear some guidance and suggestions for effective study. As part of this orientation, the director of the University of Michigan Marching Band, Professor William D. Revelli, talked about Michigan's great football tradition and the role played by the marching band. After his talk John spoke with him briefly about my flute background and asked if

there was any opportunity for me to teach in the School of Music. Professor Revelli, who also served as Chairman of the Woodwind Department, was interested because, in fact, at the time they were missing a flute teacher. He asked John to have me get in touch with him right away, which I did. I auditioned for him, he was impressed, and offered me an instructorship in flute starting immediately. I was given a studio on the sixth floor of Burton Tower and taught for the entire year until their regular teacher returned from military service.

Being on the university faculty entitled me to in-state tuition. I developed a private teaching practice, too, teaching students on Saturday mornings at the high school. We financed my studies this way. I had the opportunity to perform with groups and ensembles during the year, which gave me the chance to become acquainted with the musical culture and personalities at the university.

John also found work. Thanks to his pre-war experience in mechanical design, he obtained a job in the Department of Mechanical Engineering. In the meantime he continued to take a full class load, sometimes more. This first year was one of struggle for us, both academically and financially, but I think the challenge actually stimulated us to do better than we thought we could. John received all A grades in his courses during the first year and was offered continued employment during the summer of 1946 in the ME Department.

A Clark family picnic on Mother's Day 1946. John's parents are in the center, his brother Bob standing, Alice and Earl Watch on the far right, and John's sister Doris on the left facing the camera. I am seated between Doris and Mother Clark. Brother Chuck is missing. The others are friends. May 1946.

Mr. Georges Laurent at Tanglewood. August 1946.

In June 1946 I learned from Ruth Peacock, an old friend and an accomplished oboist from Boston, that there was an opening for a flute major to study at the Tanglewood Music Camp, the summer home of the Boston Symphony Orchestra in the Berkshires of western Massachusetts. I immediately applied for admission, as this would allow me to study with Georges Laurent, the principal flutist of the Boston Symphony, and to play in student orchestras under eminent conductors. I was accepted, and very excited. The only downside though was that I would be away on our first wedding anniversary. John encouraged me to go, anyway, realizing that this was a very important opportunity for a professional flutist. Ruth later became an oboist with the Indianapolis Symphony Orchestra.

I went and benefited greatly from the experience, and my summer at Tanglewood was also very productive for me. Mr. Laurent helped me a great deal with my flute technique and I learned some new flute literature. Playing in the orchestra conducted by several up-and-coming maestros, including the young Leonard Bernstein and Robert Shaw, gave me a lot of good experience. That summer the BSO presented the world premier of Benjamin Britten's opera *Peter Grimes* at Tanglewood. The summer was lonely without John though, and I was very happy when he visited me in July for a few days when his UM summer classes were over.

While at Tanglewood I learned that I was two months pregnant, with twins. I was not really surprised at being pregnant, but having twins was not expected. It was a bad time to have morning sickness. Being ill without the support of family or John added to my loneliness. This pregnancy did not turn out well. During a Christmas visit to my parents that year, the babies, both boys, were born prematurely and died within a day. We named them Alan and Merrill. They are buried in our family plot at the Resthaven Cemetery in West Des Moines.

During the summer of 1946 there was another important event in our lives as well. John read in a Detroit newspaper that the Michigan Air National Guard was being re-activated and was seeking pilots to fill out the squadrons. John, as I, loved to fly and the thought of returning to military flying was exciting. He was accepted largely on the basis of his multi-engine flight experience in the war. National Guard service was on weekends, so he could continue his studies and work at UM. John spent the next two years as a pilot with the 107th Bomb Squadron, MANG, as a 2nd Lt. He flew mainly the Douglas A-26 (later B-26) attack bomber, but also the North American AT-6, Beechcraft AT-11, and the Douglas C-47. To maintain their proficiency, the MANG pilots were given virtually free rein to fly anywhere and at any time they chose. With the rapid deactivation of the regular military units in those days, the National Guard squadrons became an essential element in the nation's

I am standing in front of a MANG A-26, which John flew to the 1948 Rose Bowl game. Note my WASP handbag. Wayne Co. Airport, May 1947.

defense. John took full advantage of this and made many flights around the country. Several times he flew my Powell flute to Boston, where it was made, leaving Detroit in the morning, having lunch near the flute shop, and flying back in time for me to use the flute that evening. These were all "navigational training flights." On a flight to the 1948 Rose Bowl Game in an A-26, with five aboard, he experienced an inflight emergency on New Year's Eve at the Fort Worth AAB, which almost ended in disaster. The problem resulted from the failure of flight instrumentation—airspeed and altimeter—and ice, which prevented the lowering of the aircraft's nose gear. Fortunately, being an excellent and experienced pilot, he was able to return to the base and land the aircraft safely. His companions made it to the game but John and his flight engineer remained at Fort Worth to supervise repairs to the aircraft. The full story of this flight and that of his return to Detroit through an unexpected ice storm,

A MANG North American AT-6, which John sometimes flew to Boston when he took my flute for repair. I had flown this aircraft for 600 hours in the WASP. Wayne Co. Airport, May 1947.

A picnic on an island at Clear Lake, Minnesota. L-R: me, Duke, keeping a close eye on Daddy holding the camera, John, Mother, and John's mother. September 1946.

which is equally exciting, is told in his WWII memoir, *An Eighth Air Force Combat Diary*, cited in "Selected Reading."

Before I returned to Ann Arbor from Tanglewood, John had moved to a new apartment. The landlord on Fourth Avenue had raised our monthly rent to forty dollars, which John thought was unreasonable. The new apartment was closer to campus and was larger. We shared the bath with another student couple, Bill and Dee Morris, with whom we have kept in touch over the years. Bill was a law student. The monthly rent was forty-five dollars but we felt it was worth paying because we got more living space. Like many Ann Arbor apartments at the time, ours was pretty much a makeshift arrangement. It was on the second floor and was carved out of what had originally been upstairs bedrooms. We soon found out that we also shared the apartment with a large rat that lived in our living room sofa! He would make noisy, nightly forays into our kitchen and carry his loot to the sofa where he stored it. A few weeks later the landlord, who lived on the first floor, came up one night and killed the critter in a bloody fight.

I returned from Tanglewood in late August, three weeks before fall semester classes began at UM. We took a little vacation to West Des Moines and then on to central Minnesota with Mother and Daddy, staying at a cottage on Clear Lake, near Glen. We invited John's mother to go with us. This was the first of many Minnesota summers for our family during the next fifty-seven years. Daddy and Mother had gone there regularly on fishing trips since 1920. While at Clear Lake we got word from my sister of the birth of her son, Charles Wright.

The fall of 1946 was something of a blur to me. By this time both of John's brothers and his younger sister were UM students. Home football Saturdays were really hectic. Being the only married family members, we naturally welcomed John's family to congregate at our apartment before going to the game. Every Saturday morning I taught flute at the high school and on these Saturdays I rushed back to the apartment to prepare a hasty lunch for John, his family, and their dates. John helped as much as he could. Then we would hurry off to the stadium. After the game, all would return to our place to rehash the game over whatever refreshments we had. We all enjoyed these times but they were tiring for me, especially since I was pregnant. I was glad to see the season come to an end.

During the academic year of 1946–47, John continued to get virtually all As in his courses and received the good news that he was to be given the Douglas Aircraft Company's five-hundred-dollar scholarship. He also was asked to join the research group of Professor Edward T. Vincent at the Willow Run Aeronautical Research Center operated by the university. Professor Vincent was an outstanding member of the ME faculty whom John admired. The job was just for the summer but he was asked to stay on part-time dur-

ing the following year. John was elected to the engineering honor society, Tau Beta Pi, that spring. My own studies continued to be very enjoyable and productive.

In the late summer of 1947, John and I drove with Mother and Daddy to Grand Teton National Park, where my sister and her family joined us. One notable afternoon John and I walked back about nine miles into the mountains with John and Eloise Wright to Lake Solitude. We were wearing only light clothing and street shoes. About four PM it started to snow and soon it became dark. We decided to return to camp, but in the fading light it was very difficult to follow the trail. On the way down the trail, a man with a flashlight suddenly emerged from the forest and asked if he could help us. He turned out to be a local Indian who just happened to be going our way and, besides having a flashlight, he was also familiar with the trail. With the help of our impromptu guide, we did manage to get back to the lake only to find that the last boat to our campsite had left hours before. Our guide then volunteered to lead us all the way—about three miles—to our campsite. We gratefully accepted his offer. It was about ten PM when we got back, much to the relief of Mother and Daddy who had expected us to return about six PM.

We moved once again in December 1946, this time to a real apartment. The university had recognized that married students were to become a permanent feature of college life. So, to provide adequate living facilities for them, the university built the University

John and me at the Grand Teton National Park. September 1947.

I am standing in front of our new apartment at 1437 University Terrace. September 1947.

Terrace Apartments near the University Hospital. During the summer we watched our own apartment being constructed. In September we moved in. What a relief this was! Everything was clean and new, so unlike the places we had been living in.

Although we had certainly upgraded our living quarters in most ways, rats in the new apartment building were a worse problem than we ever would have imagined possible. The apartments had been built next to the trash dump of the University Hospital (something impossible to happen these days!) where thousands of rats had taken up residence. When the weather got cold they migrated into our apartment building. At night we could hear the constant pitter-patter of their feet on our ceilings as they scampered in the spaces between floors! Occasionally, one would be caught in a trap in the basement storage room, leaving a bloody trail as it tried to escape. Ugh! On weekends, several of the fellows would take their 22-caliber rifles out to the dump to shoot the varmints. This was in the city of Ann Arbor, and next to the hospital, but no one objected. (Something else that is impossible to imagine today!) Ultimately, UM got rid of the rats in the buildings by sealing up all the openings through which they got in.

John completed his undergraduate degree in mechanical engineering at the end of the 1947 fall semester and graduated in February 1948. He had an outstanding academic record and was planning for graduate studies in mechanical engineering at MIT.

A view from the University Terrace Apartments toward the University Hospital. The rat-infested trash dump is in the foreground. Spring 1948.

John loved to play softball and was very good at it. He played with the UM Engineering Group at the Willow Run Research Center. Later, he usually played shortstop or left field, with the faculty and staff teams at MIT and after we returned to UM in 1957. May 1948.

He applied for admission after finishing his UM degree and was immediately admitted to the MIT master's degree program, starting with the fall 1948 class. A year earlier he had taken a MANG "navigation training flight" in an A-26 to Boston and interviewed at MIT to become acquainted with the institute. John worked full-time at the UM Willow Run Aeronautical Research Center until June and spent the summer at the United Aircraft Corporation's research laboratory in East Hartford, Connecticut. He arranged a plant interview there in the spring of 1948 by flying an A-26 to Rentscheler Field, the United Aircraft Corporation's airport in East Hartford. I remained in Ann Arbor until September, when we moved to Boston.

During the winter, spring, and summer of 1948, I continued my studies in the School of Music and taught flute students. This summer we reversed our roles from the summer of 1946. I stayed in Ann Arbor and

John went east. Although I was close to completing the requirements for my master's in music—lacking only the thesis—I felt that could be delayed. I did not want to stay in Ann Arbor to write a thesis while John was studying at MIT.

John returned from East Hartford the first week in September towing a closed trailer in which we packed all our worldly belongings for our move to Boston and MIT. Leaving Ann Arbor, our home of three years, was difficult as we had become accustomed to the city and the university and enjoyed our life there very much. However, John realized he needed more education if he was to work effectively in

Our last day in Ann Arbor. September 1948.

Our first home at 85 Williston Road, Brookline, Massachusetts. We shared the second floor but had a private bath. Our Chevy is parked in front. September 1948.

his field. MIT was exactly the place to study to accomplish this goal. We left Ann Arbor with fifty dollars in our pockets, which we borrowed from John's father.

Our Years at MIT

Finding a place to live near MIT was the first priority upon arriving in Boston. The second priority was getting two season tickets to the Saturday evening concerts of the Boston Symphony Orchestra. We succeeded in both efforts—finding a place to live in Brookline and obtaining good seats in the upper balcony of Symphony Hall, where the acoustics were excellent. For the next nine seasons we enjoyed these concerts. I also made contact with Mr. Laurent and arranged to continue my flute lessons with him.

In the meantime, John got settled into his

The front door of MIT at 77 Massachusetts Avenue, Cambridge, Massachusetts. John worked in the Heat Transfer Laboratory in the basement under the left portion of this building. September 1948.

course work and master's thesis research. He brought his own project with him and managed to get equipment support from the United Aircraft Corp., where he had spent the summer. He was also fortunate to become associated with a brilliant young faculty member in the ME department, Dr. Warren M. Rohsenow, who encouraged

John studying hard in our room at 85 Williston Road. October 1948.

Ed Hartell, the Heat Transfer Lab assistant, holding John's high temperature gas probe, the subject of his master's thesis. October 1948.

him in every way. John's collaboration with Professor Rohsenow in a host of research projects developed into an effective professional relationship and also personal friendship that has continued for the past sixty years.

John's field of study concentrated on the subjects of thermodynamics, heat transfer, and fluid mechanics. The MIT faculty was the best in the country, probably the world, for these topics. In addition to Professor Rohsenow, John studied with Professors Joseph H. Keenan and Ascher H. Shapiro. The demands on the graduate students at MIT were enormous, requiring hours of study each day. Being associated with some of the brightest students and faculty in the country was both stimulating and rewarding.

While John was studying and developing his laboratory research, I continued my flute practice and study with Mr. Laurent. I also found a simple, part-time job in a bookstore directly across from MIT. This was not only convenient, since John and I could drive together in the morning, but it brought in enough income to cover the cost of my flute lessons. I began gradually to make musical friendships in the Boston area, which led to playing assignments at social events and in the downtown churches.

Classes were over and final exams for the 1948 fall term were finished at MIT by the end of January. Although John had studied hard and continuously, he really had no idea how his academic achievement would compare with that of the other students. As a break from his studies, we took a short trip into New Hampshire during the first

I am practicing in our room at 85 Williston Road. December 1948.

I have just returned from a lesson with Mr. Laurent. This photo taken in front of our place at 85 Williston Road. December 1948.

On our winter break in snowy New Hampshire. February 1949.

The Massachusetts Avenue entrance to Bexley Hall. February 1949.

John studying in our Bexley Hall apartment. February 1949.

week in February. When we returned, his grades had arrived in the mail. Much to his surprise and great joy, he had received As (Hs in the MIT system) in all his subjects! This was a big boost to his morale since he had competed with the best graduate students at the best school and had come out at the top. He started the spring semester with soaring confidence!

I was invited to play principal flute in a chamber group in the performance of Mozart's "Great C Minor Mass" to be given on Easter at the Church of the Advent in Boston. The soprano soloist was Phyllis Curtin, who later sang lead roles at the Metropolitan Opera in New York City.

We moved again at the end of January to Bexley Hall, an apartment house directly across the street from MIT and next door to the bookstore where I worked. This was an improvement in living accommodations and very convenient for us both. It was, however, a short-term lease and by June we had to move again, this time back to Brookline to 152 Winchester Street, where we had a third floor flat and access to a small parking spot behind the house.

John was asked by Professor Rohsenow to join a new research project, which he was initiating at the end of classes in June in the field of boiling heat transfer. John was to serve as the project leader. This was the beginning of several decades of research on this subject and the many variations of technical studies that grew out of it. The immediate research was associated with the nuclear reactor core of the Nautilus submarine, the US Navy's first nuclear submarine. Captain Hyman G. Rickover (now an Admiral), Chief of Naval Reactors, was a frequent visitor to MIT and encouraged the staff in the research. John stayed with this project for several years at MIT.

John graduated with his master's degree in mechanical engineering at the June 1949 MIT commencement. This degree was the culmination of enormous academic effort and sacrifice. However, it gave him the key to his life's work and showed him

John and his sister Doris at the 1949 MIT commencement. June 1949.

John and me with Gordon J. VanWylen. MIT, Cambridge, Massachusetts. Summer 1949.

that his natural abilities were in teaching and academic research at the highest level. He spent the rest of his working life in this endeavor.

In the fall of 1948, John met another UM graduate, Gordon J. VanWylen, in Professor Keenan's graduate class in thermodynamics. Gordon was a doctoral candidate at MIT, a couple of years ahead of John. This meeting turned out to be a fortuitous event for us. Gordon was a dedicated Christian with an ability to explain the Christian faith effectively to believers and nonbelievers. We had many very enjoyable meetings with Gordon that year, and he led us to a more committed Christian life. Gordon went on to become a professor and

Chairman of the Mechanical Engineering Department at the University of Michigan and its Dean of Engineering. He was responsible for inviting John to join the UM faculty in 1957. Gordon retired from Hope College in Holland, MI, after eighteen years of service as its president. We continue to enjoy regular friendship with Gordon and his wife Margaret.

With our newfound confidence and optimistic prospects for the future, we decided to buy a new car. I had bought a used 1941 Chevrolet before the war and it had served us well for several years. So, this time we chose a Chevrolet four-door sedan.

The summer of 1949 was busy, but productive. John's research went well and he decided to continue for a doctorate degree. John's twenty-two-year-old sister Doris spent the summer with us, giving us the feeling of a family. She found employment

John and me beside our new 1949 Chevrolet. Boston, Massachusetts. August 1949.

Gordon VanWylen and me on our "private beach." Boston's north shore, August 1949.

at Filenes department store in Boston. We took several trips around Boston, Cambridge, Cape Cod, and the north shore. One day, with Gordon with us, we came across what we named our "private beach" just off the Boston and Maine railroad tracks north of Pride's Crossing on the north shore. For several years we returned to this spot for summer picnics and swimming and always found it empty. The relatively frequent B&M trains added to the excitement.

David Is Born

The next big event in our family was the birth of our son, David Winston Clark, on September 13, 1950, at Richardson House of the Boston Lying-in Hospital. He was a healthy boy for which we were very grateful, having lost the twins four years before. John had been promoted to Instructor of Mechanical Engineering in the fall of 1949 and was making substantial progress in his

On the beach at Cape Cod. September 1949.

doctoral studies. Until David was born I was teaching regularly, but now I put that activity on hold. John and Warren Rohsenow had by now made some significant scientific breakthroughs in their boiling research. They presented their first paper on this topic at the December 1950 annual meeting of the American Society of Mechanical Engineers (ASME) in New York City. We found a highly recommend-

Leaving the hospital with David. Boston, Massachusetts. September 1950.

Me, David, and Gordon VanWylen. Thanksgiving Day, 1950.

The proud parents and David in front of our house at 152 Winchester Road, Brookline, Massachusetts. October 1950.

ed matronly lady to take care of David so that I could accompany John to the event. Nevertheless, I was not comfortable about leaving our two-month-old baby with a relative stranger and was glad to get back home.

Our lives had become more focused on family and profession in the year since John got his master's degree and he was by now well on his way to his doctorate. His career of teaching and research at the university level seemed within reach, so we decided to take the ambitious step of finding a more permanent home. At this point I had limited my teaching to Saturdays at various public schools. There always seemed to be students interested in the flute.

Our First House—Lexington, Massachusetts

After looking at a number of existing homes we decided to build our own. Mother and Daddy loaned us nine thousand dollars at a low interest rate and we found a builder named Inge Nielson. We located an acre lot in Lexington, MA, for $1,300, secured a 4 percent mortgage from the Waverley Trust Co., and signed a construction contracts in October 1950 with Inge for a two-bedroom house, with full basement but without a garage, for $11,800. The house was completed in May 1951 and we moved in immediately. It was located at 114 Cedar Street in Lexington. The landscaping and plantings were entirely our own responsibility. John spent all his spare time and weekends in the spring, summer, and fall of 1951 moving dirt, building rock walls, and planting shrubs. It was a big job but he enjoyed it and the exercise was good for him. The New England soil provided all the stones needed for the walls.

Gordon VanWylen received his doctorate degree (the ScD at MIT) at the June 1951 MIT commencement exercises. Naturally, we attended, taking David with us in his stroller. John had become acquainted with Professor Harold "Doc" Edgerton who helped him in his research with high-speed photography techniques. "Doc" Edgerton was world famous in this field. When he saw

Mother and Daddy, David, and John in front of what would become our living room "picture window." January 1951.

Our new house in Lexington, Massachusetts. June 1952.

us at the ceremonies he took our picture.

Gordon's parents came to his graduation and we invited them out for breakfast to our new but barely furnished home in Lexington. We served breakfast on our porch with a two-by-eight board for a table. The next day Gordon's parents made us a present of a card table! We used it for a year as our main dining table. Gordon had accepted an appointment as Assistant Professor of Mechanical Engineering at the

"Doc" Edgerton's photo of us at the 1951 MIT graduation ceremonies. June 1951.

David and me in front of the Royal York Hotel, Toronto, Canada. August 1951

University of Michigan and left for Ann Arbor the following day.

Two years previous, Gordon had introduced us to the Park Street Church on the Commons in Boston. We became members in 1951 and enjoyed and benefited from its sound Christian message and commitment and from the inspiring sermons of Dr. Harold John Ockenga, its pastor. Dr. Ockenga baptized all our children.

John's master's degree paper was accepted by the ASME and he presented it at the society's 1951 Summer Annual Meeting in Toronto, Canada. We all went to the meeting and extended the trip for a brief vacation north of Toronto and then on to Niagara Falls where John's Royal Oak family met us for a day-long picnic.

John is Promoted to Assistant Professor at MIT

In September 1952 John was promoted to Assistant Professor of Mechanical Engineering at MIT. This was a great honor and encouragement for him, as he had not yet completed his doctorate degree, which is usually required in order to qualify for such a promotion. The new position brought with it an increase in salary and greater professional visibility. Warren

Rohsenow included John in some of his consulting work, and this also provided much-needed income.

The spring and summer of 1952 was the low point for us financially. To make it through this period we had to borrow $350 from the MIT Credit Union. This was the last time we ever had to do that. To furnish our house, we purchased dining room furniture on the basis of monthly payments. (Also something we've never had to do again.) We still own some of that furniture!

For the next twelve months John worked hard during the day at MIT on his doctoral thesis, teaching, and research. On two evenings a week he taught Advanced Thermodynamics at the Northeastern University Graduate School in Boston. This teaching broadened his experience and helped us make ends meet. He taught these night classes at Northeastern University for the next five years.

The remains of our Niagara Falls picnic, which we dutifully cleaned up! L-R: Mary, Bob's wife, John's mother, and me. John's sister Alice is on the bench. Niagara Falls, NY. August 1951.

David scampering around the lawn at our motel north of Toronto. August 1951.

Eloise is Born and John Graduates with His Doctorate Degree from MIT

In the summer of 1952 I found that I was pregnant again, this time with a girl, who was born on the last day of January 1953 after a hectic trip to the Boston Lying-in Hospital from Lexington. We named her Eloise-Marie. She was in a hurry to get into the world, apparently, and arrived several weeks early. She was tiny, just four pounds, and remained in the hospital for three weeks before we could take her home. John's mother came to help us.

John received his doctorate degree at the June 1953 MIT commencement. It was the successful end of a long period of intense study and the beginning of a life-long career as a university professor and engineering consultant. Both his parents came for the ceremonies and stayed with us for a couple of weeks. We celebrated the event with a family dinner at the Townline House north of Boston, one of our favorite restaurants.

During the years following the birth of the children I tried to maintain my musical activities as much as I could. I had a small group of flute students and each year was asked to play for various church or social events. In the early part of 1953 Louise Beach, a vocalist friend, and I formed a musical trio, which we named the Beach Trio. It consisted of flute, voice, and piano. Dolores Rodriguez was the pianist. Our purpose was to make ourselves available for professional appearances before groups in the Boston area. We auditioned before entertainment managers and impresarios in Boston and generated some interest. I believe we did perform a few times, but in the long run I gave it up. I really did not want to be away from the family for the times demanded by the performances.

A down side to a university career was the need to find income during the summer recesses. This was especially true for younger faculty members who were not yet established in the profession. During the summers of 1952 and 1953, John was able to find employment on MIT research projects exploring the potential and methodologies for utilizing nuclear power commercially. In the years 1954, 1955, and 1956, however, he served as a consultant

Eloise-Marie enjoying the outdoors on our lawn at Lexington. June 1953.

John, in his doctorate gown, and me at the 1953 MIT commencement. June 1953.

My professional photo for the "Beach Trio." Boston, 1953.

We made our own Christmas card this year. December 1953.

John pulling our carriage up the B&M tracks to our private beach. Eloise is riding in the carriage and David is walking. June 1955.

for the Minneapolis-Honeywell Co. and the Westinghouse Atomic Power Corp. This meant that the entire family became nomads during these summers. In 1954, while John was working in Minneapolis and living with his brother Bob, who had arranged for John to work at Minneapolis-Honeywell, the children and I lived with my family in West Des Moines. This was a good arrangement. The other years we spent the summers in a rented apartment in Pittsburgh. Beginning in 1953, John was retained as a consultant with the DuPont Company at Belle, near Charleston, West Virginia. He spent two days a month at the plant helping with problems in thermal transfer. The additional income was very welcome, as our expenses rose sharply when our last child, Peter, was born.

David and Eloise on the porch of our Lexington house. October 1954.

In front of our apartment in Pittsburgh. John's father took the picture. August 1955.

Peter, in my arms, with David and Eloise on the lawn of our Lexington home on the day we took him to the Massachusetts Mental Hospital at Woburn. He had been baptized that day at the Park Street Church, Boston, by Dr. Harold John Ockenga. October 1955.

Peter is Born

Our third child, Peter Mountain Clark, was born April 13, 1954, at the Boston Lying-in Hospital. Peter suffered from muscular dystrophy and other serious neurological and congenital defects from birth. We tried to care for him at home for eighteen months but it was a ceaseless, exhausting battle and the other two children were being neglected. In October 1955 we reluctantly placed Peter in the Massachusetts State Hospital System for the mentally retarded in Woburn, MA. He remained there for the next thirty-three years, dying in 1988 at the age of thirty-five. We buried Peter with his two brothers in the family plot at Resthaven Cemetery at West Des Moines.

John is Invited to Join the University of Michigan Faculty

Our family fortunes were enhanced dramatically in 1956. In early April John received a phone call at MIT from Gordon VanWylen in Ann Arbor. He asked if John would consider joining the Mechanical Engineering faculty at the University of Michigan, as they had an opening in his

David waiting in our driveway for the bus on his first day of school. Lexington, September 1955.

David skating on the Mill Pond at Lexington, Massachusetts. New Year's Day, 1956.

Eloise and me skating on the Mill Pond at Lexington, Massachusetts. New Year's Day, 1956.

field. Gordon explained that the College of Engineering and the ME Department wanted to upgrade the department courses to include heat transfer, John's subject. This inquiry was remarkable since John and I had prayed just the night before about guidance for his professional future. Assistant professors at MIT rarely continued their careers at the Institute and find their futures at other universities. John had been on the MIT faculty as an instructor for three years and in his present rank for four. There was little opportunity for a permanent appointment at MIT, as the Department had no tenured positions open. Hence, Gordon's call on the heels of our request for spiritual help heralded something of great significance.

John visited Ann Arbor in mid-April and was offered an appointment as full professor of Mechanical Engineering at a salary of ten thousand dollars per year, starting with the winter term, February 1, 1957. This appointment increased his salary by 33 percent and he skipped the rank of associate professor. At thirty-two, he was probably one of the youngest full professors in the history of the college. We were amazed but grateful to God for His love and concern for us. We also felt humbled by His gracious act, and it strengthened our dedication to serve as faithful witnesses to God's glory in His Kingdom on earth. John remained on the active faculty at the University of Michigan for the next thirty-two years and retired in 1988 with the rank of Professor Emeritus of Mechanical Engineering.

In June the American Society of Mechanical Engineers notified John that he had been chosen as the 1956 recipient of the Pi Tau Sigma Gold Medal Award as the "most outstanding mechanical engineer within ten years of graduation." The award was made at the ASME Winter Annual Meeting in New York in November. It was my special privilege to accompany John to the presentation. His acceptance address was titled "Science and the Spirit."

We decided to express our increased optimism by again buying a new car. Daddy had always driven a Buick so we followed in that tradition. Our new car was a 1956 Buick Special, four-door hardtop with white sidewall tires!

The summer of 1956 was spent in Pittsburgh where we had been the previous year. John continued his consulting work at the Westinghouse Atomic Power Division. John's work at MIT had made him a leader in the thermal-fluid transfer processes in nuclear power systems. He consulted in nuclear power at Westinghouse for the next twenty years and in the general field of nuclear power until 1995. In the meantime he continued his consulting work at DuPont in West Virginia and for various other firms.

We became a temporarily separated family in February 1957 when John left Lexington to join the University of Michigan faculty in Ann Arbor. John was fortunate to be invited to stay with Mrs. William T. Groves, a wonderful friend from our previous Ann Arbor days. We had met her through a music school friend of mine, Howard Hatton. She was a widow living at 1604 Morton Avenue, Ann Arbor. We also became friends with her son Bill,

Our 1956 Buick loaded for a summer at Westinghouse Atomic Power Division in Pittsburgh. Lexington, July 1956.

The children and me in the Smoky Mountains returning to Lexington with John from Pittsburgh. September 1956.

David's party on his seventh birthday on the back lawn of our Lexington house. David is far right and Eloise in third from the right. I am standing at the left. September 13, 1957.

who was about John's age and an engineering student. John later served as Bill's best man at his 1952 wedding with Betty Swift.

Because of their schooling, the children and I remained behind in Lexington while John got settled in his new position at UM and located a place for us to live when we all moved at the end of the summer. John returned twice during the semester and in June drove back to spend the summer, to sell our house and pack up to move to Ann Arbor.

The Family Moves to Ann Arbor-Dexter, Michigan

We sold our house at virtually the last minute for $24,500. The next day we packed the cars and left for Ann Arbor. The sale enabled us to repay Daddy and Mother the money they had loaned us to build the house, and still have ten thousand dollars left. This was a good start for our new lives in a new location. John had found a house of three bedrooms, a study, and garage for us in Dexter just west of Ann Arbor. It was owned by the university for use by UM faculty. We lived there until June 1960.

I had mixed feelings about leaving Boston, as I knew I would miss its rich musical culture. Ann Arbor, however, provided John unlimited professional opportunities and also was an established cultural center, as we knew from living there before our MIT days. Although I gave up teaching after we moved back in order to spend time with the children at

Our house in Dexter, Michigan, Spring 1957.

I am standing on the west side of our house in Dexter, Michigan. Later that fall when David saw this photo, bent and torn, he penned the following couplet, which I have treasured:

> *Faded photograph,*
> *Covered now with lines and creases...*
> *Pictures torn in half,*
> *Memories in bits and pieces...*

David, age eight, fall 1958.

home, I soon began playing again with groups in Ann Arbor. For ten years or more I served as the principal flute in the Ann Arbor Symphony Orchestra and in trios and quartets and sometimes at church. I served on the Board of Directors of the symphony for several years, as did John. The alumnae chapter of my musical sorority, Mu Phi Epsilon, provided another opportunity for musical fulfillment. I attended our regular monthly meeting for many years until age and infirmity prevented it.

We reestablished our membership in the University Musical Society and enjoyed their regular season of concerts at Hill Auditorium and Rackham Auditorium, which was their venue for chamber music. Another attractive event was the annual May Festival in the spring at which a major symphony orchestra presented a series of concerts over a period of five days. A great tradition had been established with the Philadelphia Orchestra performing at the May Festival for almost fifty years. It was

a great loss when these concerts were discontinued in the early 1990s. All told, I felt that if we had to leave Boston, the next best place to live for the enjoyment of musical performances was probably Ann Arbor.

John immersed himself into curriculum development and research in the ME department as soon as he returned in the fall of 1957. There was much to do and he and Gordon VanWylen began to revamp the department's graduate curriculum, starting with the master's degree program. By June 1958, a completely revised course of studies was approved for the MS degree. In the meantime John organized two grad-

John in his office in the Heat Transfer Laboratory at the University of Michigan. August 1958.

uate courses in heat transfer and outlined a research program centered on the creation of a new heat transfer laboratory. The first new faculty member for this laboratory was Dr. Vedat S. Arpaci, with whom John had worked at MIT. John supervised the doctoral research of two other graduate students, Herman Merte and Wen-Jei Yang, and had them appointed to the ME faculty and assigned to John's laboratory. This group formed a very effective nucleus for both teaching and research. By 1960 the laboratory was humming with research and graduate students. This continued for the next forty-five years. Each of the young faculty John had encouraged became internationally recognized authorities for their contributions to their field.

David entered the second grade at the Dexter schools in the fall of 1957 and Eloise started kindergarten the next year.

At that time the quality of the schools there was marginal. This concerned us, as we realized the children would ultimately be compromised for college admission without better educational preparation than we anticipated Dexter could offer. Because of this, we moved into Ann Arbor in 1960 where the schools were more satisfactory. We added a family member while in Dexter, a gentle black cat we named Jingy. She produced ninety mostly black kittens in the next sixteen years.

We Buy a House in Ann Arbor, 1960

We purchased a small house with three bedrooms and a study at 2214 Avalon Place and enrolled the children in Angell Elementary School. We still live in this same house, as of this writing, although it has been remodeled several times in the past forty-five years.

We began worshipping at the Ann Arbor Christian Reformed Church when we arrived and joined the church in 1962. This church had the same fundamental Christian message as the Park Street Church in Boston. The Ann Arbor church was founded by Gordon and Margaret VanWylen and a few friends in 1954 and held services in a small Seventh Day Adventist building on Church Street. By 1960 the church had grown and the congregation built a new church on Broadway, near UM's North Campus where the university was expanding with new dormitories and laboratories.

Our home at 2214 Avalon Place, Ann Arbor. Spring 1990.

The back lawn and stone wall John built in 1970. Spring 1990.

John had technical conferences at Boulder, CO, during the summers of 1960 and 1961 and we took these opportunities for extended family vacations. We bought a large tent and the necessary equipment and camped at the Rocky Mountain National Park and the Mesa Verde National Park, enjoying fully the scenic beauty of the west.

John has always had a great interest in public affairs and community development. He was deeply offended by the possibility that John F. Kennedy had been elected President by a fraudulent vote count in Chicago. Because of this he became quite active in the Barry Goldwater campaign in 1964. John never trusted the Kennedy family and was distressed by the Camelot portrayal given to their period of office. The defeat of Goldwater in the 1964 election was, of course, a bitter disappointment. In the years since, however, John has felt that events have shown that his doubts about

The children and me on the front steps of our new church under construction on Broadway in Ann Arbor. January 1962.

Our campsite at the Mesa Verde National Park. I am at the table and the children are in the foreground. August 1961.

the Kennedy family and the policies they promoted are justified. The election of Ronald Reagan in 1980 and the re-election of George W. Bush in 2004 were reliable indicators of the national mind-set, he believes, confirming the American position of small government, strong defense and low taxes.

A Sabbatical Leave in Munich, 1965–1966

Every seven years, faculty members at the University of Michigan are entitled to apply for a sabbatical leave of one semester. If they can find funding for an additional semester, the leave can be extended to one year. In 1964 John applied for a one-year leave, starting in August 1965. He obtained a Senior Post-Doctoral Fellowship from the National Science Foundation and an appointment as a Guest Professor at the Institute of Thermodynamics at the Technische Hochschule of Munich, now known as the Technical University. John spent the 1965–66 academic year studying optical methods in heat transfer. The institute found a house for us in the suburb of Laim, which came with a housekeeper. David and Eloise became guest students at the local gymnasiums. Before leaving Ann Arbor, we made arrangements to pick up a Volkswagen station wagon in Munich.

I had one major disappointment that year. With the house and housekeeper and the children in school I had planned to spend much of my time practicing my flute. When we arrived in Munich by air, however, my flute was stolen at the airport. It was never found. A replacement did not come until the following June. We did, however, enjoy an entire year of symphony concerts and opera for which Munich is famous.

Bavaria is a beautiful part of Germany and we traveled as much as we could. At the end

John's parents' forty-fifth wedding anniversary, July 4, 1964. L-R: John, me, John's brother Chuck, John's mother, Eloise, John's brother Bob, and David. Note the Goldwater campaign signs. Royal Oak, Michigan, 1964.

In front of our Munich house. November 1965.

Our house in Munich. September 1965.

of our stay we had driven over fifteen thousand miles through Bavaria, Germany, Austria, Switzerland, France, Spain, and Italy. Our favorite weekend trips were to the Bavarian Alps south of Munich.

John was invited by colleagues and former students to visit and lecture in Turkey, Israel, and Egypt. We traveled to these countries in January and February 1966 and enjoyed a warm reception. It was an excellent opportunity to see many of the historic places and cultural monuments of the Middle East. The political tensions that have

The children and me on the summit of Zugspitze, Germany's highest peak. October 1965.

exploded into warfare in recent times were evident then, and they did affect our travel. Unfortunately, Eloise contracted infectious hepatitis on this trip and spent six weeks in a Munich hospital after we returned.

When our year was over, we returned to the United States aboard the steamship *SS United States*, sailing from Southampton, England to New York in August 1966. Our travel to the boat took us through the low countries, across the channel, and north through England as far as Leeds. We also visited John's World War II airbase at Thorpe Abbotts in East Anglia.

In October 1966, Gordon VanWylen, who was Dean of Engineering at Michigan, asked John to become Chairman of the Department of Mechanical Engineering. John served in this capacity for two terms, leaving the chairmanship in 1974. The department benefited from his leadership, and in 1972 was ranked fifth in the nation, up from seventh, in quality of education. In

We are resting on the slopes of Alpspitze after a hard climb. Bavaria, June 1966.

David in cap and gown for the Huron High School graduation. June 1969

David at the finish of his two-hundred-meter breaststroke event in a dual meet with SMU, bringing victory to the UM Swim Team. UM, December 1969.

the fall of 1968 John organized and directed the centennial celebration of the ME department with a two-day program of honors and awards, talks, and campus tours. The principal speaker was Edward N. Cole, the president of the General Motors Corporation. As the wife of the chairman I had a number of social responsibilities and helped with the ladies' program. A hardcover book of the Centennial Proceedings was published.

David graduated from Huron High School in Ann Arbor in June 1969. He was an outstanding swimmer throughout high school and won the first points for his school in the 1969 High School State Swimming Competition.

In the fall of 1969 David entered the College of Engineering at the University of Michigan and swam during his first two years for the UM varsity swim team, earn-

Eloise in cap and gown for the Huron High School graduation. June 1971.

ing a varsity letter.

Eloise graduated from Huron High School in June 1971. She was active in music—playing violin with small string

Eloise on stage to perform the Bruch violin concerto with the Ann Arbor Symphony. June 1971.

groups and serving as concertmistress of the school symphony orchestra. She won the 1971 music competition sponsored by the Ann Arbor Symphony and performed a movement of the Bruch violin concerto at a public concert in June. That fall she entered Michigan State University as a violin major.

Our Second Sabbatical Leave in Germany—Munich and Berlin, 1972–73

John was eligible for another UM sabbatical during the 1972–73 academic year. We returned to Germany and spent six months with former colleagues at the Technical University of Munich and six months at the Technical University of Berlin. John had been influential in negotiating a faculty exchange agreement between UM and TUB and we were the first UM exchange faculty. We found a nice apartment on the eastside of Munich where John could study and write. As before, we enjoyed the out-standing symphony orchestra concerts and opera in Munich.

The children joined us at Christmas. Eloise was able to come earlier so we spent a week at St. Anton in the Austrian Alps at a ski school. Here, under the careful guidance of an Alpine ski instructor, John and Eloise improved their skiing technique.

In January we moved to Berlin and lived in an apartment building owned by the Technical University. John gave a series of lectures on Radiative Heat Transfer at the Institute of Thermodynamics which was headed by Professor Helmut Knapp. We made a good and lasting friendship with Professor Knapp, his wife Dorothee, and their family. John also worked with a young researcher, Dr. Ing Juergen Keller, who later became a renowned professor at the University of Siegen. Professor Keller and his wife Ursula are longtime friends.

In February Professor Knapp's institute took a working holiday at Krone-Platz, a ski resort in northern Italy, and invited us to go with them. We had an inspiring and

I am coming on stage as the principal flute with the Ann Arbor Symphony Orchestra for the concert in which Eloise performed the Bruch violin concerto. June 1971.

pleasant two weeks there skiing with the institute staff and faculty.

John was again invited by former students and colleagues to lecture at universities in Turkey and Israel. On this trip we visited the ancient city of Ephesus where the apostle Paul spent three years evangelizing and preaching the New Covenant given by Jesus Christ. Ephesus was also the place of the pagan temple dedicated to the Roman goddess Diana.

John at his study table. Munich, October 1972.

Doree, Our Dachsund, Joins the Family

Our European sabbatical came to an end in June. Eloise came over for a few days helping us pack and begin our journey home. While in Germany we became fond of the longhair Dachsund and bought a three-month-old miniature female in Berlin. She was sweet and well tempered and the last of her litter. Her owners had

I am on the deck of our Munich apartment having lunch. October 1972.

John and Eloise prepare for a day on the slopes with their ski group. St. Anton, Austria, December 1972.

John next to our car outside our Berlin apartment building. Spring 1973.

John's study in Berlin. January 1973.

Doree, our much-loved Dachsund. Berlin, May 1973.

named her "Doree," so we called her that, too. She lived with us for sixteen years.

We returned home aboard the Cunard liner, *HMS Queen Elizabeth II*, boarding her at Cherbourg, France, with passage to New York. Doree and our car came with us. The ship's butcher cared for Doree!

I am on the bunny slope at the Krone-Platz, Italy. February 1973.

Boating on Lake Erie and Woman Lake, Minnesota

In the summer of 1973 we decided to enjoy the wonderful boating opportunities afforded by the Great Lakes. In July we purchased a nineteen-foot, trailerable Chris-Craft "Lancer" sport boat with a two hundred HP inboard engine. We named it the *Eloise-Marie* and moored it on Lake St. Claire. We enjoyed many excursions that summer out into the lake and as far north as Port Huron. It was ideal for water skiing, so we took it up to Woman Lake, Minnesota, where we had been going for a month each summer since 1958. David and Eloise spent most of the time skiing behind the boat. We sold the boat about ten years later but bought another, which we kept all year at Woman Lake.

We spent many happy summers at Woman Lake, Minnesota, usually sharing our time there with my sister, Eloise, and her family in adjoining cabins. Our grand-children always came up, too, often for

I am sitting in the ancient marketplace at Ephesus. March 1973.

several weeks. Woman Lake became a family gathering place in the summer and has given us many happy memories. Our grandson CJ loved to spend hours skiing behind the boats on Woman Lake and became a very excellent skier like his dad.

In 1974 we decided that sailing would be a better way to enjoy the big lakes and bought a new, thirty-six foot, Pearson, slooped-rigged sailboat. We named it *Seawind.* We sailed this boat for twenty-five summers, mostly on Lake Erie. We moored the boat at the Toledo Beach Marina south of Monroe, Michigan, where we purchased the boat. For many years we sailed with our children and then with our grandchildren to Cedar Point Amusement Park near Sandusky, Ohio. They always looked forward to this annual sail and it became a family tradition. On the way back to our home marina we would stop at Kelley's Island for a few days. We sold the

boat in 1997 when, owing to age and infirmity, lake sailing became too strenuous for us. To maintain our boating life we then bought a new thirty-six foot Silverton cruiser with twin 454 "Crusader" 325 HP inboard engines, which we also moor at the Toledo Beach Marina. We named the boat *Miracle* to acknowledge my recovery from a fractured hip suffered in January 1997.

Our Final Fifteen Years at Michigan

When we returned to Ann Arbor from Europe in 1973, John felt he could better serve UM if he devoted his efforts to teaching and research. He completed the remaining year of his chairmanship and then returned to full-time faculty duty in the fall of 1974. At this time the nation was suffering from an energy crisis and the scientific-technical community focused their

The HMS Queen Elizabeth II entering Cherbourg harbor. Our car is third from the right in the center. June 1973.

The **Eloise-Marie** *in front of our cabin on Woman Lake, Minnesota, All Seasons Resort. I am in the rear seat, David is driving and Eloise is boarding. August 1973.*

Our second ski boat leaving the dock on Woman Lake, All Seasons Resort. David is driving and Susan, CJ and I are the passangers. August 1982.

Our third ski boat at its dock at All Seasons Resort on Woman Lake. August 1997.

Our grandchildren Susan and CJ Clark in front of our cabin at Woman Lake, August 1983.

Grandpa John telling CJ about "pinch bugs, tickle bugs, and belly rippers." Woman Lake, August 1984.

A family gathering at Woman Lake, L-R: me, Phil, Eloise, David, and Souise, September 2000.

efforts on utilizing energy sources that are normally ignored. John put his attention to the evaluation of solar energy, as radiative processes transmit this form of energy, a topic he had been studying for several years. He established courses of study at the graduate level in Solar Thermal Processes and Energy Conservation, including their economic evaluation, and a Solar Energy Laboratory. The courses were very popular for the next fifteen years. He expanded his efforts to consulting work with local firms and for the US Department of Energy (DOE). For a period of two years, he served part-time as President and CEO of the Central Solar Energy Research Corp. in Detroit. This organization was basically a DOE think tank for studying manufacturing methods of solar energy systems. In the meantime he continued to consult for the nuclear power industry on heat exchanger and containment problems.

David Graduates from UM, 1973

David completed his course work in Mechanical Engineering at the University of Michigan and received his BSME at the university's December 1973 commencement exercises. John had been committed to a solar energy conference in India and, unfortunately, could not attend. David began employment with the Union Carbide Corporation in Chicago where he worked for a few years before joining the engineering staff of the Onan Corporation in

Our thirty-six-foot sloop Seawind *moored to the seawall at the Harbor Beach, Michigan, Port of Refuge, August 1974.*

John and me enjoying a good Lake Erie breeze on Seawind, *July 1974.*

Minneapolis, Minnesota. He later became a designer of medical equipment for various firms in the twin cities. He retired at age fifty in the year 2000. In the following years he became certified in aircraft maintenance and inspection. He has had a lifelong interest in airplanes and has designed, built, and flown his own plane. In 2004 he purchased a 180 HP Mooney, low-wing monoplane, the first commercially built aircraft he owned.

David married Joanne Doak in March 1976 in Western Springs, Illinois. They had two children, Susan Marie (1978) and Charles John, or "CJ," (1980). The marriage was terminated in 1985. Later, David married Souise Chang.

Eloise Graduates from Michigan State University, 1977

Eloise graduated from Michigan State University in December 1977 with a major in Music Therapy. After an internship at

Our thirty-six-foot Silverton Cruiser Miracle *at Kelley's Island, May 1998.*

the Kalamazoo State Hospital, she found employment at the Lafayette Clinic in Detroit where she worked with disturbed children. She maintained an interest in violin performance. After two summers at the Aspen Center in Colorado, studying with Miss Dorothy Delay, she enrolled at Sarah Lawrence College in Bronxsville, New York, for a two-year master's degree program in violin under Miss Delay, and graduated in June 1981. For the next eighteen months she freelanced on the violin in New

David and me on our back lawn after his UM graduation. December 1973.

I am at David's wedding to Joanne Doak. March 1976.

York City, gained a good reputation, and had plenty of work. In 1983, on a contract assignment to play with the Virginia Opera at Norfolk, Virginia, she met Philip McKenzie, who played oboe and English horn in the orchestra. Their acquaintance developed and, in April 1984, they were married at the West Des Moines Christian Church where John and I were married in July 1945.

At the time of their marriage, both Eloise and Phil were members of the Virginia Symphony Orchestra and the Virginia Opera Orchestra in Norfolk. Eloise also developed a private teaching practice and had a large number of violin students.

In 1987 they made a big career change. Phil had a natural ability for people-management and Eloise developed an interest in medicine, following Phil's serious bout with cancer in 1985. To realize their ambitions they moved to Evanston, Illinois, where Phil entered the Kellogg School of

Dr. Eloise, MD, at her Rush Medical College commencement. Chicago, Illinois, June 1996.

Eloise and Phil at their wedding in the West Des Moines Christian Church with Susan Marie Clark, flower girl, and CJ Clark, ring bearer. April 1984.

Management at Northwestern University and Eloise continued her pre-med studies at Loyola University in Chicago. Phil received his master's degree in management in 1991 and Eloise completed her medical studies and received her MD degree from Rush Medical College, Chicago, in 1996. While Eloise was in medical school, Phil worked for management consulting firms, including McKinsey and Associates. They moved to Columbus, Ohio, where Eloise completed her residency in obstetrics and gynecology in 2000 at the Ohio State University Medical Center and joined a practice at Arlington Heights, Illinois. In 2003 she established her own private medical practice in Hoffman Estates, Illinois, for which

Phil set up all the administrative and management procedures.

Owing to the exorbitant malpractice insurance costs in Illinois, Eloise and Phil relocated to Thief River Falls, Minnesota. Phil became the administrative CEO of the Medical Clinic there in 2004 and Eloise joined the Clinic's medical staff in obstetrics and gynecology in the summer of 2005.

WASP Reunions, Post-Retirement Travels, Travails, and the Yankee Air Force

I have attended all the WASP reunions since 1972 and John has accompanied me since 1976. The WASPs are very social, active, and dedicated to maintaining the relevance of the history of their service. I have given many local talks and presentations about the WASPs to service clubs, church groups, veteran's organizations, etc., in recent years.

The reunions are always well attended although the membership is gradually declining, as age takes its toll.

John and I have traveled a lot since he retired from the university. These travels have mostly been in the continental United States, Maui, and Alaska, with a trip to the Shetland Islands, Scotland, and England in 1987.

Our first great-grandson, Curtis Bradley Hajek, was born to our granddaughter Susan on March 19, 1998 in St. Paul, Minnesota. He is a happy and healthy boy.

My health has been somewhat marginal for the past fifteen years but I have been fortunate to live in Ann Arbor where the medical services are excellent and extensive. In 1977 I fractured my left hip in a skiing accident and in 1993 and 2000 I had E. coli infections that required hospitalization for a month. Then in 1997 I fell at a friend's home and fractured my right hip. On a January 2003 trip to Iowa City to visit my sister, who had fractured her hip, I suffered congestive heart failure and was flown with John to Ann Arbor by air ambulance and nurse for local hospitalization and nursing home care. In April 2004 I fell at home and again fractured my left hip. This required a week in the hospital and all

I am at the 1994 WASP reunion in Washington, DC. Note the Caterpillar Club pin above my right pocket.

of the month of May in a nursing home, followed by six weeks of home care. Because of over-exposure to sunlight as a child, I have developed a dozen or more basal-cell carcinoma that required surgery. Fortunately, the University of Michigan Cancer Care Center has talented specialists for treating this problem.

Over the past fifty years in Ann Arbor we have made many good friends, two of whom I am especially anxious to mention. Professor Emeritus of Music (UM) Elizabeth A. H. Green was a friend for sixty-five years. We first met in Iowa where she had earned a reputation for excellence in school orchestra develop-

The Wall of Honor at Avenger Field, Sweetwater, Texas. I am pointing to my name in the granite. L-R: David, Phil, me, and Eloise. John took the photo. WASP Reunion, October 2000.

At the WASP Reunion in Tucson, AZ. L-R: Me, Madelon Burcham Hill, and Betty Wall Strohfus, all 44-1 WASPs. October 2002.

ment. We became reacquainted when we came to Ann Arbor in 1945. After we returned to Ann Arbor in 1957, Elizabeth gave Eloise her first violin lessons. When she died in 1995 her family asked us to perform her graveside services. Charlotte Plummer Owen was a close friend for over thirty-five years and was a musician of great attainment. She taught clarinet and saxophone privately in Ann Arbor for over forty years. Her husband, Charles, was a soloist with the US Marine Band in the 1930s and was the principal percussionist with the Philadelphia Orchestra before joining the faculty of the UM School of Music as Professor of Percussion in 1972. During WWII Charlotte was the conductor of the Women's US Marine Corps Band. She was the only woman to conduct the regular Marine Band (the "President's Own") in a public concert. For sixteen years, she conducted the Ann Arbor

John and me at the 100th Bomb Group reunion in Tampa, Florida. November 1989.

John and me on an Alaskan cruise. Summer 2000.

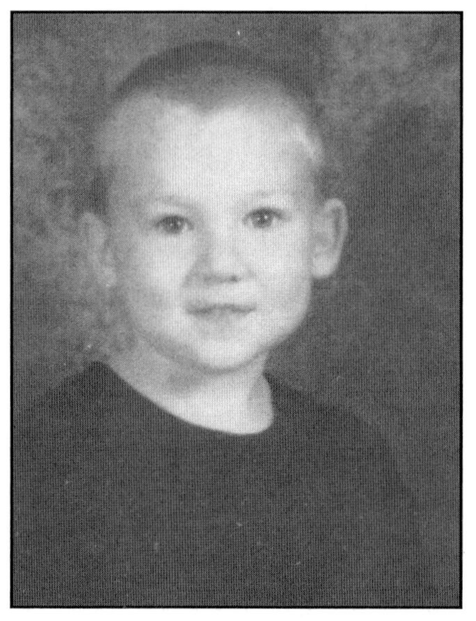

Our great-grandson Curtis, age six. May 2004.

Summer Band in weekly concerts during June and July. Charlotte died just before Christmas 2004.

At the 1940 Mu Phi Epsilon Honorary Musical Sorority Homecoming Convention in Cincinnati, Ohio, I was invited by the national president to perform as flute soloist on the Active Chapter Program Musicale. I played "Poem" by Griffes. Sixty-three years later it was my honor and privilege to sponsor the same program, "Reception and Musicale," at the Mu Phi Epsilon 2003 centennial celebration also held in Cincinnati.

In recent years John and I have become interested in the Yankee Air Force and Yankee Air Museum at Willow Run Airport near Ann Arbor. John is a Senior Life Member of the Yankee Air Force. We gave an extensive presentation of our

WWII flight experiences to the museum membership in March 2002. The Yankee Air Museum is dedicated to the history of military aviation, with special emphasis on WWII flight experiences. The Yankee Air Force restored three major WWII aircraft to flight condition: a four-engine B-17G, named *Yankee Lady*, the famous Boeing "Flying Fortress," which John flew during the war with the Eighth Air Force; a twin-engine, North American B-25 "Mitchell," named *Yankee Warrior*, the aircraft Jimmy Doolittle flew to bomb Tokyo in April 1942; and a Douglas C-47 transport, named *Yankee Doodle Dandy*. These aircraft tour the country in the summer, visiting air shows, and giving patrons the real, exciting experience of WWII flight operations. In October 2004, a tragic fire destroyed the Yankee Air Museum. Fortunately, no one was injured but the museum lost virtually all its historic documents and artifacts. Rebuilding is under-

I am with Professor Elizabeth Green, center, and Charlotte Owen on our back lawn. May 1988.

way. The flyable aircraft were saved.

After our March 2002 presentation we were thrilled to board the B-17, *Yankee Lady*, at the invitation of the officers of the museum. A few days later John was invit-

John and me and the student performers at the Mu Phi Epsilon reception and musicale, 2003 Mu Phi Epsilon Centennial Celebration, Cincinnati, Ohio. August 2003.

Yankee Lady, *the restored B-17G "Flying Fortress" of the Yankee Air Force. Willow Run Airport, Michigan. July 2002.*

ed to fly with the flight crew and was given the controls for about ten minutes. He made several slow turns north of Ann Arbor and was exhilarated by the experience. It was the first time in sixty years that he had flown a B-17.

Some Closing Thoughts...

As I finish this autobiographical memoir I want to add a few personal thoughts about living that I have found important in my life. These are intended mostly as a message to my family but may be of interest to others.

In February 2005 I reached my ninetieth birthday. My health is fragile and my sight and hearing are seriously impaired. I have experienced heart problems and fractured hips. Hence, it is with an honest understanding that I know God, in His own time, will call me home, I suppose sooner than later. I accept this without fear as God has set "eternity in my heart." I am confident of His unqualified love and His promise for eternal life with Him, as Jesus has taught

us. I believe that all my loved ones will share this with me, too, and we will be together forever.

Eternity is a long time. Because of this I have learned to consider carefully and realistically the choices presented in this life so that the peace and security of God's love can be enjoyed forever. Life on earth has always held mysteries for us, I know, and doubtless always will. There is much we do not understand. The apostle Paul reminds us of this, saying, "We look into a mirror darkly." *However, we do not lack in opportunities for a certain basic understanding about these "permanent things." The Psalmist wrote,* "The Heavens declare the glory of God and the Earth shows His Handiwork." *My own experience tells me, too, that God is always present in spirit and awaits our invitation to come into our hearts. Jesus said,* "Behold, I stand at the door and knock." *I believe it is necessary that each person be willing to open his heart and invite God to come in. This will change a person's life and open the path to eternity. God has provided prayer as an effective*

John and me in the cockpit of **Yankee Lady,** *the Yankee Air Force B-17, reliving old times! March 2002.*

means of communication for this purpose.

There are many that do not believe in the existence of God or in a moral universe. I have never had trouble with these concepts, as I believe the Holy Bible, common experience, answered prayer, personal testimony, and tradition support them. The human response to music, art, poetry, and love flows, I believe, from spiritual inspiration. Mozart recognized this when he said, "Music is the voice of God." There is a place in our lives for philosophical contemplation and discussions, of course, but I agree with C. S. Lewis that such things should not prevent "Joy from breaking through." Doubters, in my experience, often begin with skepticism and cynicism,

demanding that God prove His existence to them, thus putting themselves in judgment of God. This is not only arrogant but also unfruitful since it chokes off the channels of communication to Him, leading only to more doubt and confusion. If you start with faith, then God can enter your heart and mind and change your life, preparing your soul for eternity.

Man has always displayed a desire to become a god himself, starting in the Garden of Eden when the serpent tempted Eve. This is fundamentally a denial of God Himself and is probably the most grievous of all sins. I believe it is vital that this be recognized. In the end these issues are not really matters of the intellect alone but of *wisdom. For ordinary men, they are matters of faith. The Palmist reminds us that, "The testimony of the Lord is sure, making wise the simple."*

I have been privileged to enjoy an abundant life for which I am deeply grateful. My parents were loving, considerate, and faithful Christians who taught me early to know and love God. They provided me with a caring and secure home, the best education available, and taught me to be patient. I was fortunate to marry a man who shares these values and my views of God and eternity. We have been blessed with children, grandchildren, and a great-grandson in whom we have tried to instill the essence of the Christian faith.

My wartime service as a WASP was my one great opportunity to serve the country I love. It gave me the chance for extended personal development and to have unbelievable flying experiences. I can only describe it as an "opportunity of a lifetime." I am grateful for this, too.

John and I have traveled extensively and visited many ancient places of great renown but the most satisfying experience of all was to return home to our family and loved ones. These are the most important things in life: family, home, and friends, and to love God and one another.

Yankee Lady *at Willow Run prior to a flight to the Twin Cities, Minnesota, where our son David enjoyed an hour's flight in it as a fiftieth birthday gift from us. L-R: John, Maj. Gen. (ret) Richard C. Bodycombe, YAF chief pilot, and me. Bette Watson, YAF director of education, is fourth from the right, and Norm Ellickson, the B-17 crew chief is second from the right. Willow Run Airport. July 2002.*

OFFICERS MESS
LAS VEGAS ARMY AIR FIELD
LAS VEGAS, NEVADA

Flight Log Excerpts: 1940-44

October 17, 1940 to December 20, 1944

A. CPT Student Pilot Training
Des Moines, Iowa
October 17, 1940 to January 24, 1941

Ident. No. NC *31160*	RATING SHEET	Note.—Keep time by stages.		
Make and model *J. 3 Cub*	CONTROLLED PRIVATE FLYING COURSE	Ground Instruction Time	DUAL Hr.	Min.
Engine *French* Hp. *65*	**Stage A**	Time this flight		*30*
Time up ___ a. m. *1:35* p. m.	Minimum, 8 Hours Dual	Previous time		
Time down ___ a. m. *2:05* p. m.	Grade Maneuvers During Instruction	Total stage time		*30*
Date *10/17/40*		Total course time		*30*

Lesson No. 1. — Demonstrate and Practice

	Wind direction	Wind velocity	Judgment	Aptitude	Number of landings	Into-wind taxi	Cross-wind taxi	Down-wind taxi	No-wind taxi	Effect of controls	Straight and level flight	Turns
SW	10	3	3	1	5	5	5		4	4	5	

Check number in each column indicating student's characteristics

A	ATTITUDE	B	PHYSICAL TRAITS	C	MENTAL TRAITS	D	FLYING HABITS			E	SPECIAL FAULTS
1	Eager to learn.	1	Relaxed.	1	Alert.	1	Good coordination.	7	Good timing.	1	Cocky.
2	Cooperative.	2	Good control touch.	2	Careful.	2	Good speed sense.	8	Climbs too steep.	2	Disobedient.
3	Punctual.	3	Tired.	3	Consistent.	3	Poor coordination.	9	Skids on turns.	3	Overconfident.
4	Tardy.	4	Tense.	4	Erratic.	4	Nose too high	10	Slips on turns.	4	Overcautious.
5	Indifferent.	5	Rough on controls.	5	Forgetful.	5	Nose too low.	11	Lands too fast.	5	Irresponsible.
6	Hard-headed.	6	Airsick.	6	Mechanical.	6	Dives in glide.	12	Reacts slowly.	6	Reckless.

Above instruction given.

[signature] 39341

(Instructor's signature)   (Cert. No.)   (Rating)

Above-ground and flight instruction received.

(Student's signature (first, middle, and last names) must be signed exactly the same on all forms)   16—17685

1. First Training Flight

Ident. No. NC **3160**
Make and model **J-3 Cub**
Engine **Franklin** Hp. **65**
Time up **740** a. m. ——— p. m.
Time down **750** a. m. ——— p. m.
Date **10/31/40**

RATING SHEET
CONTROLLED PRIVATE FLYING COURSE
Stage B
Minimum, 5 Hrs.—2 Hrs. Dual Check
Grade Maneuvers During Instruction

Note.—Keep time by stages.

Ground Instr. Time	Dual		Solo	
	Hr.	Min.	Hr.	Min.
Time this flight				10
Previous time				
Total stage time				10
Total course time	9	15		10

Solo Flight

Lesson No. 1

	Wind direction	Wind velocity	Judgment	Aptitude	Number of landings	Taxiing	Take-offs	Climbs and turns	Glides and turns	Approaches (180°)	Landings
NW	10	3	3	2	3	3	3	3	3	3	

Check number in each column indicating student's characteristics

A	Attitude	B	Physical Traits	C	Mental Traits	D	Flying Habits			E	Special Faults
1	Eager to learn.	1	Relaxed.	1	Alert.	1	Good coordination.	7	Good timing.	1	Cocky.
2	Cooperative.	2	Good control touch.	2	Careful.	2	Good speed sense.	8	Climbs too steep.	2	Disobedient.
3	Punctual.	3	Tired.	3	Consistent.	3	Poor coordination.	9	Skids on turns.	3	Overconfident.
4	Tardy.	4	Tense.	4	Erratic.	4	Nose too high	10	Slips on turns.	4	Overcautious.
5	Indifferent.	5	Rough on controls.	5	Forgetful.	5	Nose too low.	11	Lands too fast.	5	Irresponsible.
6	Hard-headed.	6	Airsick.	6	Mechanical.	6	Dives in glide.	12	Reacts slowly.	6	Reckless.

Above instruction given.

_____________________ 3934
(Instructor's signature) (Cert. No.) (Rating)

Above-ground and flight instruction received.

(Student's signature (first, middle, and last names) must be signed
exactly the same on all forms) 16—17685

2. First Solo Flight

Ident. No. NC _3160_
Make and model _____
Engine _____ Hp. _65_
Time up _____ a. m. _____ p. m.
Time down _____ a. m. _____ p. m.
Date _1-5-70_

RATING SHEET
CONTROLLED PRIVATE FLYING COURSE

Stage D

Minimum, 11 Hrs.—6½ Hrs. Dual Check

Grade Maneuvers During Instruction

Note.—Keep time by stages.

Ground Instr. Time	Dual		Solo	
	Hr.	Min.	Hr.	Min.
Time this flight			3	00
Previous time	5	15		35
Total stage time	5	15	3	35
Total course time	24	25	11	50

Solo

Lesson No. 5.

Wind direction | Wind velocity | Judgment | Aptitude | Number of landings | Taxiing | Take-offs | Climbs and turns | Glides and turns | Approaches (180°) | Landings | Forced landings | Forward slip | Side slip | Dragging areas | Cross country

N | 5

Check number in each column indicating student's characteristics

A	Attitude	B	Physical Traits	C	Mental Traits	D	Flying Habits			E	Special Faults
1	Eager to learn.	1	Relaxed.	1	Alert.	1	Good coordination.	7	Good timing.	1	Cocky.
2	Cooperative.	2	Good control touch.	2	Careful.	2	Good speed sense.	8	Climbs too steep.	2	Disobedient.
3	Punctual.	3	Tired.	3	Consistent.	3	Poor coordination.	9	Skids on turns.	3	Overconfident.
4	Tardy.	4	Tense.	4	Erratic.	4	Nose too high	10	Slips on turns.	4	Overcautious.
5	Indifferent.	5	Rough on controls.	5	Forgetful.	5	Nose too low.	11	Lands too fast.	5	Irresponsible.
6	Hard-headed.	6	Airsick.	6	Mechanical.	6	Dives in glide.	12	Reacts slowly.	6	Reckless.

Above instruction given.

(signature) 39341

(Instructor's signature)   (Cert. No.)   (Rating)

Above-ground and flight instruction received.

(Student's signature (first, middle, and last names) must be signed exactly the same on all forms)   16—17685

3. First Solo Cross Country Flight

Ident. No. NC *3160*
Make and model *Cub J3*
Engine *Frank* Hp. *65*
Time up _____ a. m. *4:00* p. m.
Time down _____ a. m. *4:50* p. m.
Date *1—24—41*

RATING SHEET
CONTROLLED PRIVATE FLYING COURSE
Stage D
Minimum, 11 Hrs.—6½ Hrs. Dual Check
Grade Maneuvers During Instruction

Note.—Keep time by stages.

Ground Instr. Time	Dual		Solo	
	Hr.	Min.	Hr.	Min.
Time this flight				*50*
Previous time			*6*	*05*
Total stage time	*6*	*30*	*6*	*53*
Total course time	*25*	*40*	*15*	*10*

Dual Check or Solo as Necessary

Lesson No. 11.

Wind direction · Wind velocity · Judgment · Aptitude · Number of landings · Taxiing · Take-offs · Climbs and turns · Glides and turns · Approaches (180°) · Landings · Forced landings · Forward slip · Side slip · Dragging areas · Cross country · Approaches (360°) · Spiral approaches · Power approaches · Power landings · 30° 8's · 60° 8's · 720° power turns · Stalls · Spins

Completed Flight Test O.K.

Check number in each column indicating student's characteristics

A	Attitude	B	Physical Traits	C	Mental Traits	D	Flying Habits			E	Special Faults
1	Eager to learn.	1	Relaxed.	1	Alert.	1	Good coordination.	7	Good timing.	1	Cocky.
2	Cooperative.	2	Good control touch.	2	Careful.	2	Good speed sense.	8	Climbs too steep.	2	Disobedient.
3	Punctual.	3	Tired.	3	Consistent.	3	Poor coordination.	9	Skids on turns.	3	Overconfident.
4	Tardy.	4	Tense.	4	Erratic.	4	Nose too high	10	Slips on turns.	4	Overcautious.
5	Indifferent.	5	Rough on controls.	5	Forgetful.	5	Nose too low.	11	Lands too fast.	5	Irresponsible.
6	Hard-headed.	6	Airsick.	6	Mechanical.	6	Dives in glide.	12	Reacts slowly.	6	Reckless.

Above instruction given.

_____________ *35341*
(Instructor's signature) (Cert. No.) (Rating)

Above-ground and flight instruction received.

____
(Student's signature (first, middle, and last names) must be signed
exactly the same on all forms) 16—17685

4. Passed Flight Test

B. Private Pilot Flying
Des Moines, Iowa

				CLASS 1 DUAL Hrs. Min.	CLASS 2S DUAL Hrs. Min.	CLASS 1 SOLO Hrs. Min.	CLASS 2S SOLO Hrs. Min.
1941	NOTE: Entries are for conventional single engine land planes unless otherwise noted under remarks. TOTALS BROUGHT FORWARD →			25:40	:	15:10	:
DATE	MAKE AND MODEL	LICENSE NUMBER	MAKE OF ENGINE	:	:	:	:
				:	:	:	:
				:	:	:	:
3-4-	Cub J3	31160	Frank 65	:	:	:30	:
Mar 13	J5 Cub	NC 35789	Continental 75	:	30	:	15
Mar. 23	J3 Cub	NC 32851	Frank 65	:	:	:40	:
Mar 30	Cub J5	NC 30660	Cont 75	:	:60	:	:
			TOTALS	25:40	1:30	16:20	:15
Marie Mountain		PILOT	The Footings of These 7 Columns →				

NIGHT FLYING Hrs. Min.	INSTRUMENT FLYING Hrs. Min.	CROSS COUNTRY Hrs. Min.	TOTAL TIME ALL CLASSES Hrs. Min.	FROM	TO	REMARKS
:	:	6:00	40:50	1940 OCT-17	1941 JAN 24	Total Time C.P.T. Course —
:	:	:	:			W.A.Boyer - 39,341 C.P.T. Instructor
:	:	:	:			
:	:	:	:			
:	:	:30				W.A.Boyer C. 39341
:	:	:45		Des Moines		William Do Blake C 9986
:	:	:40		"	"	
:	:	:60				W.A.Boyer C. 39341
				I CERTIFY THAT THE ABOVE FLIGHTS WERE MADE		
:	:	:	43:45			W.A.Boyer - C.39341
Must Balance with Total Flying Time						

1. First Flight as a Licensed Pilot

NOTE: Entries are for conventional single engine land planes unless otherwise noted under remarks.				CLASS 1 DUAL		CLASS 2S DUAL		CLASS 1 SOLO		CLASS 2S SOLO	
				Hrs.	Min.	Hrs.	Min.	Hrs.	Min.	Hrs.	Min.
TOTALS BROUGHT FORWARD →				2	15			71	45		
DATE	MAKE AND MODEL	LICENSE NUMBER	MAKE OF ENGINE								
2/18/43	Cub J3	40770	Fr. 65					1	00		
2/19/43	Piper J-3	41235	Fr 65		45						
3/13/43	Piper J3	38481	Fr. 65						40		
			TOTALS	3	00			73	25		

Marie Mountain
PILOT

The Footings of These 7 Columns →

NIGHT FLYING		INSTRUMENT FLYING		CROSS COUNTRY		TOTAL TIME ALL CLASSES		FROM	TO	REMARKS
Hrs.	Min.	Hrs.	Min.	Hrs.	Min.	Hrs.	Min.			
						74	00			
						75	00			spins, stalls, chandelles, lazy 8
						75	45			Aect C. Stems Series 8's Thru C 237928
						76	25			
						76	25			

I CERTIFY THAT THE ABOVE FLIGHTS WERE MADE

Must Balance with Total Flying Time

Marie Mountain

2. Last Civilian Flight

C. US Air Force, WASP Flight Training, Sweetwater, Texas
August 10, 1943 to February 9, 1944

NOTE: Entries are for conventional single engine land planes unless otherwise noted under remarks.

				CLASS 1 DUAL		CLASS 2S DUAL		CLASS 1 SOLO		CLASS 2S SOLO	
			TOTALS BROUGHT FORWARD →	Hrs.	Min.	Hrs.	Min.	Hrs.	Min.	Hrs.	Min.
				3	00			73	20		
DATE	MAKE AND MODEL	LICENSE NUMBER	MAKE OF ENGINE	Hrs.	Min.	Hrs.	Min.	Hrs.	Min.	Hrs.	Min.
8/10/43	Fairchild PT19-A	U.S.A. -178	Ranger 175				33				
8/11/43	Fairchild PT19-A	U.S.A. -137	Ranger 175			1	50				
8/12/43	"	" "	" "			1	00				
8/13/43	"	" 140	" "				35				
8/14/43	"	" "	" "				48				
8/18/43	"	" 141	" "				42				
8/19/43	"	" 138	" "				54				
			TOTALS	3	00	5	22	73	20		

Marie Mountain
PILOT

The Footings of These 7 Columns →

NIGHT FLYING		INSTRUMENT FLYING		CROSS COUNTRY		TOTAL TIME ALL CLASSES		FROM	TO	REMARKS
Hrs.	Min.	Hrs.	Min.	Hrs.	Min.	Hrs.	Min.			
						76	35			
						76	58	Avenger Field LOCAL / Sweetwater	Texas	coordination exercises - landing takeoff - climbing and gliding turns
						77	48	LOCAL		stalls - spins climbing & gliding turns -
						78	48	LOCAL		gliding coordination - spins power on & power off stalls
						79	23	LOCAL		turn series, spins, gliding turns & coordination landing climbing turns, stall series,
						80	11	"		"
						80	53	"		usual stuff + forced landing S-turns
						81	47	"		" " " "
						81	47			

Must Balance with Total Flying Time

I CERTIFY THAT THE ABOVE FLIGHTS WERE MADE

Marie Mountain

1. First Flight as a WASP Trainee in a PT-19, Sweetwater, Texas

NOTE: Entries are for conventional single engine land planes unless otherwise noted under remarks.

				CLASS 1 DUAL		CLASS 2S DUAL		CLASS 1 SOLO		CLASS 2S SOLO	
				Hrs.	Min.	Hrs.	Min.	Hrs.	Min.	Hrs.	Min.
		TOTALS BROUGHT FORWARD →		3:00		5:22		73:25			
DATE	MAKE AND MODEL	LICENSE NUMBER	MAKE OF ENGINE								
8/20/43	Fairchild PT-19A	U.S.A. 137	Ranger 175				:46				
8/23/43	" "	" 136	" "				:35				
8/24/43	" "	" 149	" "				:55				
8/25/43	" "	" 146	" "				:24				:25
8/26/43	" "	" 175	" "				:45				:28
8/27/43	" "	" 145	" "				:19				:30
			TOTALS	3:00		9:06		73:25		1:23	

Marie Mountain

PILOT

The Footings of These 7 Columns →

NIGHT FLYING		INSTRUMENT FLYING		CROSS COUNTRY		TOTAL TIME ALL CLASSES		FROM	TO	REMARKS
Hrs.	Min.	Hrs.	Min.	Hrs.	Min.	Hrs.	Min.			
						81	:47			
						82	:33	LOCAL		usual stuff plus rect. course
						83	:08	"		parachuted safely from spin
						84	:03	"		forced landings, s-turns rectangular courses, 3 landings dual
						84	:52	"		3 landings solo, 3 landing dual
						85	:25	"		3 landing solo
						86	:54	"		x solo landing, 1 dual landing
						86	:54			

Must Balance with Total Flying Time

I CERTIFY THAT THE ABOVE FLIGHTS WERE MADE

C. H. Rowe

C-75104-41

2. "Parachute" Flight, WASP Trainee, Sweetwater, Texas

NOTE: Entries are for conventional single engine land planes unless otherwise noted under remarks.				CLASS 1 DUAL		CLASS 2S DUAL		CLASS 1 SOLO		CLASS 2S SOLO	
				Hrs.	Min.	Hrs.	Min.	Hrs.	Min.	Hrs.	Min.
1943		TOTALS BROUGHT FORWARD ⟶		3	00	26	13	73	25	28	15
DATE	MAKE AND MODEL	LICENSE NUMBER	MAKE OF ENGINE								
Sept. 28	Fairchild PT 19A	U.S.A.	Ranger 175 H.P.		:		1:05		:		:
Oct. 5	Vultee BT 15	U.S.A. 91	Wright 440 H.P.		:		:40		:		:
Oct. 6	Vultee BT 15	U.S.A. 111	Wright 440 H.P.		:	01	00		:		:
Oct. 7	Vultee BT 15	U.S.A. 90	Wright 440 H.P.		:	01	00		:		:
Oct. 8	Vultee BT 15	U.S.A. 102	Wright 440 H.P.		:	00	55		:		:
Oct. 10	Vultee BT 15	U.S.A. 86	Wright 440 H.P.		:	00	45		:		:
Oct. 11	Vultee BT 15	U.S.A. 90	Wright 440 H.P.		:	01	25		:		:
			TOTALS	03	00	33	03	73	25	28	15

Marie Mountain

PILOT

The Footings of These 7 Columns ⟶

NIGHT FLYING		INSTRUMENT FLYING		CROSS COUNTRY		TOTAL TIME ALL CLASSES		FROM	TO	REMARKS
Hrs.	Min.	Hrs.	Min.	Hrs.	Min.	Hrs.	Min.			
	:		:	04	13	135	06			
	:		:		:	136	11			
	:		:		:	136	51	Avenger Field Sweetwater, Tex.		
	:		:		:	137	51	Local		
	:		:		:	138	51	Local		
	:		:		:	139	46	Local		
	:		:		:	140	31	Local	Link Total 01:15	
	:		:		:	141	56	Local	01:15	
	:		:	04	13	141	56			

I CERTIFY THAT THE ABOVE FLIGHTS WERE MADE

Must Balance with Total Flying Time

3. First Flight in a BT-13, WASP Trainee, Sweetwater, Texas

NOTE: Entries are for conventional single engine land planes unless otherwise noted under remarks.				CLASS 1 DUAL	CLASS 2S DUAL	CLASS 1 SOLO	CLASS 2S SOLO
				Hrs. Min.	Hrs. Min.	Hrs. Min.	Hrs. Min.
1943 TOTALS BROUGHT FORWARD →				03:00	49:07	73:25	46:55
DATE	MAKE AND MODEL	LICENSE NUMBER	MAKE OF ENGINE				
Dec. 14	No. Am. AT 6	U.S.A. 276	P.+W. 650 H.P.	:	00:53	:	:
Dec. 15	North American AT6	U.S.A. 254	650 H.P. Pratt + Whitney	:	01:05	:	:
Dec. 18	North American AT6	U.S.A. 238	650 H.P. Pratt + Whitney	:	02:06	:	:
Dec. 20	North American AT6	U.S.A. 254	650 H.P. Pratt + Whitney	:	01:04	:	00:15
Dec. 21	North American AT6	U.S.A. 256	650 H.P. P. + W.	:	00:25	:	00:48
Dec. 22	North American AT6	U.S.A. 237	650 H.P. P.&W.	:	00:15	:	:
Dec. 22	N.A. AT6	U.S.A. 248	650 H.P. P&W	:	:	:	00:37
TOTALS				03:00	54:54	73:25	48:35

Marie Mountain

PILOT   The Footings of These 7 Columns →

NIGHT FLYING	INSTRUMENT FLYING	CROSS COUNTRY	TOTAL TIME ALL CLASSES	FROM	TO	REMARKS
Hrs. Min.	Hrs. Min.	Hrs. Min.	Hrs. Min.			
:	40:08	04:13	216:48	Link training total – 30:00 hours		
:	:	:	217:41	Local		
:	:	:	218:46	"		
:	:	:	220:51	"		
:	:	:	222:10	"		
:	:	:	223:23	"		
:	:	:	223:38	"		
:	:	:	224:15	"		
:	40:08	04:13	224:35			

Must Balance with Total Flying Time

I CERTIFY THAT THE ABOVE FLIGHTS WERE MADE

O. A. Martini
C – 126506

4. First Flight in an AT-6, WASP Trainee, Sweetwater, Texas

NOTE: Entries are for conventional single engine land planes unless otherwise noted under remarks.

44
19**43**

Date	Make and Model	License Number	Make of Engine	Class 1 Dual Hrs. Min.	Class 2S Dual Hrs. Min.	Class 1 Solo Hrs. Min.	Class 2S Solo Hrs. Min.
			TOTALS BROUGHT FORWARD →	03:00	65:02	73:25	56:21
Feb. 5	Fairchild PT–19A	U.S.A. 94	Ranger 175 H.P.				
Feb. 6	N.A. A.T.6	U.S.A. 252	P.+W. 650 H.P.				00:15
Feb. 6	N.A. A.T.6	U.S.A. 280	P.+W. 650 H.P.				01:25
Feb. 9	N.A. AT6	U.S.A. 235	P.+W. 650 H.P.				
			TOTALS	03:00	65:02	73:25	58:01

Marie Mountain
PILOT

The Footings of These 7 Columns →

Night Flying Hrs. Min.	Instrument Flying Hrs. Min.	Cross Country Hrs. Min.	Total Time All Classes Hrs. Min.	From	To	Remarks
06:07	44:17	58:14	306 :26	Link trainer total – 30:00 hours		
		02:33	308 :59	Sweetwater – Brownwood – Cisco – Sweetwater		
			309 :14	Local	landings	
			310 :39	"	landings	
04:39			315 :18	Sweetwater – Abilene – Big Spring – Abilene – B.S. – Swtw.		
10:46	44:17	60:47	315 :18			

Must Balance with Total Flying Time

I CERTIFY THAT THE ABOVE FLIGHTS WERE MADE

O. C. Martin – C–126506

5. Final Flight in an AT-6, WASP Trainee, Sweetwater, Texas

D. US Air Force, Active Duty, Las Vegas AAB, Las Vegas, Nevada
March 2, 1944 to December 20, 1944

DATE 19 44	AIRCRAFT IDENT. MARK	MAKE - MODEL and HORSEPOWER OF AIRCRAFT	FROM	TO	CLASS OR TYPE SeL			DURATION OF FLIGHT Total Time to Date
					315:18			315:18
3-2-44	Z-204	AT-6C -650 H.P.	Local		01:30			316:48
3-6-44	Z-207	AT-6C- 650 H.P.	"		01:30			318:18
3-6-44	Z-261	AT-6A-650 H.P.	"		01:30			319:48
3-7-44	Z-203	AT-6C-650 H.P.	"		01:20			321:08
3-7-44	Z-263	AT-6A-650 H.P.	"		01:30			322:38
3-7-44								
3-8-44	Z-274	AT-6A-650 H.P.	LQ - RL - KI - LQ		02:05			324:43
3-8-44	Z-203	AT-6C-650 H.P.	Local		01:35			326:08
3-9-44	Z-204	AT-6 C-650 H.P.	"		01:20			327:28
3-9-44								
3-10-44								
3-10-44	Z-204	AT-6C-650 H.P.	"		02:50			330:18
3-11-44								
3-11-44	Z-204	AT-6C-650 H.P.	"		02:45			333:03
3-13-44								
CARRY TOTALS FORWARD TO TOP OF NEXT PAGE					333:03			333:03

SOLO FLIGHT TIME Day	Night	Instrument	LINK	DUAL INSTRUCTION Q D	C P	as instructor or Student INSTRUCTOR	REMARKS: Each maneuver and the time spent thereon, attested to by the Instructor is to be entered in this column for all instruction received. Any serious damage to the aircraft MUST be entered here also.
180:38	10:46	44:17	30:00	128:24			
				01:30			6 landings - checkout (transition)
				01:30			8 landings - Transition
01:30							6 landings - Transition
01:20							4 landings - transition
01:30							4 " "
			31:00				
02:05							X - C
01:25							6 landings - transition
00:55		00:45		00:45			Instrument dual — transition
			32:00				
			33:00				
01:05		01:45		01:45			transition - instrument dual
			34:00				
01:00		01:45		01:45			transition - instrument dual
			35:00				
191:28	10:46	48:32	35:00	135:39			PILOT'S SIGNATURE *Marie Mountain WASP*

1. First Flight as a WASP Air Force Pilot, Las Vegas AAB, Nevada

DATE 19 44	AIRCRAFT IDENT. MARK	MAKE - MODEL and HORSEPOWER OF AIRCRAFT	FROM	TO	CLASS OR TYPE Sel	Mel		DURATION OF FLIGHT Total Time to Date
					562:45	19:15		582:00
8-121	Z-295	AT6A-650 H.P.	Local		03:30			585:30
8-13	Z-291	AT6A-650 H.P.	"		01:30			587:00
8-14	Z-291	AT6A-650 H.P.	"		01:45			588:45
8-14	Z-292	AT6A-650 H.P.	"		01:00			589:45
8-15	Z-291	AT6A-650 H.P.	"		01:20			591:05
8-15	Z-260	AT6A-650 H.P.	"		02:40			593:45
8-16	Z-260	AT6A-650 H.P.	"		00:20			594:05
8-16	Z-257	AT6A-650 H.P.	"		03:05			597:10
8-17	Z-260	AT6A-650 H.P.	"		03:00			600:10
8-17	Z-291	AT6A-650 H.P.	"		03:10			603:20
8-18	Z-291	AT6A-650 H.P.	"		02:35			605:55
8-19	Z-291	AT6A-650 H.P.	"		02:30			608:25
8-19	Z-291	AT6A-650 H.P.	"		02:25			610:50
8-21	Z-341	P-39 Q 1250 H.P.	"		00:35			611:25
8-22	Z-291	AT6A-650 H.P.	"		03:50			615:15
CARRY TOTALS FORWARD TO TOP OF NEXT PAGE					596:00	19:15		615:15

SOLO FLIGHT TIME Day	Night	Instrument	LINK	DUAL INSTRUCTION Q D	C P	as instructor or Student I Inst.	REMARKS: Each maneuver and the time spent thereon, attested to by the Instructor is to be entered in this column for all instruction received. Any serious damage to the aircraft MUST be entered here also.
406:25	10:46	55:12	37:00	152:54	13:25	156:25	
03:30							Range estimation
01:30							" "
01:45							" "
01:00							" "
01:20							" "
02:40							" "
00:20							" "
03:05							" "
03:00							" "
03:10							" "
02:35							" "
02:30							" "
02:25							" "
01:35							Checkout
03:50							R.A.
439:40	10:46	55:12	37:00	152:54	13:25	156:25	PILOT'S SIGNATURE Marie Mountain WASP

2. First Flight in a P-39 Fighter, Las Vegas AAB, Nevada

DATE 19 44	AIRCRAFT IDENT. MARK	MAKE – MODEL and HORSEPOWER OF AIRCRAFT	FROM	TO	CLASS OR TYPE			DURATION OF FLIGHT Total Time to Date
					S&L	M&L		
					779:00	22:05		801:05
11-30	Z-351	P39Q 1250 H.P.	LQ		00:35			801:40
12-1	Z-347	P39Q 1250 H.P.	"		01:25			803:05
12-1	Z-33?	P39Q 1250 H.P.	"		01:35			804:40
12-2	Z-120	TB26-4000 H.P.	LQ	DJL	~~01:25~~	01:10		805:50
12-2	Z-138	TB26-4000 H.P.	DJL	LQ	"	01:15		807:05
12-4	Z-370	P63-1550 H.P.	LQ		00:30			807:35
12-4	Z-370	P63-1550 H.P.	"		01:35			809:10
12-5	Z-139	TB26-4000 H.P.	LQ	~~DJL~~		00:35		809:45
12-5	Z-5	B17-4800 H.P.	"			00:45		810:30
12-5	Z-139	TB26-4000 H.P.	LQ	DJL		01:00		811:30
12-6	Z-129	TB26-4000 H.P.	DJL	LQ		01:50		813:20
12-8	Z-322	P39Q 1250 H.P.	LQ		01:30			814:50
12-9	Z-330	P39Q 1250 H.P.	"		01:15			816:05
12-9	Z-325	P39Q 1250 H.P.	"		01:20			817:25
12-9	Z-330	P39Q 1250 H.P.	"		01:00			818:25
CARRY TOTALS FORWARD TO TOP OF NEXT PAGE					789:45	28:40		818:25

SOLO FLIGHT TIME			LINK	DUAL INSTRUCTION		as Instructor or Student	REMARKS: Each maneuver and the time spent thereon, attested to by the Instructor is to be entered in this column for all instruction received. Any serious damage to the aircraft MUST be entered here also.
Day	Night	Instrument		QD	CP	I- Instr.	
561:35	13:05	110:40	59:25	211:30	16:15	156:25	
00:35							Test Hop
01:25							" "
01:35							" "
~~01:25~~					01:10		Administrative
					01:15		"
00:30							Test Hop
01:25	00:15						" "
					00:35		~~Administrative~~ Test Hop
					00:45		" "
					01:00		Administrative
					01:50		"
01:20	00:10						Test Hop
01:15							" "
01:20							" "
01:00							" "
571:55	13:31	110:40	59:25	211:30	12:50	156:25	PILOT'S SIGNATURE *Marie Mountain* WASP

3. First Flight in a P-63 Fighter, B-26 and B-17,
Las Vegas AAB, Nevada

DATE 19 44	AIRCRAFT IDENT. MARK	MAKE – MODEL and HORSEPOWER OF AIRCRAFT	FROM	TO	CLASS OR TYPE SeL	MeL		DURATION OF FLIGHT Total Time to Date
					807:45	29:40		837:25
12-18	Z-343	P39Q 1250 H.P.	LQ		01:30			838:55
12-18	Z-404	BT 13-450 H.P.	"		01:05			840:00
12-19	Z-406	BT 13-450 H.P.	"		01:30			841:30
12-19	Z-409	BT 13-450 H.P.	"		01:45			843:15
12-20	Z-345	P39Q 1250 H.P.	"		00:40			843:55
1945								
3-10	NC-22275	Ta-Craft — 65 H.P.	Iowa City		01:05			845:00
3-21	U.S.A. 31455	PT 19-175 H.P.	Oklahoma City	D M	04:25			849:25
3-23		PT 19-175 H.P.	" "	D M	03:40			853:05
3-27		PT 19-175 H.P.	" "	"	03:35			856:40
3-29		PT 19-175 H.P.	" "	"	05:10			861:50
3-31		PT 19-175 H.P.	" "	"	04:15			866:05
5-6	41120	Cub-J3-65H.	Local (D.M.)		01:10			867:15
5-12		T-Craft-65H.	Bay City Local		01:00			868:15
		CARRY TOTALS FORWARD TO TOP OF NEXT PAGE			838:35	29:40		868:15

SOLO FLIGHT TIME Day	Night	Instrument	LINK	DUAL INSTRUCTION QD	CP	as instructor or Student I-Inst.	REMARKS: Each maneuver and the time spent thereon, attested to by the Instructor is to be entered in this column for all instruction received. Any serious damage to the aircraft MUST be entered here also.
589:55	13:30	114:15	59:25	211:30	23:50	156:25	
01:30							Test Hop
01:05						01:05	Instruments
01:30						01:30	"
01:45		01:45					"
00:15	00:25						Test Hop
01:05							
04:25							Ferrying
03:40							"
03:35							"
05:10							"
04:15							"
01:10							
01:00							
620:20	13:55	116:00	59:25	211:30	23:50	159:00	PILOT'S SIGNATURE *Marie Mountain Clark*

4. Final Flight as an active duty WASP, Las Vegas AAB, Nevada, including some 1945 post-war flying.

Selected Reading About the WASP

(All citations are from the author's library.)

Amelia Earhart's Daughters, by Leslie Haynsworth and David Toomey, William Morrow and Co., Inc., New York, 1998; 311 pages with photos and index.

And Still Flying…the life and times of Elizabeth "Betty" Wall, by Patrick Roberts, Walking Shadow Publications, Fairbault, MN, 2003; 98 pages with photos.

An Eighth Air Force Combat Diary, by John A. Clark, First Page Publications, Livonia, MI (successor to Proctor Publications), 2001; 322 pages with photos and index.

Daughter of the Air, by Rob Simbeck, Atlantic Monthly Press, New York, 1999; 253 pages with index.

Final Report on Woman Pilot Program, by Jacqueline Cochran, Director of Women Pilots, Headquarters, Army Air Forces, Washington, D.C., 1945.

Flying the Zuni Mountains, by Ann Darr, Forest Woods Media Productions, Inc., Washington, D.C., 1994; original poems and photos.

For God, Country, and the Thrill of It, by Anne Noggle with Dora Dougherty Strother, Texas A&M University Press, 1990; 161 pages with photos.

Girls Can't be Pilots, by Margaret J. Ringenberg with Jane L. Roth, Daedalus Press, Fort Wayne, IN, 1998; 305 pages with index.

In Memoriam, Thirty-eight American Women Pilots, by Dawn Seymour, 43-5, Clarice I. Bergemann, 44-2, Jeannette J. Jenkins, 44-1, and Mary Ellen Keil, 44-2, published by Texas Woman's University, Denton, Texas, 1996; 52 pages with photos.

Jackie Cochran, by Jacqueline Cochran with Maryann Bucknum Brinley, Bantam Books, New York, 1987; 354 pages with photos and index.

Letters from Home 1944-1945, by Bernice "Bee" Falk Haydu, TopLine Printing and Graphics, Riviera Beach, Florida, 2003; 192 pages with photos.

Mary Anna Martin Wyall: WASP Letters, 1944-1945, edited by Nancy Marshall Durr for the Texas Woman's University Special Collection, Denton Texas, 1994; 63 pages with index.

On Final Approach, by Byrd Howell Granger, Falconer Publishing Co., Scottsdale, AZ, 1991; 481 pages with photos, several appendices and an extensive index.

On Silver Wings, by Marianne Verges, Ballantine Books, New York, 1991; 247 pages with photos and index.

Out of the Blue and into History, by Betty Stagg Turner, Aviatrix Publishing Inc., Arlington Heights, IL, 2001; 576 pages with photos and index.

Sister in the Sky, by Adela Riek Scharr, The Patrice Press, 1988; Vol. I: The WAFS, 531 pages with photos; Vol. II: The WASPS, 758 pages with photos and index for Vol. I and Vol. II.

Those Wonderful Women in their Flying Machines, by Sally VanWagenen Keil, 4 Directions Press, New York, 1990; 418 pages with photos and index.

We Were WASPS, by Winifred Wood with drawings by Dorothy Swain, privately published, 1994; 195 pages with drawings.

"Who were the WASP?" by Doris Brinker Tanner, The Sweetwater Reporter, Sweetwater, Texas, 1989.

Wings Over Sweetwater, by Major Bennet B. Monde, privately published, 1995; 159 pages with photos and index.

Winning my Wings, by Marion Stegeman Hodgson, Naval Institute Press, Annapolis, Maryland, 1996; 257 pages with photos.

Women Pilots of World War II, by Jean Hascall Cole, University of Utah Press, 1992; 165 pages with photos and index.

Index

(Subjects that are frequently mentioned in the text will either be omitted from the Index or have their page locations cited selectively. The first entry will usually be the page on which the subject is initially mentioned, subsequent entries dependent on textual importance.)